THE PHILOSOPHY OF DISCOURSE

THE RHETORICAL TURN IN TWENTIETH-CENTURY THOUGHT

Volume 1

Edited by

Chip Sills

Assistant Professor of Philosophy
Department of History
United States Naval Academy

George H. Jensen

Associate Professor
Department of English
Southwest Missouri State University

**BOYNTON/COOK PUBLISHERS
HEINEMANN**
Portsmouth, NH

Boynton/Cook Publishers, Inc.
A Subsidiary of
Heinemann Educational Books, Inc.
361 Hanover Street, Portsmouth, NH 03801
Offices and agents throughout the world

Library of Congress Cataloging-in-Publication Data
The Philosophy of discourse: the rhetorical turn in twentieth-century
  thought/edited by Chip Sills, George H. Jensen.
      p.   cm.
   Includes bibliographical references.
   ISBN 0−86709−286−6 (v. 1). − ISBN 0−86709−287−4 (v. 2)
   I. Sills, Chip. II. Jensen, George H.
B804.P536 1992
149′.94−dc20   91−14249
                                                                                CIP

Cover designed by T. Watson Bogaard
Printed in the United States of America
92 93 94 95 96 9 8 7 6 5 4 3 2 1

THE PHILOSOPHY OF DISCOURSE

Contents

Preface

The twentieth century has seen a protean development of the notion of "discourse." A number of challenging and contradictory discursive theories have been elaborated, attacked, and defended. These developments are stimulating but somewhat overwhelming, because of the wealth of the material and the lack of any attempt at a unitary accounting. The large number of critical vocabularies and styles descendant from the various paradigms unfortunately discourages many from entering what often seems a bewildering series of arcane debates.

The present work is an attempt to offer a useful introduction to a number of contemporary discursive models. The wealth of material has required that the work be presented in two volumes, and even so the editors have been forced to limit coverage to a representative collection of themes and persons. Volume 1 contains sections devoted to the philosophy of science, pragmatism, the Frankfurt School, the Bakhtin Circle, and the revival of rhetoric. Volume 2 contains sections devoted to structuralism and poststructuralism, hermeneutics, Cassirer, and feminism. Although most readers will probably find both volumes necessary for a more thorough introduction to the philosophy of discourse, the work has been designed so that either volume can be studied independently. The general introduction appears in both volumes.

Each volume presents chapters that concentrate, for the most part, on the work of individual figures, such as Lévi-Strauss, Foucault, or Rorty. Two of the chapters, the ones on philosophy of science and feminism, are more general, covering a group of theorists. Most chapters are elements of larger thematic sections, each of which is preceded by a general introduction. For example, the section on the Frankfurt School in Volume 1 begins with a general introduction, followed by chapters on Adorno and Habermas. By working from the introductory material to the chapters, the reader should be able to develop a broad overview of the "rhetorical turn."

This overview cannot claim to be comprehensive. Even with the expansion of this project into a second volume, we could not include a chapter on every noteworthy twentieth-century thinker who commented on the nature of discourse. Most readers will believe that some important figure has been unaccountably left out, while some lesser figure has been included. Such criticism is to be expected. In our defense, we say only that we struggled long and hard with the issue. It is difficult to select a limited number of important and representative figures, and we acknowledge that some important ones—Emilio Betti, Roland Barthes, Paul Ricoeur, Antonio Gramsci, Michael Oakeshott, Susanne K. Langer, Roman Jakobson, and James Hillman, to name a few— have been excluded. We have tried to fill in some gaps with our introductory sections.

Even though it was impossible to exhaust the richness of the "rhetorical turn," we have included enough important figures to provide the reader with a sense of this important conversation. That it is a conversation will become evident upon reading and rereading the work. The chapter on Rorty will help the reader better understand the chapter on Gadamer, and the chapter on Heidegger will help to comprehend Rorty.

It is our hope that the two volumes of *The Philosophy of Discourse* will be useful to the reader who has little prior knowledge of the "rhetorical turn," yet still be instructive for those who are actually participating in this conversation. The volumes should provide a much-needed general orientation that can serve as an entrée for more special-ized study of individual figures.

Acknowledgments

These volumes could not have been completed without the help of many people. We would like to express our appreciation to our authors, many of whom told us, "This is the hardest thing I have ever written." We appreciate their willingness to cut massive rough drafts and clarify difficult concepts.

We wish to thank those who suggested authors for individual chapters: Hans Kellner (Michigan State University), Robert Detweiler (Emory University), Richard Rorty (University of Virginia), Allan Megill (University of Iowa), Robert Paul (Emory University), Martin Jay (University of California–Berkeley), Ian Hacking (University of California–Santa Cruz), and Ben W. McClelland (University of Mississippi).

We also wish to thank those who generously agreed to supplement our knowledge by reading and critiquing rough drafts: Ron Jackson (Emory University), Kathryn Kirkpatrick (Emory University), Janet Summers (University of North Carolina–Greensboro), Walter Adamson (Emory University), Sheryl Gowen (Georgia State University), and Chris Zervos (Purdue University–Calumet).

For his general support, we wish to thank Donald McCloskey (University of Iowa).

For their patience and support, we wish to thank our respective wives and children.

THE PHILOSOPHY OF DISCOURSE

General Introduction

Chip Sills

To speak of the "rhetorical turn" in contemporary discourse is to risk further eroding an already well-worn turn of phrase by creating yet another variant. There are no shortages of "turns" proposed, discovered, announced, and disseminated in the contemporary discursive jungle. Richard Rorty started it all with his influential *Linguistic Turn*, a collection of essays in the tradition of recent linguistic analysis, in 1967. Rorty's Introduction to this work stressed the tension between the modernist quest for a neutral methodology and the specific substantive assumptions—such as methodological nominalism—endemic to linguistic philosophy.[1] Since then, patient readers have received numerous updates. Geoffrey Hartmann, for instance, posited a "hermeneutic turn" initiated by Hegel.[2] Since the exploitation of charming and world-disclosing turns of phrase is a fundamental element in any rhetoric, it was only a matter of time before the self-reflexive mania of contemporary intellectual culture hit upon the strategem of turning the various devices of rhetorical practice on the rhetoric of modernity itself. The resulting "rhetorical turn" was heralded by the editors of *The Rhetoric of the Human Sciences*, which announced itself as a preliminary report of this movement.[3]

It is tempting to characterize the rhetorical turn as the "big picture," as the synthetic entity that includes and continues the twentieth-century emphasis on language in a more comprehensive mode. From this point of view, the rhetorical emphasis on the pragmatics of communication completes the more formalist inquiries of linguistic and hermeneutic analysis and *Verstehen*, which then appear as but partial manifestations. But the self-consciousness implied in the rhetorical turn also implies the ironic reminder that such a characterization is itself the instantiation of a strategy—often called "Hegelian"—that can be seen as a rhetorical

1

gambit, one that has come under heavy criticism. Let us begin, then, to introduce this newcomer by adopting the strategy of simply examining the constituent terms of the phrase: "rhetoric" and "turn." The account that follows will hopscotch around vast cultural icons and clichés, giving only preliminary and contentious indications of one way to view the rhetorical turn, but I may crave indulgence from the reader, for any statement of introduction announces by its title that it is only a fragment, indicating a greater account to follow.

Rhetoric is an ancient discipline currently experiencing a phoenixlike rebirth. Not so long ago, the term "rhetoric" was perhaps most often associated with empty verbiage and long lists of obscure terms whose purpose was to provide names for formally distinguishing various poetic operations, for naming the parts of a discourse, for classifying the elements of persuasion, for classifying genres or prescribing which moves were appropriate to those genres. "Rhetoric" was also supposed to prescribe appropriate mechanisms for composing and delivering speeches. But the current rebirth of intense interest in rhetorical concerns is perhaps best understood as a recrudescence of the ancient warfare waged for millennia between philosophy and rhetoric.

A good case could be made for the proposition that Western philosophy first took form as an effort to distinguish itself from rhetoric. There is no question that Socrates himself was popularly considered by many of his contemporaries to be a sophist, a master of rhetoric who attracted an admiring entourage of listeners and codisputants. But Socrates was a rhetorician with a difference — he showed a sustained and subtle interest in exploring the limits of rhetorical principles in the pursuit of truth. In the process, he succeeded in initiating a problematic separation of the philosophical project — said to be an inquiry after truth — from that of rhetoric — said to be a discipline that explores the dynamics of persuasion as the manipulation of opinion. Plato's *Gorgias* has Socrates analyzing rhetoric as a rather disreputable enterprise, essentially a subdivision of the art of pandering.[4] But Plato was evidently dissatisfied with this somewhat dismissive judgment and returned to the problem of properly relating philosophy and rhetoric in the *Phaedrus*. This dialogue begins with a humorous restatement of the earlier position, dramatically realized by Lysias's speech in favor of giving love to the nonlover — the theme of the speech itself is already a very specific and open instance of pandering, in the most obvious and provocative sense. The lustful nonlover has commissioned a speech from Lysias to win the favor of some attractive young man, and Lysias has graciously complied. But Socrates does not take the opportunity thus offered to repeat the charges made in the *Gorgias*. Instead, he first meets Phaedrus's challenge to outdo Lysias's effort with a speech of his own, directed towards the same thesis: it is better to give one's love to a person who is not in love with you. His *daimon* then warns him that he has blasphemed love, and Socrates makes amends with the famous speech about love as a form of divine madness, with the power to lead both lover and beloved towards the truth—which is seen explicitly as a divine realm. He then goes on to consider more closely the relations of philosophy and rhetoric, arguing that philosophy and "true rhetoric" are inextricably linked. We are invited to interpret his recantation of his earlier speech as also being a recantation of his earlier dismissal of rhetoric. Philosophy, in employing the dialectical method, both ensures that its results are true and embodies the rhetorical approach best calculated to achieve adherence to the truth found. So truth and persuasion are joined for Socrates; philosophy and rhetoric are synthesized.

This uneasy synthesis was not maintained, however, and for good reason. Philosophy in general has upheld the distinction between opinion (*doxa*) and truth (*episteme*), and sophists/rhetoricians have in general denied that this distinction can be given any nondogmatic or trans-contextual validity. As Blumenberg points out, "Rhetoric belongs to a syndrome of skeptical assumptions."[5] Since the truth that philosophy seeks is *universal*, the devotees of rhetoric have marked their disagreement with this project by deploying the skeptical tropes that oppose the assertion of universal truths by pointing out the equal plausibility of differing "truths," or arguing that philosophical pretensions to absolute truth invariably involve arbitrary assumptions (the trope of hypothesis), an infinite regress in justification, or begging the question (the trope of circular reasoning). All this achieved canonical expression by the second century A.D. in the work of Sextus Empiricus.[6] In fact, however, the skeptical approach shows the *necessity* of the opposition between philosophy and rhetoric, as much as it undermines the positive assertion of any specific version of philosophical truth, for Sextus Empiricus reduces the problem of justified knowledge to the following dilemma: every object of apprehension seems to be apprehended either through itself—immediately—or through something else—via mediation. But nothing, evidently, is apprehended through itself, because everything is (potentially, at least) an object of controversy. And if something is taken to be apprehended through something else, then the tropes of hypothesis, infinite regress, and circularity see to it that no certainty is available here, either. Philosophy, in the widest sense, tends to choose the first alternative, and seeks a truth that is self-grounding. This is the motivation for the endless philosophical quests for "presuppositionlessness" and "neutral methodology." Rhetoric, on the other hand, is inherently other-oriented, and provisionally adopts whatever is at hand in order to develop its persuasive strategies. The skeptical dilemma is more damaging to philosophy, inasmuch as philosophy maintains its project of seeking truth. Rhetoric, by adopting a more modest criterion of practical persuasion via opinion, seems more at home in a skeptical environment, and confines itself to analyses of the media by which persuasion is effected. Rorty's more recent outlook begins to look like the reprise of a viewpoint formulated eighteen centuries ago.

The skeptic's use of the word "trope" (often misleadingly translated as "mode") provides the best opportunity for examining the second term of our title: "turn." For a trope is, among other things, a turning, as when we refer to the phototropism of plants (turning to the light) or even simply the "tropics" (where the sun annually "turns" at the solstices). Troping also variously implies movement, change, innovation, stratagem, adaptation, transfer, difference, exclusion, inclusion, merger, and identity.[7] The rhetorical turn can thus be viewed as yet another attempt to renew the creative tension between philosophy and rhetoric, involving all the tropal dimensions listed above. If the synthesis of philosophy and rhetoric has proved problematic, so has the effort to keep the disciplines separate. Philosophy of rhetoric, the effort to achieve systematic and comprehensive understanding of the proper use of rhetorical terms and procedures, has frequently shown a telos towards first principles, while no philosophy has ever been able to completely dispense with the apparatus of persuasion. In this regard, the above-mentioned tendency for philosophy to experiment with various attempts to achieve a "neutral" *methodical* explication of its theses (thus claiming not to rely on any rhetorical presuppositions) seems remarkable, and indeed constitutive of much of what has been termed "philosophy." From Spinoza's method of deduction from definition and axiom to more recent positivist flirtation with mathematicological formalism, to the various strategies anthologized in Rorty's collection, philosophy in the age of modern science has shown a recurring tendency to claim the rhetorical higher ground of a neutral truth-securing method. In the wake of Goedel's theorems, however, which are arguably only the restatement of the skeptical objections of Sextus Empiricus in mathematical form, this claim looks more and more threadbare.[8] Odd as it may seem, even mathematics arguably has rhetorical elements in its procedures.[9]

The contemporary recrudescence of rhetorical interest can be seen, then, in the context of the decline of the fortunes of scientific philosophy, which developed itself amid the most extreme and strenuous efforts to positively banish all rhetorical elements from its presentation. Paul De Man has collected representative statements from early modern philosophers, documenting their uniform hostility to rhetoric. Descartes, Locke, Hobbes, Condillac, and Kant all made efforts to distinguish rhetoric from proper philosophical procedure.[10] Reading through these manifestos, one cannot escape a certain feeling of irony: in the midst of proclaiming a skeptical assault upon the religious, political, and philosophical legacy of the past, these thinkers uniformly belittle the discipline of rhetoric, which our analysis thus far has shown to be most congenial with skeptical assumptions. The discrepancy coalesces around the issue of science. Mathematicological procedures find their intuitive justification in the fact that they prove so valuable in extending the limits of mechanistic natural science. Other attempts to ground natural philosophy in such a way as to justify the success of Newtonian mechanics show a similar ambivalence about skepticism: one was *not* permitted to be skeptical about the Newtonian world-picture. When Bishop Berkeley, in correspondence with Samuel Johnson, cited logical reasons for doubting crucial elements of Newton's account, Johnson's reply was a blank incredulity that Newton could be wrong.[11] And, in general, early modern philosophy is often taught as an attempt to establish a mode of knowing certainty that could maintain itself in the face of skeptical considerations. From this point of view, the rhetorical turn could be seen as the development of tendencies present at the outset in modern philosophy. Still, compared with the place of honor held by rhetoric in the medieval intellectual world, the decisive rejection of rhetoric in the early modern period must be considered one of its defining characteristics, and the rhetorical turn of today appears as a "return of the repressed."

The *locus classicus* of the confrontation of skepticism and scientific philosophy has long been held to be the critical philosophy of Immanuel Kant. Kant's problem was to somehow guarantee the rational acceptability of the Newtonian world-picture in the face of Hume's skeptical objections. The everyday world of sense-perception seemed to depict a world of real objects, extended in space and enduring in time, a world that seemed to follow Newton's laws of motion and gravitation. Yet our perceptions were not immediately revelatory of these objects, but depended on our own sensory apparatus, which organized the "signals" arriving from the real objects into "ideas" (this, at least, was the view of thinkers as disparate as Locke, Leibniz, Berkeley, and Hume).[12] It is only with these "ideas" that we are in immediate contact. Kant's ingenious solution was to deny (along with the skeptical tradition) that we have any knowledge of "things in themselves" apart from our perception of them, while at the same time arguing that the "objectivity" we seek (so our knowledge can be actually true) is available on *this* side of the phenomena, so to speak, as a rationally deducible set of categories of understanding that guarantee the possibility of any experience whatsoever. Any possible experience is organized automatically by the categories of our "transcendental unity of apperception." These categories, happily enough, fit Newtonian conceptions very neatly. Kant's philosophy may owe some of its enduring appeal, despite its difficulties, to its proposed arrangement of skepticism, experience, and truth. Precisely some such arrangement was required as an ideological justification of physical science, which claims a skeptical methodology (it purports not to rely on political, philosophical, or religious dogma, and it experiments, or subjects its hypotheses to skeptical testing) while at the same time making claims to truth and basing its justification on the commonplace experiences of a technological society.[13]

It is not widely appreciated how deeply Hegel's critique of Kantian philosophy and the Newtonian science that formed its motivation was informed by (1) Hegel's abiding concern with confronting and answering the objections of the ancient skeptics to objective knowing, and (2) his realization that this concern required "a new concept of science."[14] At issue is a "method" that is viewed as integral to, rather than externally imposed upon, the subject matter. Hegel's work, while acknowledged as immensely seminal, is rarely taken seriously on its own terms. The rhetoric of "absolute knowing" is typically viewed with incredulity (and often, faint condescension) as a last-gasp effort at a final metaphysics of Being (in the Aristotelian tradition) or Consciousness (in the Cartesian tradition). The fact that neither of these interpretations bears serious scrutiny is a measure of the sorry state of Hegel scholarship in contemporary academic culture. Even while the breathtaking events in the Soviet Union and Eastern Europe are being heralded as "Hegel's revenge," few observers are aware that a real confrontation with Hegel's contribution to philosophy requires a recognition of how his reconception of philosophic "science" involves a subtle and searching treatment of the relations of philosophy and rhetoric.[15] The most promising new directions in Hegel interpretation are redirecting attention to the importance of rhetorical considerations in Hegel's notion of *Bildung*, to the key role that the tropes of ancient skepticism played in Hegel's overall view of opposition and negation in the advancement of knowledge, and to a more nuanced appreciation of the rhetoric of "absolute knowing."[16] The absence of reference implied in the term "absolute" warns us not to take *anything* as a fixed and final reference-point for the construction of a comprehensive view of the world. But, paradoxically, we cannot make *any* beginning without incurring some debt of reference, some acknowledgment that something appears to be the case. At issue is whether it is useful to proceed along the assumption that what appears is in some sense, finally, conducive to a comprehensive account about all that is the case. Here Hegel and pragmatism (which has taken of late an openly rhetorical turn) are in agreement. At the very least, thought after Hegel should know enough to think "rhetoric" every time we hear the word "method"!

With Hegel, the transition from modernism to postmodernism is already in question. This can be scrutinized in terms of the issue of foundationalism. It seems to us that "modernist" foundationalism is different from traditional foundationalism in an important way that needs to be elucidated. In brief, the difference is that the modernist foundational project proceeds *after* a radical skeptical gesture that makes (or seeks or claims to make) traditional *metaphysical* foundationalism impossible. Modernist theory no longer looks for an "objective" reality behind the appearances, but seeks through various methodological strategies (tending always toward positivism, which is most clear and intransigent about this dismissal of metaphysics) to "found" certain knowledge on *this* side of the appearances. Alternatively, "certainty" and "truth" themselves are scrapped as viable strategies for organizing knowledge, and one resigns onself to some version of probabilism. Postmodernism, viewed most broadly as the acceptance of this situation, is then the final blow against *any* project of foundations. If Hegel, for instance, is seen as identifying speculative reason as the "absolute" foundation for reality, then his project comes under postmodern attack. But the very peculiarity of Hegel's vision is that the "absolute" becomes determinate, intelligible, only through the comprehensive inspection and critique of all foundational schemes. In this sense, Hegel's work has served as a strategic resource for many subsequent antifoundational projects.[17] And the postmodern attack on foundations has itself bifurcated into two general tendencies: one that keeps vigilant watch on any attempt to reestablish foundations of any sort, and another that takes the inability to establish any *single* foundation as a license to use any and all foundational discourses as seems convenient.

Hegel was, if never really refuted, certainly bypassed and ignored. Marx, of course, genuinely attempted to overcome Hegel dialectically.[18] But the subsequent development of Western ideology, including Marxism, owed less to any sense of "dialectics" than to triumphant scientism, which developed from neo-Kantianism to logical positivism. The separation of fact and value and the acknowledgment of physical science as the paradigm of genuine knowing have served as almost unchallenged arbiters of rational discourse until recently.[19] The rhetorical turn can be seen as the attempt to undermine the hegemony of positivism via a reconsideration of rhetoric. The Marxist variants of the rhetorical turn have had to fight a war on two fronts: in addition to criticizing discourse — including positivism — as the ideology of the (bourgeois) rulers, the more intelligent (and democratic) Marxist critics have always had to bear with the atrocities being committed daily in the name of "Marxism." Writing in the spring of 1990, when practical revulsion against the pretensions of Marxist hegemony has swept so much of the communist world, it seems difficult to credit the long and sympathetic hearing that Marxist ideology has received (and continues to receive) in the Western Academy. But surely one advantage Marxism accorded to theorists of discourse was its proposal to analyze discourse as ideology: as the rationalization of a complex historical configuration of interests, divided conveniently into the thought that rationalized the proprietors and the thought that gave marching orders to those indentured to struggle against the proprietors in the name of the coming socialist configuration. That most Marxist theorists were in no sense proletarians has always given the role of Marxist theoretician (beginning with Marx) an odd redolence of uninvited pretender, a role seemingly congenial to academics and intellectuals generally.

The rhetorical resources subsumed under Paul Ricoeur's "hermeneutics of suspicion" have thus played an ambivalent role in introducing the rhetorical turn. Nietzsche and Freud, besides Marx the most brilliant and compelling practitioners of the genre, have also played the role of radical critic, only to find their insights codified and institutionalized. Nietzsche, master of rhetoric that he was, ambiguously combined a form of fatalistic positivism (the "eternal return") with a straightforward attack upon the Western project of metaphysical truth and an unparalleled awareness of the protean powers of language to construct alternative realities. By radically distinguishing between "life" and "language," however, Nietzsche trades on just those metaphysical oppositions that he wishes to overcome.[20] Yet Nietzsche's incomparable rhetorical power, together with his uncompromising hostility to bourgeois culture, has attracted many who wanted an alternative to Marxism that embodies a stance intransigeantly opposed to the culture of modern liberal capitalism. Nietzsche has had a well-documented influence on many thinkers of this century, including several dealt with in these volumes. Heidegger, Foucault, and Derrida, at least, owe enormous debts to Nietzsche's example. The idea that discourse should be considered finally an art form, a spontaneous creation of the will to power, continues to have great appeal to many.

The final hermeneut of suspicion, Freud, also had an influential contribution to the interpretation of signs, and deserves mention as an introducer of the contemporary rhetorical turn. Freud first gained wide acceptance for his work with *The Interpretation of Dreams*, and the psychoanalytic art/science/therapy he founded is based upon a regressive hermeneutic analysis of neurotic *symptoms* disclosive of a dynamically repressed unconscious life.[21] Where Marx had interpreted human culture as formed by the antagonistic impulses of class struggle, and Nietzsche had analyzed culture as will to power, Freud saw an immortal battle between life and death instincts within the individual, and a constitutive struggle between the conflicting demands of instinct and communal life. Freud's interpretive discourse also implied an interpretation of discourse: the motivations and discursive counters of our conversations were to be understood as sublimated reenactments of primal scenes whose fantasy-memories formed the unconscious parameters of our possible experience.

All three of the hermeneuts of suspicion were modernist in opposing classical transcendence: the traditional Judeo-Christian interpretation that the ultimate purpose of discourse was the task of reconciling revealed truth with the experiences of finite life. Yet even the radical immanentism of these modernist critics maintained various covert ties to transcendence. Marx's classless utopia, Nietzsche's superman, and Freud's not-so-surreptitious self-identification with Moses all betokened an inability to rest easy in contemporary Western culture. It may be that the relatively uncritical view each of them took towards natural science is symptomatic of this inconsistency. Since the nineteenth century, as the first chapter of this work attests, science has lost much of its lustre as the one "natural" explanation of the way things are, and has come to disclose many of the same inconsistencies and intractable difficulties that have characterized other disciplines of knowing.

The fact that Freud's name is often immediately linked with that of Jung, as a fellow pioneer of depth psychology, brings out some of the pathos of the transition from the modern to the postmodern. Where Freud was forthright in his opposition to any future for religious "illusion," Jung thought he discerned in the traumas of irreligious modernity the outlines of a psychological quest for wholeness deserving of respect and requiring an imaginative reconstruction. Where one tendency of postmodernity follows Freud in denying recognition to any further traffic with the absolute, another follows Jung in countering that any and all such traffic is justified by psychological necessity. Where Freud, like an Old Testament prophet, places an interdict on any further theology—a gesture that makes any religion in effect a form of idolatry—Jung responds that precisely our lack of a culturally reinforced faith makes the equal access to any and all modalities and symbols of faith permissible.[22] It is noteworthy that further development of archetypal psychology since Jung's death has included its own "rhetorical turn": James Hillman closes his *Re-Visioning Psychology* with a call for a return to Renaissance rhetoric and neo-Platonist panpsychological consciousness.[23]

Another avenue to the contemporary rhetorical turn is twentieth-century semiotic theory, which can be viewed as having a twofold origin in the work of Charles S. Peirce and Ferdinand de Saussure. Peirce's contribution is dealt with in the chapter contributed by Peter Skagestad, so I will not comment on it here. Saussure contributed an influential analysis of the semiotic dynamics of language that is still being exploited and debated. Briefly, Saussure argued that the *sign* could be understood only when analyzed into its component parts: signifier (the perceptible sign itself, the word or gesture or mark) and signified (the concept intended).[24] The analysis has spawned a great interpretive and critical literature. Saussure claimed that the signifier had a "horizontal" relationship of *signification* — it indicated a "lack" or relationship to its concept, only accessible via other signs — as well as a "vertical" relationship — its *reference* or denotation of some aspect of experience. Poststructuralist semiotics has characteristically denied access to the vertical dimension, by arguing that it doesn't exist or cannot be known via signification. The play of surfaces is all we have; the illusion of depth characteristic of Western thought since Heracleitus is denied. The post-Hegelian war against comprehension is being fought on every front.

These comments may serve to place the rhetorical turn in some preliminary context. Perhaps they are best summarized by the statement that we are now more willing than before to realize that whenever we speak of "discourse," we are ineluctably on rhetorical terrain.

Notes

1. Richard Rorty, ed., *The Linguistic Turn: Recent Essays in Philosophical Method* (Chicago: Univ. of Chicago, 1967). Rorty defines "methodological nominalism" thus: "The view that all questions which philosophers have asked about concepts, subsistent universals, or 'natures' which (a) cannot be answered by empirical inquiry concerning the behavior or properties of particulars subsumed under such concepts, universals, or natures, and which (b) can be answered in *some* way, can be answered by answering questions about the use of linguistic expressions, and in no other way." (p. 11)

2. Geoffrey Hartmann, *The Fate of Reading and Other Essays* (Chicago: Univ. of Chicago, 1975), p. 120.

3. John S. Nelson, Allan Megill, and Donald N. McCloskey, *The Rhetoric of the Human Sciences: Language and Argument in Scholarship and Public Affairs* (Madison: Univ. of Wisconsin, 1987).

4. Here I am following the discussion of Walter Hamilton in his Introduction to his translation of the *Phaedrus, Phaedrus and Letters VII and VIII* (Hammondsworth, Middlesex: Penguin, 1985), pp. 7–18.

5. Hans Blumenberg, "An Anthropological Approach to Rhetoric," in Kenneth Baynes, James Bohman, and Thomas McCarthy, eds., *Philosophy: End or Transformation* (Cambridge, Mass.: MIT, 1987), pp. 429–58.

6. Sextus Empiricus, *Outlines of Pyrrhonism*, trans. R. G. Bury (London: Heinemann, 1976).

7. The literature on tropes is immense and growing. See, for starters, Mark Johnson, ed., *Philosophical Perspectives on Metaphor* (Minneapolis:

Univ. of Minnesota, 1981); Kenneth Burke, "The Four Master-Tropes," Appendix D of *A Grammar of Motives* (New York: Prentice-Hall, 1945), pp. 503–17; Hayden White, *Metahistory* (Baltimore: Johns Hopkins Univ., 1973) and *Tropics of Discourse* (Baltimore: Johns Hopkins Univ., 1978); and Hans Kellner, *Language and Historical Representation: Getting the Story Crooked*, part III (Madison: Univ. of Wisconsin, 1989), pp. 189–264; for a more inclusive bibliography, see Chip Sills, *The Myth of Reason: Is Hegel's 'Logic' a Speculative Tropology?* 1988 diss. Emory University.

8. See John Kadvany, "Reflections on the Legacy of Kurt Goedel: Mathematics, Skepticism, Postmodernism," *Philosophical Forum*, 20 (Spring 1989), pp. 161–81.

9. This has been argued by Philip Davis and Reuben Hersh in Nelson, et al., *Rhetoric of the Human Sciences* (Madison: Univ. of Wisconsin, 1987), pp. 53–68.

10. Paul De Man, "The Epistemology of Metaphor," in Sheldon Sacks, ed., *On Metaphor* (Chicago: Univ. of Chicago, 1979), pp. 11–28. De Man treats Locke, Condillac, and Kant, but similar statements by Descartes and Hobbes are well known. One noteworthy exception to this hostility to rhetoric is the great Neapolitan philosopher and rhetorician Giambattista Vico, whose recent vogue is itself a symptom of the rhetorical turn.

11. George Berkeley, *Principles, Dialogues, and Correspondence*, ed. Colin Turbayne (New York: Library of Liberal Arts, 1965), pp. 215–42.

12. The "common sense" philosophy of Thomas Reid, now enjoying a bit of a renaissance, was noteworthy in its insistance that we *do*, for all practical purposes, immediately perceive external objects. Reid thus denies the premise that makes skepticism seem invincible—the premise that all we have to deal with immediately are the *appearances* of external objects. See his *Inquiry Into the Human Mind on the Principles of Common Sense* (1764).

13. It is of course a matter of controversy within the scientific community whether or not science makes any metaphysical claims to truth. Many, if not most scientific practitioners, conditioned by positivist protocols, would deny that the "truths" of science have any more than a pragmatic standing. But the rhetorical situation is quite different. Science is widely held by many of its practitioners and by virtually all contemporary official organs of authoritative discourse to be *the* authoritative discourse—the paradigm of what truth means.

14. Michael Forster's *Hegel and Skepticism* (Cambridge, Mass.: Harvard Univ., 1989) is a welcome recent exception to the habitual minimizing of this aspect of Hegel's project. Hegel makes the claim for a "new form of science" in several places. See, for example, *Science of Logic*, trans. A. V. Miller (New York: Humanities Press, 1969), pp. 27ff. and 53ff.; *Philosophy of Right*, trans. T. M. Knox (Oxford: Oxford Univ., 1967), pp. 1–2.

15. See John H. Smith, *The Spirit and Its Letter: Traces of Rhetoric in Hegel's Philosophy of 'Bildung'* (Cornell: Cornell Univ., 1988). While Smith is agnostic at best about the continuing value of Hegel's speculative philosophy, his study broaches in a serious and scholarly way the issues of philosophy and rhetoric in Hegel's work.

16. In addition to the works of Forster and Smith, see Chip Sills, "Is Hegel's *Logic* a Speculative Tropology?" *Owl of Minerva*, 21:1 (Fall 1989), pp. 21–40.

17. See, for instance, Henry Sussman, *The Hegelian Aftermath* (Baltimore: Johns Hopkins Univ., 1982), for an exploration of post-Hegelian philosophy and literature as selective exploitation of various Hegelian tropes. Exploration of Hegel as an antifoundational thinker has been undertaken by William Maker in "Reason and Modernity," *Philosophical Forum*, 18:4 (Summer 1987), pp. 275–303; and by Richard Dien Winfield in "The Route to Foundation-Free Systematic Philosophy," *Philosophical Forum*, 15:3 (Spring 1984), pp. 323–43.

18. See Richard Bernstein's *Praxis and Action* (Philadelphia: Univ. of Pennsylvania, 1971), especially Part I, for a reasoned defense of this reading.

19. Gillian Rose, in *Hegel Contra Sociology* (London: Athlone, 1981), offers a succinct summary of the continuing and pervasive influence of neo-Kantian assumptions in contemporary thought.

20. This argument is made forcefully in Stephen Houlgate, *Hegel, Nietzsche, and the Criticism of Metaphysics* (Cambridge: Cambridge Univ., 1986).

21. Sigmund Freud, *The Interpretation of Dreams*, trans. J. Strachey (New York: Avon, 1968).

22. This opposition, together with the analysis of the culture taking shape under its pressures, is given brilliant exposition in Philip Rieff's *Triumph of the Therapeutic: The Uses of Faith After Freud* (Chicago: Univ. of Chicago, 1987); the 1987 edition contains a new Preface by the author. See also Peter Homans, *Jung in Context* (Chicago: Univ. of Chicago, 1980), for a complementary discussion.

23. James Hillman, *Re-Visioning Psychology* (New York: Harper Colophon, 1975).

24. See Ferdinand de Saussure, *Course in General Linguistics*, trans. W. Baskin (New York: McGraw-Hill, 1959); also Oswald Ducrot and Tzvetan Todorov, eds., *Encyclopedic Dictionary of the Sciences of Language*, trans. C. Porter (Baltimore: Johns Hopkins Univ., 1983), pp. 95–105, which contains useful bibliographies. Perhaps the most trenchant and accessible introduction to contemporary semiotics, including Saussure's contribution, is Walker Percy's "A Semiotic Primer of the Self" in *Lost in the Cosmos*, (New York: Washington Square, 1984), pp. 86–126. Percy refuses to grant the postmodern ontological distinction between "signified" and "referent" that underwrites so much of contemporary semiotic discourse; his realism in this regard is refreshing; while undoubtedly unsatisfactory to many, it enables semiotic discourse to escape the nominalistic quandaries of contemporary theory. See also his "The Divided Creature," *Wilson Quarterly*, 13:3 (Summer 1989), pp. 77–87.

Science, Realism, and Pragmatism

Introduction

Chip Sills

The "modern" world is perhaps most characteristically described as that world in which science has replaced religion as the ultimate authority on the nature of reality. But what is science? The fact that the question itself has become a problem as much as a cultural banality defines the postmodern condition. Answers to this question can be used to locate positions along differing axes of contemporary inquiry. The chapters that follow begin to address some of the most controversial issues in contemporary views of science, as well as introduce the reader to high points in contemporary history and philosophy of science. Here in this introduction, however, it is appropriate to offer a more general overview.

To address the most salient issues in contemporary philosophy of science, it is useful to distinguish between realism and pragmatism. Realism is the view that there is an objective reality "out there" that just is whatever it is, independent of our conception of it. While it is in some sense made accessible by our senses, it is not reducible to sensory inputs. Pragmatism is the view that one need not have a comprehensive epistemological justification for one's attitudes and opinions, together with the claim that the contexts within which given questions arise and find solution are sufficient (and all we can legitimately expect) for reaching the proximate certitude that enables us to function practically in the world. If something "works," then we are justified in utilizing it until something better comes along. Viewed in these terms, the postmodern crisis in science can appear as the growing tension between the pragmatic and realist tendencies in science, and the corresponding difficulty in maintaining both simultaneously.

It was not always so. Today's pragmatist/realist schizophrenia is best seen in historical perspective. Let us recall the fabled, heroic years near the beginnings of what is usually called the "scientific revolution."

15

Modern science began, according to most accounts, with a twofold imperative: (1) to look toward the work actually being done by craftsmen and technicians in their efforts to solve specific technical problems, and (2) to develop theoretical means for expressing scientific truths free of the encumbrances of past religious and philosophical authorities.

In order to understand the first point, it is useful to recall that Galileo in fact spent much of his time working with sailors, gunners, and artisans; some of his colleagues were men like Niccolo Tartaglia and Giovanni Benedetti, who had no university education at all, but were self-taught engineers. Yet Tartaglia's work in ballistics (it was Tartaglia who first ascertained that 45 degrees of elevation ensures the maximum range for a projectile fired from a cannon) and Benedetti's in free fall (it was Benedetti who first argued, against the prevailing Aristotelian doctrine, that bodies of unequal weights fall at equal speeds) were decisive in inspiring Galileo's work.[1] Francis Bacon, one of the most celebrated early propagandists of science, advised his readers to look to "the mechanical arts," for they "are continually growing and becoming more perfect." This is contrasted with the sterile disputations of the philosophers, whose wisdom "can talk, but it cannot generate, for it is fruitful of controversies but barren of work."[2] From Bacon we also inherit the inspiring notions that the progress of the sciences is bound up with the progressive easing of the burdens of human life and that the society of the scientists is a democratic one — the way is open to anyone, regardless of social caste, to become a competent practitioner — something already being demonstrated by researchers like Tartaglia and Benedetti, as well as many other technical innovaters who were taking advantage of the printing press to introduce a whole new class of authors and literature into circulation.

The second point, that scientific theory should be permitted to develop free of unnecessary philosophical and religious encumbrances, is somewhat murkier. On the one hand, it is evident that modern science could never have developed in its present form without ridding itself of Aristotelian doctrine. And the polemical theme that scientific inquiry should remain free of philosophical or religious inhibition remains a powerful one. But this did not mean, even to Galileo and Bacon, that the progress of science was unconnected with the problem of truth. Quite the contrary — both avowed that it was because of their zeal for truth that they struck out in new directions. So philosophy, as disciplined inquiry into the nature of truth, has always had an uneasy and problematic relation to the truth that science is pursuing. For science is not — at least to Bacon and Galileo — merely a collection of interesting discoveries about which techniques work best to secure certain technical goals, but is rather the rational and systematic investigation of nature. Just as Socrates claimed that his disciplined dialectical inquiry gave a methodical basis for philosophy, so scientists have claimed that the virtues of their method suffice to secure certain knowledge — "justified true belief," to borrow from Plato. From its beginnings, then, the modern scientific project has tended to conflate a rhetorical denunciation of philosophical authority with the adoption of a specific philosophical attitude — for scientific realism is a species of metaphysical realism. This internal fault line can be followed in the subsequent history of science.

The pragmatist strain is evident in Bacon's and Galileo's privileging of the actual technical innovations being perfected by their contemporaries, even when these innovations seemed to fly in the face of the most authoritative theory available. The pragmatist feels comparatively little embarrassment if competent technical design — efficient adaptation to technical ends — exists alongside great theoretical confusion. A realist, however, thinks that inherent in the experimental approach employed by science is the belief that the world is as it is, independent of our concerns or attitudes towards it, and that experiment is the trying of a case before the supreme impartial tribunal — nature as it is. It is this faith in the reality and independence of nature which makes universal scientific laws actually *true*. It is evident that both Bacon and Galileo were also realists, for they saw scientific experimentation as submitting hypotheses to the adjudication of nature. In its origins, then, the modern scientific project was *both* pragmatic and realistic in its approach, and saw the two attitudes as inherently complementary. If theoretical confusion was present, or anomalous experimental results attained, the scientific faith was that further refinement of the universal laws, better instruments of observation, or new discoveries about the interimplication of phenomena would serve to clear up the situation. The technical efficiency aimed at by the pragmatist would ultimately be explained by real universal laws describing the actual structure of nature.

One of the best ways to enter the world of contemporary philosophy of science is to investigate how it was that realism and pragmatism became increasingly difficult to maintain simultaneously. This is important, because the everyday common-sense conception of the scientific project still takes for granted that science can be approached both realistically and pragmatically, while theorists at the cutting edge of physics are engaged in a fundamental debate over just this issue.

What happened between Galileo's time and our own to complicate the issue? Science continued to develop along the lines pioneered by Galileo and Bacon: we associate the spectacular successes of classical physics with a combination of the inductive experimentation argued for by Bacon (despite his rather crude conceptions and confused experimental practice) and the complex blend of theoretical innovation, experimentation and mathematical formalism practiced by Galileo (for example, the formula for the acceleration of gravity in a vacuum as being $s = kt^2$ where s = distance, t = time and k = an experimentally derived constant). Newton's laws of motion and universal gravitation continued the process of developing a mathematical formalism which expressed physical interactions, and James Clerk Maxwell's equations demonstrated the fundamental identity of electrical and magnetic phenomena. The discoveries of Newton and Maxwell were paradigm examples of the drive to bring all experimental and observational data under a small number of universal laws whose activity could be given precise mathematical formulation. After Maxwell's work in the mid-nineteenth century, many believed that continued reductionism and formalism would inevitably result in a comprehensive unification of physical laws. Hand-in-hand with these theoretical advances went an unprecedented level of technical innovation. The latter part of the nineteenth century was the high tide of scientific and technological self-confidence.

What happened to call this progress into question? Very briefly, a few key assumptions of classical physics and the mathematicological formalism in which its presuppositions were expressed came under serious doubt. And this attack should not be seen as originating outside the scientific enterprise, but represents more a self-unraveling, an apparent redirection of the scientific project from within. I am referring, of course, to the discovery of the quantum and the subsequent development of quantum mechanics, the theory of special relativity, and Goedel's undecidability theorems. Max Planck's efforts to solve the so-called black-body problem were a classic example of creative hypothesis and experimental confirmation. Yet his results led to the development of quantum mechanics, which made the classical dream of universal mechanical calculability seem in principle out of the question. Einstein's relativity theory overthrew the notion that the universe must be conceived as deployed in Euclidean space. Goedel's theorems demonstrated that the logical bases of mathematics involve contradictory axioms.

The situation that has evolved in the wake of these innovations looks something like this: the weird world of quantum mechanics has convinced many physicists that there is no point in talking about "reality" outside of observation.[3] Thus, physicists like Niels Bohr and Werner Heisenberg have led a movement in contemporary physics towards pragmatism and away from realism. The idea is that, since the existing quantum mechanics adequately provides for the best working knowledge we can have, this is all that scientists need. Since this physics bears no evident relation to any specific conception of an underlying "deep" reality—or rather, its paradoxical results can be interpreted in a bewildering variety of mutually contradictory ways—

the efficient move is to pitch the notion of reality. Scientists can still devise experiments, communicate results with each other, and help develop technical applications without ever claiming to know the nature of the "deep reality" responsible for the quantum results. Many versions of this tendency deny that there is any sense to the notion of deep reality. This trend bears striking parallels to the logical positivist movement in philosophy, which similarly denied any meaning to metaphysical statements and suggested that we regard questions of meaning as questions about verifiability. On the other hand, a determined minority of physicists, like Einstein, David Bohm and John Bell, have affirmed that the belief that physical theory reflects reality is a necessary spur to further theoretical innovation, and that our present state of theoretical impasse need not be the final word. A major sticking point for the realists is the apparent existence of faster-than-light correlations between phenomena, a result supposedly impossible according to Einstein's own relativity theory. The "quantum interpretation problem" — the problem of how to *interpret* the quantum phenomena — is made thorny by the fact that a large number of apparently incompatible interpretations of why quantum mechanics works the way it does are equally consistent with all the experimental data.

To recapitulate, then, the theoretical innovations in the first thirty years of this century have brought about a definite bifurcation between realist and pragmatist approaches to physical science. In a nutshell, the development of science along the lines originally proposed has led to a theoretical unraveling, the consequences of which are still being felt and assessed.

One option in this situation is to argue that scientific reason and practice have been improperly or too narrowly conceived. Drawing on Romantic criticisms of the scientific project — "we murder to dissect" — theorists from Alfred North Whitehead to Gregory Bateson and Ilya Prigogine have contended that science must be reconceived on a more organic and holistic basis.[4] This tendency resumes Hegel's critique, that mechanistic physical science rests on arbitrary presuppositions that do not permit a comprehensive account of reality to emerge. The recurring problem for this tendency is to provide an adequate account for the undeniable technical competence of science within the proposed larger conception.

Other options include denying that *any* nonarbitrary "science" is possible. Science is thus viewed as a peculiar syndrome of rational, practical and rhetorical options which serves to elevate and justify certain approaches to inquiry while suppressing others. Feminist and political critiques of science exploit the possibilities of this approach. Based on a Nietzschean "will-to-power" analysis, such theories, from Heidegger to Foucault to contemporary feminist criticism of science, see in the drive for comprehensive explanation a sinister imperialistic urge. Science is criticized for rhetorically cloaking this urge in its insistence upon objectivity and value-neutrality. The recurring problem for this tendency is to explain how its skeptical arguments concerning science connect with its systematic arguments concerning the logic of oppression.

The *cultural* consequences of this impasse are of course enormous. We began by asserting that the postmodern condition can be expressed as the situation where the status of science is simultaneously a cultural banality — science is the repository of reliable truth — and at the same time science is itself called into question. Science had come to be perceived as the one legitimate paradigm for real knowledge about reality. The combination of science's own doubt about the "reality reference" of its own activity, together with criticisms from within and without science about the way it had gone about its work, opened up a space from which a large number of critical projects have been launched. When science challenged religion, the painful process of losing the comfort of one form of ultimate authority was assuaged by the claims and comforts offered by the other. Today, however, no rival authority is available to take the place of science, and the consequences of a general cultural devaluation of science (if such is in the offing) have yet to be assessed.[5] Questions about the "scientific" status of science, about political and/or gender biases built into the very structure of inquiry have raised a skeptical challenge to certain knowing unparalleled since the time of Sextus Empiricus, whose *Outlines of Pyrrhonism* has an amazingly contemporary ring.[6] Whether science will continue to maintain its ideological hegemony into the future despite these challenges, whether it will come to be devalued as simply the complex of rational and technical structures best suited to utilitarian technological calculation, or whether some new enlargement of scientific reason will absorb these conflicting tendencies, are all questions raised by the contemporary situation of scientific inquiry.

Notes

1. See Morris Berman, *The Reenchantment of the World* (Ithaca: Cornell Univ., 1981), pp. 59–60.

2. Francis Bacon, from Preface to *The Great Instauration*, in Peter Gay, ed., *The Enlightenment: A Comprehensive Anthology* (New York: Touchstone Books, 1973), pp. 47–48.

3. Note, for instance, physicist John H. Wheeler's comment, "No elementary phenomenon is a real phenomenon until it is an observed phenomenon." Reported in Nick Herbert, *Quantum Reality: Beyond the New Physics* (Garden City, N.Y.: Anchor, 1985), p. 18.

4. Whitehead's views are presented most accessibly in *Science and the Modern World* (New York: Free Press, 1967); Bateson's in *Mind and Nature: A Necessary Unity* (New York: Bantam, 1980); Prigogine's in *Order Out of Chaos*, with Isabelle Stengers (New York: Bantam, 1984). There is a growth industry today in "new science" theorizing, of varying quality. A useful overview, with good bibliographic notes, is in David Ray Griffin, ed., *The Reenchantment of Science* (Albany: SUNY, 1988), especially his Introduction, pp. 1–46.

5. The most important attempt to date to assess the *cultural* consequences of the triumph of scientific analysis over faith in religious authority is still probably Philip Rieff's *The Triumph of the Therapeutic: The Uses of Faith After Freud* (Chicago: Univ. of Chicago, 1966; new edition, with new preface, 1987). Rieff's hostility to dialectical reason makes him apparently dubious about the possibility that internal contradictions in the logic of science can be rationally addressed.

6. Sextus Empiricus, *Outlines of Pyrrhonism*, trans. R. G. Bury, Loeb Classical Library (London: Heinemann, 1976).

1

Negating Positivism
Language and the Practice of Science

Michael H. Shank and David Vampola[1]

For much of its history, science has been associated with the search for certain knowledge — in a word, for truth. Indeed, in Greek antiquity and the Middle Ages, "science" (*episteme, scientia*) meant "certain knowledge." After the outlook of the Scientific Revolution of the sixteenth and seventeenth centuries became entrenched, the English word "science" eventually acquired a more specific connotation asssociated with the search for truth about the *natural* world in particular. Continental European languages still retain the broader connotations of the term.

Long before the twentieth century, reflections upon the nature of science frequently were self-conscious about the importance of language. Indeed, science conceived as a search for truth has been, and continues to be, closely associated with the use of *formal* languages, such as formal logic and mathematics. These languages are called "formal" because the connections between statements formulated in them are believed either to hold or not to hold by virtue of their form rather than their content.

To anyone engaged in a search for truth, formal languages appear especially attractive. Since they offer clear-cut rules that purport to separate correct procedures and inferences from erroneous ones, in principle they can help to distinguish true statements from false ones. Thanks to their rules, the formal languages are normative. They set standards (e.g., they specify which deductions are legitimate) and they create sharp boundaries (e.g., between truth and falsehood, between

22

the propositions that count as scientific knowledge and those that do not).

The association between formal languages and scientific knowledge goes back at least to the late fifth and fourth centuries B.C. Plato identified *episteme* with the certainty of knowledge accessible to dialectic (what we would now call logic). His student Aristotle was deeply impressed by the power and certainty of mathematical proof and logical deduction; he first succeeded in codifying formal logic in his theory of the syllogism, which occupies a prominent place in his theory of science.[2] If the premises of a syllogism are true, and the form of the syllogism is correct, the conclusion follows necessarily from the premises and is also true. Logic, then, seems to compel assent — it leaves no room for discussion.

To appreciate the appeal of formal languages as instruments of science, it is useful to contrast logic with rhetoric. Aristotle defined rhetoric as "the faculty of observing in any given case the available means of persuasion."[3] Since persuasion implies both an audience and a definite goal, the rhetorician must pay attention to considerations that go beyond formal ones. By contrast with the abstract and universal point of view of formal logic, the goal of persuasion gives rhetoric a decidedly pragmatic cast, which relaxes the stringent criteria of formal logic. To persuade, the orator needs premises that *seem plausible*, and arguments that *seem valid*. If the premises are true, and the arguments valid, so much the better; but if not, the *appearance* of truth and validity to the audience may be sufficient to bring the audience to the orator's point of view. By virtue of this compromise and its practical ends, therefore, rhetoric as traditionally understood has little to do with a picture of science that countenances only true premises and conclusions.[4]

Aristotle's success in formalizing logic helps explain his enthusiasm for logic as the language of science. This understanding of scientific knowledge as akin to a formal deductive system has proved to be both very influential and resilient among the cultures that developed in the shadow of Greece. For lack of space, however, we pass over the logical heyday of the late Middle Ages, the renewed interest in rhetoric during the Renaissance, the upheavals in the history of science and philosophy between the seventeenth and nineteenth centuries, and leap to the early twentieth century. In this century in particular, the interface between language and science has proved to be very rich, drawing on a great variety of philosophical traditions and academic disciplines.[5] Under the circumstances, we have renounced the goal of exhaustiveness and chosen instead to concentrate on a few elements that have stimulated or worried the Anglo-American tradition in the philosophy of science.

Logical Positivism

In Western intellectual circles of the late nineteenth century, natural science had emerged as *the* privileged way of knowing. During the same period, Gottlob Frege's attempts to clarify the relation between logic and mathematics stimulated new developments in logic during the late nineteenth and early twentieth centuries. Logic moved out of its time-honored context — ordinary language — and into the rigorous world of quasi-mathematical relationships.

In the atmosphere of exhilaration about the new logic that grew out of Frege's work, a new school of thought arose — logical positivism (also called more descriptively "logical empiricism"), a philosophical program founded by the Vienna Circle in 1928. Like Aristotle before them, the members of the Vienna Circle saw in the newfound rigor, formality, and power of the new logic of their day the ideal tool with which to give an account of scientific knowledge. Like Aristotle, the logical positivists hoped to connect science with the achievements of contemporary logic, and thus give the natural sciences a firm philosophical foundation. They were less interested in the changeable aspects of science (such as its content, or the displacement of one theory by another) than in its generalizable and formalizable features.[6] The logical positivists also had a corollary goal — and here they were very unlike Aristotle: they wanted to eliminate all metaphysical statements from science and philosophy. They attached the label "metaphysical" to all propositions that made claims about existence without "demonstrable" empirical grounds for doing so.[7]

A profound concern with language thus pervades the positivist program, both in its constructive aspects (the attempt to strengthen the link between science and the rigorous formal framework of mathematical logic) and in its critical aspects (the attempt to banish meaningless language from science and philosophy).

The following account selects from the logical positivists' program a few elements that illustrate both their view of language and the role they assigned to linguistic considerations when thinking about science. These elements are: the distinction between theoretical terms and observational terms; the principle of verification (or later, confirmation); the distinction between sense and nonsense; and the unity of science.

Theoretical and Observation Terms

The language of science (by which the logical positivists usually meant the *physical* sciences) comprises terms of two distinct kinds: theoretical terms and observation terms.[8] Observation terms refer to objects in the world, to the data of sensation and experience that provide the foundation for genuine knowledge. By contrast, theoretical terms on their own tell us nothing about the world, only about connections and meanings. They function like definitions. Newtonian mechanics, for example, includes theoretical terms such as "acceleration," "force," and "mass." Symbols for these terms appear in various formal relationships, such as $F = ma$ (Newton's second law), from which yet other formal relationships may be derived using the laws of mathematics and/or logic. These theoretical terms, symbols, and relationships are abstract. They can be manipulated in equations in blissful ignorance of any connection to the "real" world of experience, just as we can divide both sides of the expression $2x = y$ by 4 without knowing what x and y stand for. Not until the term "force" is connected to "observation terms" (such as the fact that the needle on my bathroom scales points to 172 when I stand on it) does F have empirical significance — significance about the world of experience (i.e., my weight).

A theory, then, uses formal language to express a set of relationships between theoretical terms. Since the terms in it initially have no observational content, such a theory is sometimes called an "uninterpreted calculus." To tell us anything at all about the world, the theoretical terms must be interpreted — connected to "observation terms," which in turn signify objects and phenomena in the world of experience.

This view of science assumes that there are several kinds of language. First, there is an unproblematic observation language that allows us to talk about sense experience in a neutral manner, untainted by theory. Second, there is a theoretical language that is formal and abstract, with high standards of truth. Finally, there must be "correspondence rules" that specify the connection between observation terms (172 on the scales) with the theoretical terms (F in $F = ma$).

In this account, the correspondence rules play a crucial role. They allow the theoretical terms, which otherwise are disembodied abstractions, to soak up empirical content. Hence, they give theories a chance to be more than just elaborate constructions in our minds or on paper. Thanks to these rules, theories may in fact tell us something about the world. Conversely, the correspondence rules allow the rigor of formal relationships in the theory to trickle down to the claims of the world of experience. The great hope here is that the formal rules about truth and falsity, which hold in the theory, will continue to hold when the correspondence rules link the theoretical terms to the world. Once the theoretical and observation terms are connected, it becomes possible to use deduction to draw conclusions from the theory, and yet have those conclusions signify something about the world of experience. By linking the theoretical terms to the observation terms, the correspondence rules in principle make possible a science that is at once logical (and hence truth preserving) and empirical (and hence true to the world).

Verification

How can one know whether a theory is "true-to-the-world"? If the correspondence rules are working properly, in principle one should be able to *test* a theory — to find out whether the formal relationships in it are verified (confirmed) or falsified (refuted) in the world of experience. If the theory is verified or confirmed, we at last will possess some of the true knowledge of nature that science (understood as a search for truth) set out to find.

Not all theories will be verified. Some theories will be falsified or disconfirmed. They must either be modified or thrown out. Other theories can never be subject to verification, and can therefore never be scientific. For example, they may contain metaphysical terms, which (according to the logical positivist account) by definition bear no relation to the world of experience, and are therefore meaningless. For such terms, no correspondence rules will ever be found.

For the early logical positivists, then, verification was a necessary criterion for science. Thanks to verification, one could (a) know that a scientific theory was true, and (b) distinguish true scientific theories from false or unverifiable theories. The point deserves emphasis because, even though the requirement of verifiability at first glance may seem self-evident, verification in fact presents serious problems.

Demarcation Between Sense and Nonsense

For the logical positivist, verification is a tool that distinguishes statements that make sense (whether they be true or false) from those that are nonsensical (meaningless). Statements with empirical content ("this apple is blue") are in principle verifiable; they have a determinate meaning and therefore make sense (whether or not they are true or false). Metaphysical statements, which are devoid of empirical content, are in principle unverifiable (e.g., the soul is immortal). They are therefore meaningless and nonsensical. Propositions that make sense, on the other hand, may lay some claim to constituting knowledge. For the logical positivists, the distinction between sense and nonsense is closely associated with the distinction between science and nonscience.[9] This account presupposes a very formal picture of language, one in which poetic or metaphorical language can find little room.

The Unity of Science

If verification can indeed identify theories that are true (scientific) and distinguish them from those that are false or nonsensical, then as more true theories emerge, in principle we can show the latter are logically connected with one another. It should then be possible eventually to construct a single unified account of the world that brings together all the verified (and hence true) theories. All of the latter, thanks to the correspondence rules, can be reduced to or translated into physical concepts, which in turn rest firmly on experience. In other words, there is fundamentally only one kind of knowledge — knowledge that passes the logical positivist test — and science is it.[10]

The logical positivist account of scientific knowledge includes several seductive elements. It strives for truth, objectivity, and clarity, and who can oppose that? It tries to join the rigor of formal languages with the nonformal observation language that provides access to the world of experience into a unified whole that not only deals with the world, but also seeks to be universally true. In verifiability, logical positivism claims to have found a "litmus test" that separates the sheep of scientific knowledge from the goats of metaphysics. And it holds out the hope that all the sheep belong to the one and only true flock — the unity of science.

Logical positivism was a normative philosophy of science. It isolated criteria for scientific knowledge, and did not hesitate to use them — e.g., to label as unscientific whatever did not meet those criteria. It was also a static philosophy of science: today, its formal methods and tests seem most convincing when applied to established science with an analyzable structure, not to science on the cutting edge or science in the making.

So long as philosophers focused primarily on the structure of scientific theories, on the connections between scientific terms and the world — in other words, so long as science was analyzed from "still" photographs, parts of which were occasionally retouched — many branches of science plausibly could be seen as quasi-axiomatic systems with a deductive structure. In such a context, formal logic held the promise of clarifying our understanding of science.

Some people continue to find this approach enticing. But philosophers of science who are historically minded and/or intrigued by science as a changing phenomenon find the positivist perspective very problematic, for it contributes little to the question, "How does science change or grow?" Techniques suited to understanding a photograph cannot fully do justice to a movie.

Criticisms of Logical Positivism: Popper and Wittgenstein

During the last two generations in particular, historically oriented philosophers of science have taken a critical look at logical positivist tenets and assumptions. Their work owes much to two other Viennese philosophers, who each spent the latter part of their careers in England,

Ludwig Wittgenstein at the University of Cambridge, and Karl Popper at the London School of Economics. In some accounts, both thinkers are sometimes associated with the Vienna Circle. In the case of Wittgenstein, this association is apt, for his early work both antedated the logical positivist program, and helped move it forward. In Popper's case, however, the connection is more misleading. In the end, however, both thinkers undermined key elements of logical positivism, albeit from very different philosophical positions. For ease of presentation, we discuss Popper's work first even though Wittgenstein was his elder.

Karl Popper

For the logical positivists, part of the rationale for distinguishing observation terms from theoretical terms came from their empiricism. Empiricists believe that knowledge is obtained by induction from experience — by collecting empirical evidence into generalized laws. The terms used to describe experience, therefore, have a special status: they provide the foundations for knowledge, the context for the verification of theories.

In his influential *The Logic of Scientific Discovery*, Popper submitted these assumptions and the positivist requirement of verification to critical scrutiny.[11] Popper recognized the force of the long-familiar skeptical view that no amount of empirical evidence can ever fully justify an inductive generalization; the latter, therefore, cannot be completely verified by checking its consistency with the real world. For him, such an "ideal" model of scientific discovery, which relies upon induction and then confirms its generalizations with some procedure of verification, not only fails to reflect actual scientific practice, but is logically flawed.

According to Popper, knowledge accumulates (and hence science grows) only by first making bold hypotheses; the consequences (or predictions) of these hypotheses are then put to the test. Although it may be tempting to call "true" any hypothesis that passes the test of verification, this would be a mistake. We can never know with certainty that an hypothesis is true; we can only know for sure that it is false, when a prediction derived from the hypothesis is *not* confirmed by experience.[12] But it is not enough to propose an hypothesis; in addition, one should try to falsify it by discovering appropriate counterexamples. The falsified hypothesis must then be replaced with a broader, more comprehensive one that not only takes the counterexample into account but also makes additional testable claims. Attempts should then be made to falsify the new hypothesis, and so on. In Popper's view, the ability to formulate hypotheses and also the opportunity to criticize them are central to the development of science. Paradoxically, knowledge grows not by observation and verification, but by "conjectures and refutations," as Popper entitled another of his books.

Popper also believed that language helped make criticism and hypothesis formation possible. In the case of criticism, language is the means through which information is made public. Only when information becomes public can it be open to critical scrutiny. Without language our hypotheses would remain private, and therefore could never be corrected or replaced. With the means of widespread publication, furthermore, scientific hypotheses can be spread to the widest possible critical audience. The larger the audience, according to Popper, the greater the possibility that someone will falsify a theory. Critical refutation leads to the growth of knowledge, hence the wider the publication of hypotheses, the greater the potential growth of our store of scientific knowledge. In addition, language can also promote hypothesis formation by mediating the thought processes of imagination. One of the best ways to cultivate and stimulate the imagination, according to Popper, is story telling: "It is one of the novelties of human language that it encourages story telling, and thus creative imagination. Scientific discovery is akin to explanatory story telling, to myth making and to poetic imagination."[13] Thus elements that the logical positivists dismissed as metaphysical (or meaningless) may play a crucial role in hypothesis formation. For Popper, then, the distinction between science and nonscience is not identical to the distinction between sense and nonsense (metaphysics). Rather a statement is unscientific if it is not falsifiable (that is, if there is no way of specifying how it might be tested).

Although myth making is important for scientific discovery, myths also play a role in forming ideologies. In intellectual history, one encounters not only scientific revolutions but also major ideological shifts. Popper recognized that sometimes there may be a relationship between ideological and scientific revolutions, although the aim of each might be different. For example, "the Copernican and Darwinian revolutions were *ideological* in so far as they both changed man's view of his place in the Universe. They clearly were *scientific* in so far as each of them overthrew a dominant scientific theory: a dominant astronomical theory and a dominant biological theory."[14]

Another difference between Popper and the logical positivists, then, lies in Popper's reluctance to dismiss the importance of ideology in creating conjectures. Popper believes that some scientific revolutions bear no relationship to changes in ideology (e.g., the work in electromagnetism by Faraday and Maxwell, and the establishment of quantum mechanics by Heisenberg and Born).[15] What is less clear is whether changes in the conceptual frameworks of science have deeper ideological roots than Popper's work has recognized. Indeed the demarcation between ideology and science may not be as clear as Popper would wish.

In spite of his differences with the logical positivists, Popper shares with them one important belief, namely that science is fundamentally one. If science grows by conjectures and refutations, it is because each new theory or conjecture must be more comprehensive and richer than the one it replaces (e.g., as when Newtonian mechanics was replaced by relativistic mechanics, of which the former is a special case).

Popper's criticisms did much to help undermine the assumptions of the logical positivists, but not primarily because he was interested in language. On the contrary, Popper has not disguised his irritation with philosophers who spend their time analyzing language rather than dealing with what he saw as the one truly important philosophical problem: "the problem of understanding the world—including ourselves, and our knowledge as part of the world."[16] One of his targets may have been his older Viennese contemporary, Ludwig Wittgenstein, who was profoundly interested in language.

Ludwig Wittgenstein

Of the many diverse critics of the logical positivist program, few have made a greater impact on the development of thought in the twentieth century than Ludwig Wittgenstein. In the early phase of his work represented in the *Tractatus Logico-Philosophicus* (1921), Wittgenstein in some ways appears to be a forerunner of the logical positivist position. For example, he attempted what may be construed as a demarcation criterion between sense and nonsense. In his preface to the *Tractatus*, he wrote: "The whole sense of the book might be summed up in the following words: What can be said at all can be said clearly, and what we cannot talk about we must pass over in silence."[17] According to the *Tractatus*, linguistic clarity results from a study of the logical form of propositions. Here Wittgenstein implies that for anything to count as a knowledge claim, it must be analyzable in terms of the logical system that was developed by Gottlob Frege and Bertrand Russell. Natural science, in turn, consists of the "totality of true propositions."[18] Hence, if natural science is to count as knowledge, it must also meet the demands imposed by the system of formal logic; if any statement does not meet these requirements, then it cannot be part of natural science. Unlike the positivists, however, Wittgenstein attached great importance to areas "whereof one could not speak," among which he included ethics and aesthetics. Indeed he even used the term "nonsense" (i.e., beyond language) in relation to some of his own propositions.[19]

Crucial to the program put forth in the *Tractatus* is a theory of meaning based upon the correspondence between a "picture" (*Bild*) and objects in the world.[20] Every true proposition forms a logical picture of the actual state of affairs expressed by the proposition. In other words, the proposition "Socrates is mortal" can be analyzed into the logical form, "There is an object named 'Socrates' and this object does not live forever." This logical form, if it is to be taken as true, must correspond to an actually existing situation in the world. Although Wittgenstein did not invoke the language of observational and theoretical terms here, he emphasized the role of correspondence between actually existing objects and their "pictures." What this relationship of correspondence really consists in was a problem that would concern Wittgenstein later in his life.

As he eventually acknowledged, one difficulty with this picture theory is that some symbolic behaviors (hand gestures, for example) are meaningful, yet they cannot be analyzed in terms of a logical form and its relationship to existing states of affairs. In the posthumously published *Philosophical Investigations* (1953), Wittgenstein advocated a position that could account for the apparent meaningfulness of both symbolic behaviors and linguistic expressions. Here he moved away from a theory of meaning based on the correspondence between propositions and the world; instead he attempted to explain how we come to understand the meaning of expressions. How do we comprehend meaning? According to the *Philosophical Investigations*, we understand the meaning of an expression by following a rule. For example, we understand the meaning of "prime number" by following the rule "a prime number is any number that is divisible only by itself and 1." Similar rules can be established for expressions in ordinary language.[21]

Although Wittgenstein is mainly interested in how "understanding" relates to "meaning," there is here an implicit theory of meaning that has consequences for our picture of science. Rules, or conventions, can bestow meaning on expressions. Indeed we cannot, according to Wittgenstein, talk intelligently about meaning without recourse to a consideration of rules. Meanings are not some kind of mysterious things in our minds; rather, they are to be found in the linguistic conventions that we all follow.

The importance of the position that Wittgenstein advocated in the *Philosophical Investigations* has several ramifications for logical positivism. First, observation language cannot be clearly separated from theoretical language.[22] All terms in the language are governed by linguistic rules; hence no expression is ever completely "uninterpreted." The meanings of "force," "mass," and "172" when I step on the bathroom scales make sense only within a given context.

Second, the notion of "meaning" as use, or "rule following," also has important implications for the requirement of verifiability. By what method can I know that I am applying the formula $F = ma$ correctly? Verification, in the logical positivist's sense, cannot be of much help here, since I may be mistaken about the rules that define the variables in the world of experience. But if the meanings of these terms are established by their context and their use, they no longer provide an infallible and invariant standard for testing scientific laws.

Finally, some of Wittgenstein's followers believe that he brought about a major change in twentieth-century thought by shifting the agenda of philosophy in the *Philosophical Investigations* away from traditional questions of ontology and metaphysics to inquiries concerning the *way* we think about understanding and meaning.[23] In philosophy (and philosophy of science), this change appears as a shift away from establishing the truth-content of propositions and toward a consideration of the method by which we define the very criteria for using the term "true." One radical extension of Wittgenstein's views has led to a form of relativism, in which the task of epistemology and philosophy of science is only to specify the conditions under which scientific terms are defined. From this perspective, since the linguistic rules that we follow are context dependent, and since contexts can change over time, no method will guarantee that scientific expressions themselves remain invariant.

Logical positivism had focused predominantly on the structure of fully developed scientific theories and on the logical connections between scientific concepts. The travail involved in developing these theories was not a concern central to understanding the nature of science. The positivists seemed more interested in trying to understand science as a generic mature adult, and less interested in either individual differences or development (conception, pregnancy, birth, childhood, adolescence, etc.). In their different ways, both Popper and Wittgenstein criticized logical positivism for this "ideal" way of viewing science, knowledge claims, and language. For Popper, the growth of science had to be tied to its practice in history, to an ongoing succession of conjectures and refutations. For the Wittgenstein of the *Philosophical Investigations*, meanings are established through rule following and context, and not through metaphysical speculation. In recent years the philosophy of science has pursued these new directions by turning away from a strictly formalist approach and by paying more and more attention to both history and context. To illustrate the shift, we turn to Thomas Kuhn and Paul Feyerabend.

Two Philosophers of Scientific Practice: Kuhn and Feyerabend

The interest in scientific practice in more recent philosophy of science reflects the conviction that any decent account of science ought to pay attention not only to the final product, but also to the process and the practice of science. To learn about scientific practice, one can study the way scientists behave today, or turn to the history of past scientific practice. Indeed one would be well advised to do both, lest one unwittingly assume that scientific practice has not changed over time.

Although they are by no means alone in doing so, Kuhn and Feyerabend have used the history of science to focus attention on issues of scientific practice and have also managed to change the way philosophers think about science. As we shall see, linguistic concerns are tightly interwoven into their work.

Thomas Kuhn

Friends and foes alike agree that Kuhn's *The Structure of Scientific Revolutions* (1962) marks a turning point in the philosophy of science of the late twentieth century, certainly by virtue of the questions it raises, if not the answers it provides. The work illustrates an approach to scientific discourse that stands on its head the outlook of logical positivism — and even that of Popper.[24] Particularly striking is the frequency with which Kuhn appeals to scientific practice, to historical illustrations of scientific change, and to the behavior of scientific communities to challenge positivist assumptions.

Yet Kuhn is far from rejecting all positivist emphases. Formalisms continue to play an important role in his picture of science, and he readily concedes the importance of understanding their connection with the world of experience. But he is convinced that the positivist assumptions about language in particular misrepresent the various ways that the sciences develop and that scientists work.

Attention to language and scientific discourse enter Kuhn's argument at several points. On the negative side, linguistic concerns pervade his criticism of the logical positivist program; on the positive side, they permeate his analysis of scientific change and the behavior of the scientific community. Finally, Kuhn uses linguistic analogies at several crucial junctures, most notably in his account of scientific practice.[25]

The negative points first. Like Popper and other critics of the logical positivist schema, Kuhn doubts that one can draw a sharp distinction between observation language and theoretical language. What we see are not bunches of sense data that cohere into unambiguous facts, which an observation language then reports neutrally and univocally. Rather, an act such as seeing, for example, is a complex whole, in which sense data are intertwined with theoretical presuppositions. The point may be illustrated in simplistic fashion by Jastrow's duck-rabbit, popularized by Wittgenstein's *Philosophical Investigations*. Since the same sense datum (the line drawing) may be "seen" now as a duck, now as a rabbit, seeing clearly involves more than simply bare sense data.[26] As N. R. Hanson aptly put the matter, "there is more to seeing than meets the eyeball."[27] If observation language is tainted by theoretical elements, how can it be the neutral ground on which to base "objective" comparisons betwen theories?

Conversely, the theoretical language of science is *not* devoid of empirical content until the former gets the latter "from the bottom up" (through connections to an observation language via correspondence rules). Kuhn argues that, contrary to the logical positivists, some empirical content enters the symbolic generalizations of science prior to any direct empirical testing.[28] Although the logical positivists think of scientific formalisms as "uninterpreted calculi" without empirical content, this is not the case in practice. In fact, the process of deciding which formalisms are likely to apply to a specific problem — an important acquired skill — involves a sifting and winnowing that draws upon empirical considerations, and yet occurs before any experimental testing. Thus it is not the general formalism $F = ma$ that appears in problems involving free fall, the simple pendulum, and so on; these are treated by different, more specific formalisms, at an intermediate level of generality and closely connected with an empirical situation.

Not surprisingly, then, Kuhn sees problems with the correspondence rules that allegedly link the distinct theoretical and empirical realms in the positivist account of science. For one thing, scientists themselves are often hard-pressed to identify such rules, and seem unaware of their importance. Moreover, correspondence rules rest upon a view of language that thrives on univocal one-to-one correspondences between concepts and objects. (According to the later Wittgenstein, for example, language does not function in this fashion.) Kuhn concedes that philosophers who examine scientific practice may well be able to *construct* such correspondence rules (which implies that they do not exist ready-made), but at the risk of obscuring and distorting significant features of scientific activity.

What are these features? Popper had presented science as a kind of permanent revolution, constantly geared to the falsification of existing dogma and the production of new, improved (i.e., more encompassing) conjectures. In contrast, Kuhn argues that the day-to-day science that accounts for the bulk of scientific activity resembles puzzle solving much more than revolution. "Normal science," as Kuhn dubbed it, consists of attempts by scientists to solve new problems by drawing upon established patterns and procedures (exemplars or "paradigms") that have proven successful in the past. Far from being revolutionary, then, normal science thrives by adhering to a received orthodoxy, which forms the basis for both graduate teaching and research in a given field.[29]

During the course of normal research, however, one puzzle may prove impossible to solve in accordance with the established procedures dictated by the paradigm. Although initially only a minor irritant, this recalcitrant "anomaly" may soon be joined by other anomalies, which become a thorn in the flesh of the entire field and generate a state of crisis. Science now enters a revolutionary phase. To make sense of the anomaly, some scientists may suggest radical solutions that are logically incompatible with the accepted paradigm, and therefore imply a rejection of it. Whereas such proposals would not get very far during normal scientific activity, during the state of crisis they are taken more seriously. Eventually an influential segment of the field may agree that one of the new proposals has succeeded in solving not only the problem that precipitated the crisis, but also much more. Defenders of the old paradigm and proponents of the new solution argue with each other for a while, and try to convince each other that they are right. Some change their minds; others never do. Vocal support for the old paradigm fades as the new solution becomes enshrined as the new paradigm.

The revolutionary phase has ended, and normal scientific practice resumes, now based upon the new paradigm. Eventually new textbooks appear, which usually downplay the profound disjunction between the old and new paradigms, emphasizing instead the continuities between them as milestones in the cumulative progress of science. Graduate students are trained to think and solve problems in terms of the new exemplar, which now raises new sets of questions to be answered in accordance with the new prescriptions.[30] Normal science, then, typically represents the ordinary state of scientific activity in a given field; revolutionary science is less frequent. In brief, Kuhn sees "scientific development as a succession of tradition-bound periods punctuated by non-cumulative breaks."[31]

The controversial term "paradigm" plays a pivotal role in Kuhn's scheme, since it both characterizes normal science and is the linchpin of scientific revolutions. First, according to Kuhn, the concept of a paradigm both replaces and improves upon several elements of the positivist account. Second, and most specifically, this usage of the term suggests views of language that deserve our attention.

In his *Structure*, Kuhn used the term "paradigm" in many different ways, which some analytically oriented philosophers found confusing. In response to criticisms, he later distilled these various meanings into two primary ones.[32] The more specific sense of paradigm is that of "exemplar" or "shared examples of successful practice." This is the sense that was used above, for the sake of clarity, to summarize Kuhn's scheme.[33] The more comprehensive sense of paradigm Kuhn has renamed "disciplinary matrix," by which he means the body of elements to which most practitioners of a specific scientific discipline are committed. This general sense includes exemplars as only one of its elements; other elements mentioned by Kuhn are models, values, and symbolic generalizations.[34] This sense is much more global, more akin to the notion of a worldview.

Kuhn's analogy is rooted in grammar. For example, to conjugate a regular verb with a root ending in −a, students of Spanish or Latin memorize the conjugation of one verb (*amo, amas*, etc.). This verb becomes a paradigm, a pattern that allows the student successfully to conjugate other verbs ending in −a by imitation, without relying upon a long list of rules. Like its grammatical counterpart, the scientific "paradigm" or exemplar not only provides a pattern that has successfully solved one problem, but it also helps practitioners identify new problems, which they try to solve in conformity with the paradigm.

The paradigm also does more than this. Once established, it becomes part of the common heritage that practitioners of a specific discipline or subdiscipline share — the concepts, theories, models, instruments, and methods to which they are committed, and which distinguish them as a group from other groups. The paradigm as exemplar is a leading element, but only one of the elements, that identifies practitioners as members of a specific scientific discipline. Taken together, all of these elements constitute the more general sense of "paradigm" as "disciplinary matrix."

From the point of view of discourse and language, several elements of Kuhn's scheme stand out. The metaphor of paradigm is of course linguistic. More importantly, Kuhn's use of the term has drawn attention to scientific pedagogy, particularly to the role of the textbook in science — a relatively neglected aspect of scientific language. The textbook embodies the current scientific orthodoxy in a form that will efficiently pass on to students the traditions and values of the scientific community. For in Kuhn's scheme, the sciences are traditions. They are part of the historical process, which is why they must be understood historically, and not merely logically. This point was largely irrelevant to the schemes that focused on formal languages as the key to an atemporal scientific truth. Notwithstanding the formalisms they often contain, textbooks are far from being neutral channels of knowledge. Whether self-consciously or not, they communicate specific values and adopt a particular point of view on the history of science — a point of view suited to the purposes of scientific education rather than historical understanding. In particular, textbooks often transform the meandering goatpaths of history into rectilinear highways, and erect smooth bridges to skim over the deep fault lines of revolutionary paradigm shifts.

In spite of its flaws from a historical point of view, the textbook is a successful pedagogical tool. In particular it "aim[s] to communicate the vocabulary and syntax of a contemporary scientific language."[35] It thus plays a crucial role in shaping the thinking of new students and passing on to them the paradigm qua disciplinary matrix. Indeed the latter functions very much like a language, for it outlines the boundaries of a community of discourse and outlook. The disciplinary matrix provides the framework in terms of which scientists in a given field speak about their field, think about their field, and see the world. The possession of this common language or dialect marks off — in part — one group of specialists from another, which by comparison seems to "talk funny." This is the reason why Kuhn can speak of the crisis phase of his scheme (when the old paradigm comes under fire) as a "communication breakdown."[36] During a crisis, adherents of different paradigms no longer share a common language with respect to the specific scientific problems that matter most to them, even though they belong to the same field.

Formal languages seem particularly inadequate to the task of accounting for circumstances such as these. Even though formalisms may conveniently summarize the results of an established science, they do little to illuminate the process by which a new paradigm or theory comes to replace an old one. Far from being compelled by the power of proof (which is the forte of formal languages), changes in allegiance are, according to Kuhn, more akin to a religious conversion or a *Gestalt* switch. He repeatedly emphasizes that there is no algorithm (read: algorism)[37] that leads ineluctably to a given position, or settles disputes quickly to the satisfaction of all. Indeed disagreements among reasonable people remain long after the controversy seems to have ended. Far from being the result of a formal process, the settling of arguments in science reveals a much more open-ended approach to language and a much more complicated process of give-and-take than the one suggested by the early logical positivist account.

As has been hinted above, Kuhn's understanding of science gives a prominent role to scientific communities, with which the notion of "paradigm" is tightly intertwined. It is the scientific community that takes a particular exemplar or paradigm as a prominent part of its language. But it is also the scientific community that adjudicates changes in its language. Instead of being static and carefully defined like a formal language, the language of the scientific community is in flux. Sometimes new terms are invented; sometimes old terms take on new meanings. For example the term "mass" was assigned to what Newton called "quantity of matter." In the equations of Newtonian mechanics, "mass" represents a constant of proportionality or a conserved quantity; later, in relativistic mechanics, however, "mass" became a variable and a quantity convertible with energy. Any logical inference or mathematical derivation that would start from Newtonian mass and reach a result about relativistic mass would be, strictly speaking, fallacious (even though some textbooks try to do so).[38] But since "speaking strictly" is precisely what formal languages are all about, logical inferences fail in cases such as this.

It is in part because of logical chasms of this sort between old and new paradigms that Kuhn has called such paradigms "incommensurable." By this, he does *not* mean that the latter cannot be compared by any means whatever. Rather he means that adherents of the two paradigms "cannot ... resort to a neutral language which both use in the same way and which is adequate to the statement of both their theories."[39] The debate takes place between people who, entrenched in their own worldviews, must translate as best they can the worldview of the opponent into their *own* language. They must do so because there is no neutral language into which both theories can be translated. Whatever else this process may be, it is certainly not formal. To understand how it works, therefore, one must examine the "techniques of persuasion" that lead to such nonlogical shifts.[40] When formal logic fails and persuasion is required, the skills and techniques of rhetoric suddenly begin to loom large.

Kuhn's interest in nonformal approaches to language, his emphasis on the importance of scientific practice centered on shared exemplars rather than formal rules, his identification of the scientific community as the bearer of a tradition couched in a particular language and passed on in its textbooks, his suggestion that techniques of persuasion take precedence over logical compulsion in attempts to settle scientific arguments—all of these themes suggested to Kuhn's critics that he was portraying science and scientific change as irrational, subjective, relativist, and ruled by "mob psychology." Behind these charges, which Kuhn adamantly denies,[41] often lies the assumption that if *formal* criteria cannot account for theory choice, the latter must be irrational. Again this is an inference that Kuhn rejects: even in the absence of a shared neutral language that would make formal comparisons possible, he argues, one can still provide good reasons for selecting one theory over another. But to understand those reasons, it will be necessary to examine "to a previously unprecedented depth, the manner in which language fits the world, asking how terms attach to nature, how those attachments are learned, and how they are transmitted from one generation to another by members of a language community."[42]

Linguistic concerns thus underlie key aspects of Kuhn's thought: his criticism of his predecessors, his understanding of scientific change, his analysis of scientific education, his insights into the social dimensions of the scientific enterprise, and his directions for future research.[43]

Kuhn's emphasis on the role that techniques of persuasion play within the scientific community has helped lay the foundation for new work in the philosophy and sociology of science in the last twenty years. As he remarked in the final words of the famous Postscript (1969) to the *Structure of Scientific Revolutions*: "Scientific knowledge, like language, is intrinsically the common property of a group or else nothing at all. To understand it we shall need to know the special characteristics of the groups that create and use it."[44] These are suggestive words, however leery Kuhn himself may be of the direction in which they have been pushed.

Paul Feyerabend

Surveys of recent philosophy of science often mention Feyerabend's name in the same breath as Kuhn's. Indeed both men (sometime colleagues in the Philosophy Department at Berkeley) criticize the logical positivist program on similar grounds. When the common foe is removed, however, their points of view differ in interesting ways.

Whereas Kuhn started out as a theoretical physicist who turned into a historian of science, Feyerabend is a philosopher of science who has wandered from technical issues in the philosophy of quantum mechanics to broader questions about the position of power that science now occupies in modern society.

Feyerabend's most famous work, *Against Method: An Outline of an Anarchistic Theory of Knowledge*, is an unconventional book from its title page (which includes a footnote) to its index (there is an entry for "wicked remarks"). Using argumentation, harangue, invective, and humor, the book seeks to persuade the reader that, contrary to widespread opinion, science does not possess a foolproof method that gives it a cognitive edge over other kinds of inquiry. There is no single scientific method of a logicodeductive sort. Indeed the only methodological prescription that scientific practice does not violate at every turn is "anything goes."[45]

If this is so, how have people come to believe that science possesses a distinctive and powerful method? Feyerabend points to a strong element of rhetoric in the scientific argumentation that seeks to defend new positions. His favorite case study is of Galileo. When Galileo's arguments are examined according to strict logical criteria, the arguments are not compelling: they are counterinductive (that is, "inconsistent with well-established hypotheses and/or well-established facts"[46]), based upon incomplete evidence, and so on. According to Feyerabend, Galileo's arguments succeeded not because they were logically compelling, or because he had a corner on a unique method, but because he was a superb propagandist and rhetorician.[47]

For Feyerabend, the axiomatic, logicodeductive approach to science misses the boat on several counts. First, for him as for Kuhn, it distorts the history of science and contemporary scientific practice: scientists do not in fact make their cases using flawless logic, nor do they convince their peers on such grounds. Second, the decision to see science in logicodeductive terms singles out one system of logic from the several available and gratuitously calls it normative. Third, to make science amenable to treatment by this one preferred system, the logicodeductive approach tries to suppress from its account the very features of science that are responsible for its progress, such as the influence of the "muddleheaded" Pythagoreanism of Philolaus on Copernicus.[48]

In short, the treatment of science by the canons of formal logic yields a sanitized and idealized picture of science that bears some resemblance to science, to be sure, but not enough to understand how it is practiced. In Feyerabend's own analogy, one cannot hope to understand how a real automobile operates by first building a little toy automobile and then studying it carefully.[49]

Feyerabend suggests that to understand science, one first must become an anthropologist of sorts: "the anthropological method is the correct method for studying the structure of science"[50] — an intriguing endorsement in a book entitled *Against Method*. Scientists constitute a set of tribes with peculiar worldviews; to find out what they think, one must live with them, watch them, listen to them, examine both what they say and what they do. Without having at hand enough anthropological evidence for the behavior of scientists and especially their ways of thinking, it is pointless to attempt a "rational reconstruction" of science.

Indeed Feyerabend is fond of chiding most philosophers of science for their lack of firsthand experience of science.[51] Any self-respecting anthropologist would carry out field work before making pronouncements. Yet most philosophers of science would not think of doing so: as scientific rationalists, most believe that logical tools suffice to understand what science is all about.[52]

Feyerabend clearly considers pragmatic considerations to be of preeminent interest here: the subject of the investigation is science as it is practiced — not science as it ought to be, or science as it might appear in a completely axiomatized form, or science reduced to "minipractice." Significantly Feyerabend's advocacy of greater attention to scientific practice is intimately connected with his attack on the preferred status that philosophers of science bestow upon the axiomatic, logicodeductive approach. Indeed both views go back to Feyerabend's assumptions about language. The logician's constant demand for "clarification" (read: tailoring to fit logical criteria) stifles scientific discovery. Lack of clarity is to be expected when one enters new territory:

> Just as a child who starts using words without yet understanding them, who adds more and more uncomprehended linguistic fragments to his playful activity, discovers the sense-giving principle only *after* he has been active in this way for a long time — the activity being a necessary presupposition of the final blossoming forth of sense — in the very same way the inventor of a new world view (and the philosopher of science who tries to understand his procedure) must be able to talk nonsense until the amount of nonsense created by him and his friends is big enough to give sense to all its parts.[53]

Indeed, on Feyerabend's view, the historical emergence of formal logic depended on the prior existence of a body of argumentative practice that could serve as grist for its mill.[54] In brief: let practice flourish, and sense will eventually emerge.

Not surprisingly, this analysis of the problem of scientific method is of more than academic interest; Feyerabend sees in it practical, indeed political, consequences. Science has achieved unprecedented status in modern society. It has become an authority. It controls vast amounts of public funds. It tells people what they may or may not believe or investigate. Science has achieved this imperious and imperial position thanks to widespread belief in the special virtues of its unique methodological clothes. But, Feyerabend argues, there are no such clothes; the naked emperor looks rather a lot like everyone else.

Science, then, should not receive special financial treatment or become enshrined as the new dogmatism. It should have to fight in the political and educational arena, just like other disciplines. We have now come full circle: for the political arena is par excellence the domain of rhetoric. Let arguments be put forward, and maybe accepted — but not before they have been scrutinized, analyzed, and rebutted.[55]

Whereas the critical aspects of Feyerabend's arguments share strong similarities with those of Kuhn, his claims involve a normative aspect that is more ambiguous in Kuhn. The norms, however, are suggested by Feyerabend's radically democratic political philosophy. Science *should not* be receiving the preferential treatment usually accorded to it; it should not be exempted from scrutiny by the most vociferous critics (as it was until a generation ago); it should be more pluralistic, and less dogmatic.

Here an interesting difference between Kuhn and Feyerabend appears. Like Popper, Feyerabend does not like normal science, because it is a tradition that has become enshrined as a dogmatism. It is very important to note that he does not oppose tradition for its own sake, however. On the contrary, the pluralism to which he aspires would be impossible without vigorous debates *between* traditions. Within science and without, he thus bemoans both the despotic rule of one tradition over all others, and the syncretistic assimilation or watering down of distinctive traditions (e.g., the vernacular mass of modern Catholicism as indistinguishable from mainstream Protestantism, etc.).

Views such as those of the later Wittgenstein, Kuhn, and Feyerabend have stimulated renewed interest in the sociology of science and, in some circles, a rapprochement between sociology of science and philosophy of science. Wittgenstein had stressed the importance of context for understanding meaning; social context in particular therefore seemed to call for attention. Kuhn's work pointed to scientific communities as crucial agents in both the preservation of scientific traditions and the eventual success of scientific revolutions. And Feyerabend's analyses and polemics drew attention to science as both a culture that demanded the attention of anthropologists, and a form of knowledge with political as well as social dimensions. These suggestions have helped to stimulate thinking in new directions that can only be discussed in summary fashion here, but they deserve to be mentioned briefly because issues of language and speech play a central role in their accounts of science.

Language, Social Interaction, and Science

The views of Ludwig Wittgenstein on establishing meaning through an appeal to rules have left a clear mark on recent sociology of science. David Bloor sees Wittgenstein's philosophy as a foundation for examining how scientific terms are established through social (hence also linguistic) convention. In Bloor's view, Wittgenstein "treated cognition as something that is social in its very essence. For him, our interactions with one another, and our participation in a social group, were no mere contingencies. They were not the accidental circumstances that attend our knowing; they were constitutive of all we can ever claim by way of knowledge."[56] In Bloor's appropriation of Wittgenstein, scientific expressions do not have a special, "privileged" status that gives them precedence over any other cognitive claims made by a given community. All such expressions have their particular rules, which govern their internal consistency and "appeal" to the community's members.

Wittgenstein's views motivate what Bloor calls the "Strong Program" in the sociology of science. The "Strong Program" asserts that the sociology of science should be:

1. Causal, that is, concerned with the conditions that bring about belief or states of knowledge.

2. Impartial with respect to truth and falsity, rationality or irrationality, success or failure. Both sides of these dichotomies will require explanation.

3. Symmetrical in its style of explanation. The same type of cause

should explain, say, true as well as false beliefs.

4. Reflexive. In principle its patterns of explanation would have to be applicable to sociology itself.[57]

The inclusion of the first tenet of this quartet is not controversial; virtually any social theory should include causal explanations. The problem, naturally, is how a proponent of the "Strong Program" can specify which specific conditions cause "belief or states of knowledge." Wittgenstein's views on cognition and language provide general support for this first tenet, that is, all beliefs are in some sense formed (or "caused") by following a rule, but a large number of case studies would be needed in order to demonstrate convincingly what this principle signifies in practice.

Tenets two and three are more controversial. The philosopher of science Larry Laudan, for example, has questioned whether impartiality and symmetry are necessary for a sociology of science. He notes that there is no strong reason why development of a true theory requires the same social explanation as that of a false one.[58] This need for "unity of explanation" is a descendent of the logical positivist mentality, and is indicative of the way recent social interpretations continue to be influenced by long-term intellectual traditions.

Finally, reflexivity remains a problem for any social explanation of science. A critic might ask: How is a social interpretation of the development of science exempt from also being explained in terms of social conditions? This last problem is the most difficult for the "Strong Program" to solve, and remains an open and lively area of research.[59]

Another recent approach to the philosophy and sociology of science agrees with Bloor that scientific terms can only be defined through social interactions. The followers of the so-called second phase of the "Strong Program," however, believe that anthropological and ethnographic methods of observation in the laboratory itself are the best guide for understanding the development of scientific language. According to Harry Collins, one of the primary proponents of this view, "it is actually possible to locate this process [of knowledge production] in scientific laboratories, in letters, conferences and conversations."[60]

In an essay on scientific experimentation, Collins at first seems to be concerned with the definition of scientific truth and the ways in which objects of scientific investigation can be "socially constructed" through language. In Collins's work, as in much philosophically interesting sociology of science, the emphasis has moved from ontological and epistemological questions to examinations of the process of disseminating scientific ideas. In this discussion he attempts to delineate two models (or "images") that explain the production, validation, and transfer of knowledge: the algorithmical and the enculturational.

In the algorithmical model, the production of knowledge is treated as a kind of computer program. If all the steps are followed in replicating another person's research, then the identical experimental results should be obtained. Once validated in this way, the experimental results (as knowledge) are "transferred" from one experimental group to the general scientific community. If similar results are not reported, then some information may have been left out in one or more steps of the experimental procedure. As Collins states, this search for missing information has led to the "discovery of competitive secretiveness, incompleteness of the journal article and so on."[61] Here it is not only the explicit features of language, but also what scientists do *not* discuss in print that becomes worthy of attention.

In contrast to the algorithmical model, the enculturational model denies that scientists can ever develop an effective general measure for deciding which steps or procedures are relevant for determining the outcome of a particular scientific investigation. As members of a learned culture, all we can determine are the relevance and the parameters of steps and procedures. The problem of transferring scientific knowledge then becomes one of a scientist learning about the culture (in terms of meanings and practices) through interactions with other scientists. Collins illustrates this point by noting that "it was found that a scientist who was to learn to build a successful copy of a laser nearly always needed to spend some time in close interaction with another who had built one."[62] This process is similar to what Wittgenstein maintained about the establishment of meaning though rules. It is by learning to follow the rules for building a laser that a scientist comes to understand what a laser is.

The use of the enculturational model can illuminate more than the manner in which an individual scientist learns to construct instruments. Experimental procedures, which help define what counts as valid scientific claims (and thus knowledge), are also determined by inter-actions in the scientific community. These interactions, which are manifested in the discourse of scientists in the laboratory, can be investigated by social scientists and linguists in much the same way that ethnographers have examined the discourse of non-Western peoples. Of paramount importance here is the view that the discourse of scientists no longer has a "privileged" cognitive status above that of any other social or cultural group.

Feyerabend had suggested that an anthropological approach to the activity of the tribe of scientists would help elucidate what science is about, and how its language functions. Although they seem unaware of Feyerabend's advocacy of such a project, Bruno Latour and Steve Woolgar have given full expression to the methods of ethnography in their book *Laboratory Life*, which takes anthropological procedures into the laboratories of the Salk Institute. The language of scientists in a working situation reveals their cognitive assumptions about "objectivity." The workers in these laboratories are, according to Latour and Woolgar, "constantly performing operations on statements; adding modalities, citing, enhancing, diminishing, borrowing, and proposing new combinations."[63] Scientific development, therefore, is not simply the accumulation of facts that consequently generate laws. It is a linguistically mediated process that involves the interactions of scientists. Contrary to what scientists themselves claim, they are not, in the view of Latour and Woolgar, mere discoverers of "facts," but rather "readers and writers in the business of being convinced and convincing others." Indeed Latour and Woolgar assert that they were "able to portray laboratory activity as the organisation of persuasion through literary inscription."[64] One result of this attempt at persuasion "is the occasional conviction of others that something is a fact."[65] Latour and Woolgar argue that this "something," which was originally a statement (that is, a linguistic artifact), becomes a fact when it used by others after having been wrenched out of its social context, stripped of its temporal qualities, and enshrined in a persuasive scientific article. In brief, then, a study of the laboratory reveals that facts too are socially constructed.

In contrast to the emphasis on informal communication in earlier sociology of science, in the work of Latour and Woolgar both laboratory life and the production of scientific knowledge revolve around formal documents. Laboratory apparatus and animals, conversations, discussions, arguments, annotations, the reading of journals, and the writing of articles — all of these tools and activities either use, or are geared to, the production of scientific articles.[66] It is the scientific article that mediates between the narrower social context of the laboratory and the larger community of scientists.

In other words, rhetoric, as "the organization of persuasion," plays a leading role in science, from the direction of scientific investigation in the context of a laboratory, through the construction of a scientific fact, to the persuasion of colleagues far and near.

Science, Ideology, and Discourse

The presence of rhetoric in science raises the question: what are the motivations behind these persuasions? For some philosophers and historians of science, the answer lies in investigating ideology.

The "social construction" of science through language is only one direction that some recent philosophers, historians, and sociologists of science have taken. These scholars are increasingly aware that scientists' use of language can help identify the ideologies and social relations that underlie science. Steven Shapin is one of the foremost researchers in this area. In an important article on the reception of phrenology in Edinburgh, for example, he has shown that the debate between phrenologists and antiphrenologists was framed in the language of "insiders" and "outsiders."[67] The phrenologists were attempting to "break into" the medical establishment controlled by the antiphrenologists; hence at one level the debate was over the "content" of medicine itself, but at another level the terms of the debate hid a deeper social conflict between two groups of medical practitioners.

Concerns about gender also loom large in studies that emphasize the role of language and ideology in science. In *Reflections on Gender and Science*, Evelyn Fox Keller has examined certain biases based upon gender that have arisen in seemingly "objective" scientific investigations. Behind her work lies an attempt to revise traditional epistemological questions. She argues that objectivity, which is the aim of scientific knowledge, has two possible orientations. The first, which she calls "static objectivity," begins with a strict "severance" of the knowing subject from the domain of objects in the world. This view is bound with an ideology of power and control. Since the followers of this view have "objectified" and alienated the world from possible care and concern, they are free to control it. In addition, the viewpoint of "static objectivity" does not allow an "openness" for the scientists' response to the natural world. This epistemological position, she argues, limits human experience.

"Dynamic objectivity," on the other hand, "aims at a form of knowledge that grants to the world around it independent integrity but does so in a way that remains cognizant of, indeed relies on, our connectivity with the world."[68] In "dynamic objectivity" the chasm between the knower and the known is bridged, much to the benefit of the knower. This relationship between subject and object is "not unlike empathy, a form of knowledge of other persons that draws explicitly on the commonality of feelings and experience in order to enrich one's understanding of another in his or her own right."[69]

The model of static objectivity, which stresses control and aggression, represents some of the tendencies commonly associated with masculinity. The central role of this model in the mentality of scientific investigation can be seen, according to Keller, in the language that scientists use. She observes that "problems, for many scientists, are to be 'attacked,' 'conquered,' or 'licked.' If subtler means fail, one resorts to 'brute force,' to the 'hammer and tongs' approach."[70] Scientists do not use nearly as often the language of "dynamic objectivity," which emphasizes new points of view and new possibilities for research. For Keller, the exclusion of "dynamic objectivity" (which is in some ways identified with popular conceptions of "femininity") from the scientific mentality may limit our knowledge of the world. Divesting science of the destructive metaphors of "static objectivity" might, she argues, open up new avenues of scientific investigation.

The insights of Keller with respect to the difference between a "masculine" and a "feminine" epistemology (which in turn could effect the process of scientific explanation) appear also in the writings of Sandra Harding. Harding has drawn upon the empirical work of developmental psychologist Carol Gilligan, whose *In a Different Voice* has supported a distinction between masculine and feminine views of moral rationality. One of the implications of Gilligan's work is to show that "a rational person, for women, values highly her abilities to empathize and 'connect' with particular others and wants to learn more complex and satisfying ways to take the role of the particular other in relationships."[71] Men, on the other hand, value autonomous agency and the ability of individuals (who are estranged from the social fabric) to make correct decisions.

The question, of course, is whether these ideals of moral rationality are translatable into the realm of scientific investigation. Harding suggests that they may have import for the problem raised by Kuhn and Feyerabend concerning the disjunction between rationalized logics of scientific justification and actual scientific practice. The actual practice of science, according to Harding, may be somewhat akin to the feminist conception of rationality, which attempts to adjudicate between competing views or frameworks. The feminist position, furthermore, sees much more complexity in the moral domain than the "autonomous" male perspective. It may be that the practice of science is more sensitive to principles of "relatedness" and "complexity" than the image of science put forward by those who have attempted to provide a structure for explaining why scientific changes occur. Harding's emphasis on the importance of feminist ideals of rationality suggests, moreover, a connection with contextual theories of meaning and the social dimension of scientific practice. "Relatedness" implies that individuals do not act or think in isolation; rather the group and social life must be recognized as having great importance. With Popper and advocates of the "Strong Program" in the sociology of science, the feminist critique of positivism agrees that scientists are not autonomous individuals who uncover simple truths. In the work of Keller and Harding, description and explanations of the world may be more complex than the positivists will allow.

Epilogue

Not all contemporary philosophers or historians of science are convinced that every aspect of logical positivism should be abandoned. Some philosophers of science continue to debate questions such as: is there some invariant structure of scientific explanation? under what conditions are general scientific laws confirmed or refuted? In short, scientific knowledge abstracted from the messiness of its historical context remains a focus of investigation that draws upon the tools of the formal languages.

For a growing number of scholars, however, the framework for understanding science has changed so much that formal techniques seem inadequate, if not altogether inappropriate. Having abandoned the image of science as a socially (and hence linguistically) neutral quest for truth, they tend to see science as a set of practices bound by their context. To this group, the tools of rhetorical analysis seem better suited to the task of understanding what scientific activity is, and how it has changed.

Notes

1. We wish to thank Jean Chambers, David Lindberg, and Margaret Schabas for helping us improve what we wanted to say.

2. Aristotle's *Prior Analytics* contains his formal logic; the *Posterior Analytics* his theory of science.

3. Aristotle, *Rhetoric*, Book I, ch. 2, 1355b25.

4. This highly schematized summary emphasizes general trends and distinctions. Among the interesting exceptions: Alcuin (eighth century) sees dialectic and rhetoric as species of the genus logic (Wilbur S. Howell, *Logic and Rhetoric in England, 1500–1700* [Princeton: Princeton Univ., 1956; New York: Russell and Russell, 1961], pp. 33–34), while there is also evidence for a view of rhetoric that focuses on explanation and teaching as distinct from persuasion (see Robert J. Connors, "Rhetoric of Explanation: Explanatory Rhetoric From Aristotle to 1850," *Written Communication*, 1 [1984], pp. 189–210).

5. For an excellent overview, see Jan Golinski, "Language, Discourse and Science," in R. C. Olby, G. N. Cantor, J. R. R. Christie and M. J. S. Hodge, eds., *Companion to the History of Modern Science* (London: Routledge, 1990), pp. 110–23.

6. See for example the opening paragraphs of Rudolph Carnap's preface to the first edition of his *Der logische Aufbau der Welt* (Berlin: Welt-Kreis Verlag, 1928); translated as *The Logical Structure of the World* (Berkeley: Univ. of California, 1967).

7. See Julius R. Weinberg, *An Examination of Logical Positivism* (Paterson, N. J.: Littlefield, Adams, 1960), ch. 6, pp. 175ff.

8. For the logical positivists, the distinction has its most proximate roots in the early Wittgenstein: logic is tautologous, and therefore tells us nothing about the world; see Weinberg, *An Examination of Logical Positivism*, p. 81; Ludwig Wittgenstein, *Tractatus Logico-Philosophicus*, trans. D. F. Pears and B. F. McGuinness (London: Routledge and Kegan Paul, 1961, 1974), 6.1, 6.11, 6.111 (p. 59).

9. It is important to bear in mind that the distinction between science and nonscience does not always map onto the distinction between sense and nonsense, even though the two are sometimes presented as equivalent. For Karl Popper, some of the hypotheses that qualify as nonsensical in logical positivist terms do indeed prove fruitful for scientific theorizing.

10. "There are not different sciences with fundamentally different methods or sources of knowledge, but only *one* science. All knowledge finds its place in this science and, indeed, is knowledge of basically the same kind; the appearance of fundamental differences between the sciences are the deceptive result of our using different sub-languages to express them." Rudolf Carnap, "The Old and the New Logic," in A. J. Ayer, ed., *Logical Positivism* (New York: Free Press, 1959), p. 144.

11. The German original, *Logik der Forschung*, appeared in 1934; the English translation first appeared in 1959.

12. Assume that *p* implies *q*. According to elementary logic, if we find that *q* is the case, we cannot claim that *p* is necessarily the case (for it might also be true that *k* implies *q*). We can only know for sure that if *q* is *not* the case, our initial hypothesis (*p* implies *q*) is false (i.e. if *not-q* is the case, then *not-p* is the case).

13. Karl Popper, "The Rationality of Scientific Revolution," in Ian Hacking, ed., *Scientific Revolutions* (Oxford: Oxford Univ., 1981), p. 87.

14. Ibid., p. 100.

15. Ibid., p. 101.

16. See the preface to the first English edition of *The Logic of Scientific Discovery* (London: Hutchinson, 1959), p. 15.

17. Ludwig Wittgenstein, *Tractatus Logico-Philosophicus*, trans. D. F. Pears and B. F. McGuinness (London: Routledge and Kegan Paul, 1961, 1974), p. 3.

18. Ibid., 4.11 (p. 25).

19. For example, *Tractatus* 6.522 (p. 73): "There are indeed things that cannot be put into words. They *make themselves manifest*. They are what is mystical." And also 6.54 (p. 74): "My propositions serve as elucidations in the following way: anyone who understands me eventually recognizes them as nonsensical, when he has used them — as steps to climb beyond them. (He must so to speak throw away the ladder after he has climbed up it.)"

20. For more on this, see Wittgenstein, *Tractatus* 2.1 ff.

21. Discussions of "rule following" and its relationship to meaning appear throughout the *Philosophical Investigations* (New York: Macmillan, 1953), but are especially prominent in sections 53–56 and 193–211.

22. Moritz Schlick was an especially strong advocate of this distinction; see for example his "The Foundation of Knowledge" (1934) (in A. J. Ayer, ed., *Logical Positivism*, pp. 209–27). Other members of the Vienna Circle, such as Otto Neurath, were more skeptical; see Neurath's "Protocol Sentences" (1932–33) (in A. J. Ayer, ed., *Logical Positivism*, pp. 199–208).

23. This view is implied in the work of Stephen Toulmin and Peter Winch.

24. Nevertheless the book continues to be published as a part of the "International Encyclopedia of Unified Science," of which Carnap was one of the editors.

25. In each of these cases Ludwig Wittgenstein's philosophy of language as presented in his *Philosophical Investigations* casts a long shadow over Kuhn's work.

26. Thomas Kuhn, *The Structure of Scientific Revolutions* rev. ed., (Chicago: Univ. of Chicago, 1970), p. 126; and "Second Thoughts on Paradigms" [1974], in Kuhn, *The Essential Tension: Selected Studies in Tradition and Change* (Chicago: Univ. of Chicago, 1977), pp. 293–319.

27. Norwood Russell Hanson, *Patterns of Discovery: An Inquiry Into the Conceptual Foundations of Science* (Cambridge: Cambridge Univ., 1958), p. 7.

28. Kuhn, "Second Thoughts on Paradigms," in *Essential Tension*, pp. 300–301.

29. For Popper's criticisms of this view, see his "Normal Science and Its Dangers," in Imre Lakatos and Alan Musgrave, eds., *Criticism and the Growth of Knowledge* (Cambridge: Cambridge Univ., 1970), pp. 51–58.

30. Kuhn, *Structure*, p. 137.

31. Ibid., p. 208.

32. The many senses of paradigm are enumerated in Margaret Masterman, "The Nature of a Paradigm," in Lakatos and Musgrave, eds., *Criticism and the Growth of Knowledge* (Cambridge: Cambridge Univ., 1970). Kuhn's clarifications appear in a Postcript to the revised edition of *Structure* (Chicago: Chicago Univ., 1970) and in his "Second Thoughts on Paradigms." Paul Feyerabend has come to Kuhn's defense on this point, arguing that the obscurity and opacity that some philosophers have seen in Kuhn's notion of paradigm reflects not the inadequacy of Kuhn's analysis, but an unreasonable demand for simpleminded clarity in a context that is very complex; Feyerabend, "More Clothes From the Emperor's Bargain Basement: A Review of Laudan's *Progress and Its Problems*," *British Journal for the Philosophy of Science*; also in Feyerabend, *Problems of Empiricism: Philosophical Papers*, vol. 2 (Cambridge: Cambridge Univ., 1981), p. 236.

33. Some aspects of Copernican heliocentrism illustrate the paradigm-as-exemplar: it offers a solution to some puzzling problems (e.g., the order and retrograde motion of the planets), but also raises new questions (e.g., how to explain rectilinear free fall on a moving earth).

34. Kuhn, "Second Thoughts," p. 297ff; *Structure*, pp. 182ff.

35. Kuhn, *Structure*, p. 136.

36. Ibid., pp. 210ff.

37. This is the correct English spelling of a term derived from the name of the tenth-century mathematician al-Khwarizmi. The term "algorithm," which Kuhn and almost everyone else uses, is nonsense from an etymological point of view (since it is based on a misleading similarity with the word "logarithm," which has two Greek roots, not an Arabic one). The perpetuation of this mistake is a perfect example of the way in which the textbook tradition, after seizing "logarithm" as its paradigm, has succeeded in disseminating and conferring an aura of normalcy upon an error that even etymological pedants can no longer properly characterize as egregious.

38. See Kuhn, *Structure*, p. 102, where he discusses "derivations" from relativistic to classical mechanics. Some texts even "derive" $E = mc^2$ from the classical work equation; see Richard Weidner and Robert Sells, *Elementary Modern Physics*, 2d. ed., (Boston: Allyn and Bacon, 1968), p. 90.

39. Kuhn, *Structure*, p. 201.

40. Ibid., p. 152.

41. Dudley Shapere, "The Structure of Scientific Revolutions," *Philosophical Review*, 73 (1964), pp. 383ff.; Karl Popper, "Normal Science and Its Dangers," in Lakatos and Musgrave, eds., *Criticism and the Growth of Knowledge* (Cambridge: Cambridge Univ., 1970), esp. pp. 55ff. For Kuhn's rejection of these charges, see his "Reflections on My Critics," also in Lakatos and Musgrave, p. 234.

42. Kuhn, "Reflections on my Critics," p. 235.

43. Under the circumstances, it is perhaps fitting that Kuhn's latest current institutional home is the Department of Linguistics and Philosophy at MIT.

44. Kuhn, *Structure*, p. 210.

45. Feyerabend, *Against Method*, pp. 23ff.

46. Ibid., p. 29.

47. There is a strong reflexive element in Feyerabend's case, of course. In the index of *Against Method*, the entry for "rhetoric" reads "1–172"—the entire book.

48. Feyerabend, *Against Method*, pp. 255–56, 304–5.

49. Feyerabend, *Problems of Empiricism*, vol. 2, p. 129.

50. Feyerabend, *Against Method*, p. 252.

51. For example, Feyerabend, "More Clothes," p. 237.

52. "Scientific rationalists assume that scientific practice, and the practice of thinking in general is based on simple laws and standards, and must be based on such standards, and that both can be treated exhaustively by discussing the simple slogans for expressing them and the logical relations between the slogans: one can understand science, and for that matter any fruitful line of thought, without participating in it." Feyerabend, in the 1980 postscript to the reprinting of his review of Wittgenstein's *Philosophical Investigations* (1952, 1955); in his *Problems of Empiricism: Philosophical Papers*, vol. 2 (Cambridge: Cambridge Univ., 1981), p. 129.

53. Feyerabend, *Against Method*, pp. 256–57.

54. Ibid., p. 257.

55. Ibid., pp. 300–304. These arguments are developed in his *Science in a Free Society*.

56. David Bloor, *Wittgenstein: A Social Theory of Knowledge* (New York: Columbia Univ., 1983), p. 2.

57. David Bloor, *Knowledge and Social Imagery* (London: Routledge and Kegan Paul, 1976), p. 5.

58. Larry Laudan, "The Pseudo-science of Science?" in James R. Brown, ed., *Scientific Rationality: The Sociological Turn* (Dordrecht: D. Reidel, 1984), see pp. 53−67.

59. For more on this, see the discussion in Steve Woolgar, *Science: The Very Idea* (London: Tavistock, 1988), pp. 91−95.

60. Harry M. Collins, "The Replication of Experiments in Physics," in Barry Barnes and David Edge, eds., *Science in Context* (Cambridge, Mass.: MIT, 1982), p. 94.

61. Ibid., p. 95.

62. Ibid., p. 97.

63. Bruno Latour and Steve Woolgar, *Laboratory Life: The Construction of Scientific Facts*, 2d ed., (Princeton: Princeton Univ., 1986), p. 86.

64. Ibid., p. 88.

65. Ibid., p. 105.

66. Ibid., pp. 45−53; for recent work on the experimental scientific article, see Charles Bazerman, *Shaping Written Knowledge: The Genre and Activity of the Experimental Article in Science* (Madison: Univ. of Wisconsin, 1988).

67. Steven Shapin, "Phrenological Knowledge and the Social Structure of Early Nineteenth-Century Edinburgh," *Annals of Science*, 32 (1975), pp. 219−43.

68. Evelyn Fox Keller, *Reflections on Gender and Science* (New Haven: Yale Univ., 1985), p. 117.

69. Ibid., p. 117.

70. Ibid., p. 123.

71. Sandra Harding, "Is Gender a Variable in Conceptions of Rationality? A Survey of Issues," in Carol C. Gould, ed., *Beyond Domination: New Perspectives on Women and Philosophy* (Totowa, N.J.: Rowman and Allan Held, 1984), pp. 52−53.

2

C. S. Peirce
Discourse and Semiotic
Peter Skagestad

Although Charles Sanders Peirce (1839–1914) enjoys the dubious reputation of a "philosophers' philosopher," he was not himself a professional philosopher, as that term is understood today. Peirce was the product of a culture and an educational system that did not slice up the world of the intellect in quite the same way as do twentieth-century university curricula. In Peirce's formative years there were as yet no graduate schools in the United States, and Peirce was thus not trained as an academic specialist. His highest academic degree was a B.S. in chemistry from the Lawrence Scientific School at Harvard; however, Peirce's training in mathematics certainly rivaled his training in chemistry, and his original contributions to mathematics arguably place him among the leading mathematicians of his age.[1] Yet he did not make his living from either chemistry or pure mathematics. Apart from a four-year stint as a lecturer of logic at America's first graduate institution, Johns Hopkins, from 1879 to 1883, Peirce's vocation was that of astronomer, attached to the U.S. Coast Survey from 1861 to 1891. While teaching logic, he also performed pioneering psychological experiments, including the classic Peirce-Jastrow experiment, which undermined Gustav Fechner's hypothesis of a "threshold" below which the senses cannot discern small differences in stimuli.[2] Peirce spent the last twenty-three years of his life as a private scholar, lecturing occasionally and writing prolifically on mostly philosophical subjects. During these years, he generally preferred to refer to himself as a "logician." While Peirce made extensive, pathbreaking contributions to formal, mathematical logic, he always understood the concept of logic more broadly, to include the study of methods in general. His career as a whole may be characterized by the following autobiographical statement from the fragment titled "Concerning the Author":

> From the moment when I could think at all, until now, about forty years, I have been diligently and incessantly occupied with the study of methods [of] inquiry, both those which have been and are pursued and those which ought to be pursued. (CP 1.3)[3]

The same fragment nicely summarizes Peirce's philosophical outlook, known as "fallibilism," as well as its underlying temperament, that of a man who prided himself on never being certain of anything:

> Only once, as far as I remember, in all my lifetime have I experienced the pleasure of praise — not for what it might bring but in itself. That pleasure was beatific; and the praise that conferred it was meant for blame. It was that a critic said of me that I did not seem to be *absolutely sure of my own conclusions.* ... Indeed, out of a contrite fallibilism, combined with a high faith in the reality of knowledge, and an intense desire to find things out, all my philosophy has always seemed to me to grow. (CP 1.10; 1.14)

If today this fallibilism appears less as a distinctive philosophy than as part of the philosophical outlook in general, this is in no small measure due to the largely indirect influence wielded by Peirce's thought on present day philosophy.

The Doctrine of Signs

While current interest in the study of signs is to a large extent directly inspired by the French semiological school and its deconstructionist offshoot, there is a growing recognition that the intellectual framework of the ideas now being imported from France was an American export in the first place. This recognition has in recent years been greatly aided by the work of the noted Italian semiotician Umberto Eco, who constantly acknowledges his indebtedness to Peirce, as well as to Peirce's American successor Charles Morris.[4] If Peirce is not the founder of semiotic, he is certainly the first modern thinker to have taken seriously John Locke's obscure and mostly overlooked suggestions, in the closing paragraphs of *An Essay Concerning Human Understanding*, that the sciences be classified as physical, practical, and semiotic, and that, since words are our most important species of sign, logic be regarded as the preeminent branch of semiotic.[5] Following Locke, Peirce defined *semiotic* as "the doctrine of signs," and he devoted a large part of his career to spelling out in detail that doctrine and its implications for the various sciences and, more especially, for philosophy.

Peirce's major writings on semiotic stem from the 1890s and early 1900s, but the core of his theory is found in the doctrine of thought-signs presented in his articles and manuscripts from the period 1867–1868. By a "sign" Peirce meant, broadly speaking, anything capable of standing to somebody for something in some respect (CP 2.228). To stand in this relation *to somebody* is to be subject to interpretation in this person's mind, and this process of interpretation, Peirce insisted, is the creation in the interpreter's mind of a new sign, which Peirce labeled the "interpretant" of the original sign (ibid.). For instance, if a particular sensation leads me to infer that a given object is red, the sensation will have served as a sign to me of the object in respect of color. To say that it has served as a sign to me is to say that I have interpreted it, that is, it has been replaced, in my mind, by a different sign of its object, to wit, by the perceptual judgment: "The object is red." This judgment is in turn a sign, capable of further interpretation by myself or, should I choose to utter it, by other minds. The capacity to be thus transformed into a new sign is an essential attribute of signhood. Peirce may not have coined the phrase "every decoding is another encoding," but he certainly conceived the idea and made it a centerpiece of his theory of signification, cognition, and discourse.[6]

In "On a New List of Categories," published in 1867, Peirce introduced his famous trichotomy among the three chief types of signs, or *representations*, as Peirce called them at this stage:

> First. Those whose relation to their objects is a mere community in some quality, and these representations may be called *likenesses* [later, *icons*].
>
> Second. Those whose relation to their objects consists in a correspondence in fact, and these may be termed *indices* or *signs*. [The term *signs* was soon to be extended to cover all representations.]
>
> Third. Those the ground of whose relation to their objects is an imputed character, which are the same as *general signs*, and these may be termed *symbols*. (CP 1.558)

For instance, a weather vane is an index, a painted portrait is an icon, while a photograph is both an icon and an index. The weather vane indicates the direction of the wind by virtue of having a causal connection of a certain kind to its object, the wind. A painted portrait signifies a person by resembling that person.[7] A photograph signifies by means of both relations. I may recognize a photograph as a picture of John Doe because it looks like John Doe. But because of what I know about photographic processes, the photograph may signify also in the absence of perceived similarities—indeed, it may signify by means of putative *dissimilarities*: the photograph may tell me, for instance, that John Doe has lost weight since I last saw him. The photograph then functions as an index. There is a causal chain—albeit a complex one—through which the light reflected off Doe's face has produced the image on the photograph in my hand. This is not to suggest that photographs do not lie. The practice of retouching has, from the very beginning, made photographs highly fallible indices. (Similarly, a weather vane might be so constructed, by accident or design, as to systematically mislead us about the wind direction.) But one potential implication of modern digital-imaging technology is that photographs may soon altogether cease to signify indexically. An example of a symbol, finally, would be a word, in so far as it signifies by means of a purely conventional relation to its object. An onomatopoeia (e.g., "thud," "whisper," "gargle," "fricative") is both a symbol and an icon, while an exclamation—whether of pain, sorrow, joy, or surprise—may be both a symbol and an index. The use of "ouch," rather than "uff da," to signify pain is purely conventional, but one can normally tell from a particular utterance of "ouch" whether this utterance was caused by pain experienced by the speaker and, if so, by roughly how intense a pain it was caused. It should be noted, if only in passing, that this sign relation—that of the index—has lately come into focus in the philosophical discussions of indexical reference during the last twenty years.[8]

While it is not made explicit in 1867, Peirce's trichotomy of types of sign naturally arises from his definition of a sign, formulated as follows in 1868:

> Now a sign has, as such, three references: first, it is a sign *to* some thought which interprets it; second, it is a sign *for* some object to which in that thought it is equivalent; third, it is a sign, *in* some respect or quality, which brings it into connection with its object. (CP 5.283)

While every sign, by definition, possesses all three references, signs may nonetheless be classified according to their predominant mode of signification. A sign may signify *primarily* through its relation to an interpreter (symbols), through its equivalence, in the mind, to its object (icons), or through its extramental connection with its object (indices). The irreducibly triadic nature of a sign gives rise to a great many other triads in Peirce's semiotic, of which we shall here only note the subdivision of semiotic into three distinct sciences of signs:

> The first would treat of the formal conditions of symbols having meaning, that is of the reference of symbols in general to their grounds or imputed characters, and this might be called formal grammar; the second, logic, would treat of the formal conditions of the truth of symbols; and the third would treat of the formal conditions of the force of symbols, or their power of appealing to a mind, that is, of their reference in general to interpretants, and this might be called formal rhetoric. (CP 1.559)

While Peirce here appears to restrict the scope of these sciences to symbols, a later manuscript (from 1897) makes the same distinctions with respect to signs in general, now also called "representamina": "In consequence of every representamen being thus connected with three things, the ground, the object, and the interpretant, the science of semiotic has three branches." The first branch, *pure grammar*, "has for its task to ascertain what must be true of the representamen [sic] used by every scientific intelligence in order that they may embody any *meaning*." The second branch, logic proper, is "the formal science of the conditions of the truth of representations." The third branch, *pure rhetoric*, has for its task "to ascertain the laws by which in every scientific intelligence one sign gives birth to another, and especially one thought brings forth another" (CP 2.229). While Peirce's nomenclature in this case has not taken root, this distinction is central to the theory of signs later elaborated by Charles Morris. As Morris has put it, the three correlates of the triadic sign relation — "sign vehicle," "designatum," and "interpreter" — give rise to the three dimensions of semiosis, which are studied, respectively, by *syntactics*, *semantics*, and *pragmatics*.[9] These terms rapidly gained wide currency — partly, no doubt, because they were adopted early on by Rudolph Carnap and thus became common coin for otherwise distantly separated schools of thought.[10]

The classic statement of the philosophical ramifications of the Peircean doctrine of signs remains the series of articles published in the *Journal of Speculative Philosophy* in 1868. Peirce here elaborates his semiotic model of discourse and thinking in the context of arguing, first, that people lack a number of mental faculties traditionally attributed to them and, second, that as a consequence of these "incapacities" certain standard epistemological assumptions have to be abandoned. The mental faculties that Peirce feels have been wrongly attributed to people include these four:

1. We have no power of introspection, but all knowledge of the internal world is derived by hypothetical reasoning from our knowledge of external facts.
2. We have no power of intuition, but every cognition is determined logically by previous cognitions.
3. We have no power of thinking without signs.
4. We have no conception of the absolutely incognizable. (CP 5.265)

In these articles Peirce draws on the psychology of Wilhelm Wundt to argue in detail that we have no reason to assume the existence of such things as intuitions; knowledge is not grounded in anything immediately given, whether to the intellect or to the senses.[11] His strategy is to examine, one by one, the various psychological phenomena that seemingly testify to the existence of intuitions, and to show in each case that the phenomenon in question is more simply explained to result from an inferential process. Such a process, though of finite duration, cannot necessarily be traced back to its logical beginning in a finite number of inferential steps; rather, when analyzing the reasons for my belief that, for example, an object in front of me is red, I approach the ground of my belief asymptotically, without ever reaching a point at which I am entitled to say simply, "I believe it because I see it" (CP 1.538). This is not to deny that my belief that the object is red may be *caused* by the fact that the object is red; what is denied is that this fact is something I can directly intuit. All cognition is "semiosis," or sign-interpretation, whereby an external sign gives rise, in the cognizing mind, to a more determinate sign that itself is capable of further interpretation *ad infinitum*.

Since all thought is essentially interpretation, there are no indubitable first premises. Everything we know is known through the mediating process of sign-interpretation; there is nothing directly and immediately given, either to the intellect or to the senses. Among Peirce's general conclusions, the following two are of particular interest. First, Cartesian doubt, so far from being an indispensable prolegomenon to philosophy, is in fact a perfectly futile exercise. We all have beliefs that we are unable to doubt simply because it does not occur to us that they *can* be doubted. These beliefs carry no special epistemic warrant, but neither can we get rid of them by pretending to doubt everything. The person who goes through the motions of facing the skeptical dilemma will not in fact consider the dilemma resolved until he has recovered all the beliefs he pretended to give up at the outset, that is, until he has found some highly doubtful beliefs with which to justify beliefs he never doubted in the first place. This is "as useless a preliminary as going to the North Pole would be in order to get to Constantinople by coming down regularly upon a meridian ... Let us not pretend to doubt in philosophy what we do not doubt in our hearts" (CP 5.265). Here, in a nutshell, is the outlook Peirce was later to baptize "critical common-sensism." There is only one vantage point from which to philosophize, and that is the point at which we actually find ourselves when we begin the study of philosophy (CP 5.265). Epistemology, in particular, has no access to a fixed point of departure from which it can either underwrite or undermine the totality of our knowledge claims; it can be pursued only from within the body of our current beliefs, such as they are. As has been noted by Israel Scheffler, both the position taken by Peirce and the very wording in which it is expressed importantly foreshadow characteristic positions of Wittgenstein, Russell, Popper, and Neurath.[12]

Second, the Cartesian criterion of truth, namely subjective certitude, is vacuous. Peirce formulates this criterion as follows: "Whatever I am clearly convinced of, is true," and he goes on: "If I were really convinced, I should have done with reasoning and should require no test of certainty" (CP 5.265). The Cartesian criterion, then, becomes available only when there is no longer any need for it. The criterion also runs counter to the spirit of modern science, where the subjective certainty of one individual counts for nothing unless he can persuade others to agree with him. A novel theory is held on probation until it has secured the consensus of all inquirers. *Until* this consensus has been reached, the author's subjective certainty does not affect the probationary status of the theory; *after* consensus has been reached this certainty becomes irrelevant because there is nobody left who questions the theory:

> We individually cannot reasonably hope to attain the ultimate philosophy which we pursue; we can only seek it, therefore, for the *community* of philosophers. Hence, if disciplined and candid minds carefully examine a theory and refuse to accept it, this ought to create doubts in the mind of the author of the theory himself. (CP 5.265)

The philosophical position at which Peirce had arrived in 1868 was, first, a thoroughgoing fallibilism that did not recognize any authoritative "bedrock," "foundations," or "first principles." Second, it was a communitarianism whose exact contours remain to be drawn. Peirce clearly locates objectivity squarely in the social realm, but that is so far too vague a statement to be very enlightening. It must be noted that Peirce is *not* saying that consensus — even among disciplined and candid minds — is a test or criterion of either truth or objectivity. Once consensus has been attained, there is no further demand for any test or criterion. Rather, Peirce is hinting something about the *meaning* of truth. In the 1868 article he explicitly addresses the meaning of the closely related concept of reality, in these words:

> The real, then, is that which, sooner or later, information and reasoning would finally result in, and which is therefore independent of the vagaries of me and you. Thus, the very origin of the conception of reality shows that this conception essentially involves the notion of a COMMUNITY, without definite limits, and capable of a definite increase of knowledge. And so those two series of cognition — the real and the unreal — consist of those which, at a time sufficiently future, the community will always continue to re-affirm; and of those which, under the same conditions, will ever after be denied. (CP 5.311)

Peirce's attack on foundationalism clearly presages the social constructivism that appears so novel when encountered in the writings of Richard Rorty and others about a hundred years later. So far, however, we have only drawn the outlines of Peirce's positive doctrine. For further elucidation we turn to Peirce's doctrine of meaning, formulated in the late 1870s and later baptized "pragmatism."

Peirce's Pragmatism

Peirce's doctrine of meaning was first set forth in what has become his most widely read — and most widely misunderstood — article: "How To Make Our Ideas Clear," published in *Popular Science Monthly* in 1878. This is the place where Peirce first put in print the principle he was later to refer to as "the pragmatic maxim": "Consider what effects, that might conceivably have practical bearings, we conceive the object of our conception to have. Then, our conception of these effects is the whole of our conception of the object" (CP 5.402). While early commentators interpreted this statement as a somewhat crude and obscure anticipation of the "verifiability criterion of meaning" later popularized by the logical empiricists of the Vienna Circle, that interpretation is hardly taken seriously anymore.[13] Closer to the mark is an observation made by A. J. Ayer, that the pragmatic maxim anticipates Karl Popper's falsificationism.[14] In Popper's view, the "content" of a statement is defined by the class of "potential falsifiers" of the statement: the more occasions there are for proving a statement false (if it is false), the more the statement says.[15] While Popper avoids talking about "meaning" — presumably to stay clear of some of the philosophical pitfalls that tripped up the logical empiricists — it is worth noting that, in his view, "content" is defined, not by a class of objects referred to, but by a class of potential actions and their consequences, namely the actions that would falsify the statement were it false. Peirce's principle has also gradually come to be recognized as a close relative of the speech-act approach to language analysis adumbrated by the later Wittgenstein and explicated in greater detail by J. L. Austin.[16] In this approach meaning — or at least one *kind* of meaning — is located in the relation of words to the actions performed by certain utterances and, beyond, to the social norms and practices which permit or mandate a given utterance to count as a given action, rather than in the relation of words to their objects.

Peirce's basic idea was that there are several levels at which to understand a word or statement; in the 1878 article he distinguishes three "grades of clearness," which clearly correspond, respectively, to the syntactic, the semantic, and the pragmatic levels of semiosis. We all understand the word "real," for instance, in the sense that we are able, in ordinary, familiar cases, to distinguish what is real from what is imaginary. This familiarity with ordinary instances of a concept constitutes the most rudimentary level at which to understand a word. We understand the word better if we are able to relate it to our other ideas by means of a formal definition; at this level we understand the real as that which is what it is independently of what anybody may think about it. This definition only helps bring order among our ideas;

it does not help us distinguish the real from the unreal in those hard cases where everyday familiarity with the word does not suffice; the definition does not help us determine, for instance, whether such things as forces, fields, genes, species or historical periods are real or unreal. To tackle such questions we must apply the pragmatic maxim and move to what Peirce called the third grade of clearness. We must ask ourselves what action we would take to determine whether something is real, and what consequences we would expect to follow if the thing is real, as opposed to what would follow if it is not real. In other words, we must locate the word "real" within the matrix of social practices that give the word its fullest meaning, the most relevant practices being, in Peirce's view, those followed by experimental science. Suppose scientific inquiry were to go on indefinitely; if, in the indefinite long run of inquiry, our belief in, for example, the force of gravity were never refuted, then gravity is real. The real, then, is that which would still be thought to exist in the hypothetical final opinion after all the resources of experimental science should have been exhausted. If a particular belief will stand its ground no matter how long we go on refining and applying the experimental method, then it will make no sense to deny that that belief is grounded in reality. To understand the word "real" in this sense is to understand it pragmatically. A pragmatist, in Peirce's sense, is someone who is not satisfied that he has fully understood a word until he has been able to relate it in this manner to possible human actions and their consequences.

We shall note here two important implications of this doctrine. First, there can be no such thing as absolute precision. We understand a term like "electricity" pragmatically by relating it to the scientific practices in which the term is embedded. So, the more scientists learn about electricity, the more they are able to mean by the word "electricity" (CP 5.313; 7.587). As has been noted both by H. Wennerberg and by W.B. Gallie, there is thus no hard-and-fast distinction between knowing the meaning of a word like "electricity" and knowing a number of facts about electricity.[17] The more we know about the world, the more we are able to mean with our words, and the greater precision we are able to attain in our discourse. Perfect precision is therefore bound to be as elusive as omniscience.[18] While this conclusion follows from the pragmatic maxim, it is also an obvious corollary of the earlier doctrine of signs: to be a sign is to be capable of being transformed into a more determinate sign, et cetera. In Gallie's paraphrase: "More simply, communication is something which can only be done at all because it can always be done better than it ever actually is done."[19] So, while the pragmatic maxim is offered as a method of *reducing* vagueness — making our ideas clear — it would be a fundamental misunderstanding to believe that this or any other method can *eliminate* vagueness or even that the latter would be a desirable goal: "Perfect accuracy of thought is unattainable — *theoretically unattainable*. And undue striving for it is worse than time wasted. It positively renders thought unclear."[20]

Far from being part of the pathology of discourse, vagueness is an essential condition for any significant discourse to take place. Since what a statement means to me depends on the factual information I possess, it follows that a perfectly precise statement would be intelligible only to someone who shared my stock of information. And I could have nothing to communicate to such a person that he or she did not already know. Since vagueness and ambiguity have long figured as the villains in texts on "informal logic," it is interesting to find the above conclusion drawn by one of the founders of modern formal logic. It is also interesting to find that a similar argument for the essential communicative function of ambiguity has been made by that other founding father of modern logic, Bertrand Russell:[21]

> It would be absolutely fatal if people meant the same things by their words. It would make all intercourse impossible, and language the most hopeless and useless thing imaginable, because the meaning you attach to your words must depend on the nature of the objects you are acquainted with, and since different people are acquainted with different objects, they would not be able to talk to each other unless they attached quite different meaning to their words.

Russell was very far from being a pragmatist, and he was in various respects critical of Peirce; but in this one respect the two appear to have been of one mind. I must emphasize "appear to," since this particular passage falls somewhat below Russell's customary standard of clarity.

Second, Peirce's pragmatic method, as here adumbrated, implies a particular conception of truth, albeit a different one from the more famous pragmatic conception of truth formulated by his friend and fellow pragmatist William James. Peirce agreed with Aristotle that truth is to say of that which is that it is, and of that which is not that it is not. He would also undoubtedly have agreed with the latter-day logician Alfred Tarski that to say that the sentence "Snow is white" is true is to say neither more nor less than that snow is white. Peirce believed that truth is the correspondence of a statement to the stated fact or, more generally, the agreement of a representation with its object (CP 5.553–54). Truth is correspondence to facts in precisely the same sense that reality is that which is what it is independently of what anybody may think about it. These are both formal definitions belonging to the second level of understanding — the second grade of clearness, as Peirce put it. In more modern terminology, the correspondence definition specifies the *semantics* of the word "truth." What the correspondence definition does is relate our idea of truth to our ideas of fact and of statement. It thus helps bring order among our ideas, but it does not give us a clue to how to go about seeking truth. Nobody expects a definition of truth to provide a criterion of truth, but a pragmatist will insist that we have not fully understood the word "truth" until we understand truth, inter alia, as something it makes sense to spend time and effort searching for. The reason this is a problem is that, on one level, "we think each one of our beliefs to be true, and, indeed, it is mere tautology to say so" (CP 5.375). For instance, suppose I believe, as I do, that "pure" snow is white. Then, I necessarily believe that the statement "Snow is white" is *true*, and also that it is a *fact* that snow is white. Having a belief, taking a statement to be true, and taking the facts to be thus and such, are simply three different characterizations of the same state of mind. So, on the purely semantic level, while there may be a distinction, there is no *difference* between the truth and whatever I happen to believe. To spell out the difference, we must move to the third level of understanding — to the level of pragmatics. How do we go about ascertaining truths? By taking recourse to reasoning and experience, in hard cases by employing the scientific method (or methods). What happens when we employ these methods? Some beliefs are dropped, new ones are formed, and the new beliefs tend to command broader agreement than the old ones — that is very largely the reason what the selection of the new beliefs consists in. Now let us take this process to its logical limit. Suppose that, on some question, we were to arrive at a universal consensus, and suppose also that this consensus would never be broken even if scientific inquiry were to go on forever. It would, on these suppositions, make no sense to say that the consensus opinion was nonetheless false. What could this mean? It cannot mean that there is some recalcitrant fact which might turn up, were we to probe further; this possibility has been ruled out by hypothesis. The truth, then, is the final, universal opinion towards which scientific inquiry would lead us, were it to be carried out in the indefinite long run. At the risk of repetition, to say that truth is the final opinion is not to deny that truth is correspondence to facts; it is an attempt to spell out more precisely what, for practical purposes, "correspondence to facts" means.

We are now in a position to specify more clearly the nature of the communitarianism indicated at the end of the last section. The concept of truth — like the cognate concept of reality — is a social concept. We may formally define it as "correspondence to facts," but we can understand this correspondence pragmatically only in terms of a consensus emerging from particular kind of discussion. A hermit would be able to understand the concept of truth only by hypothetically placing himself in a social context where opinions are uttered, questions asked and answered, reasons offered and rebutted, and so on. It does not follow that the truth can ever be equated with any consensus actually arrived at. Any consensus actually arrived at in any given community is liable — indeed, likely — to be broken as soon as the limits of the community are expanded to include groups heretofore excluded. Any actual consensus must therefore be regarded as provisional in nature. In Peirce's controversial mathematical analogy, the final opinion that constitutes the truth is the limit that the actual consensus approaches as the size of the community approaches infinity.[22]

Belief and Rationality

While Peirce evidently does not relativize truth to any existing consensus, a no less far-reaching relativism may appear to be implicit in the pragmatist perspective — namely a relativism of meaning, including the meaning of the word "truth." Why is it that what we pragmatically understand by truth is whatever will be the outcome of free and open inquiry? The most obvious, and least satisfactory, answer is simply that free and open inquiry is part and parcel of *our* way of life. The pragmatic maxim directs us to locate the concept of truth within the matrix of our relevant social practices; if those practices were different, the pragmatic maxim would lead us to a different pragmatic concept of truth. As Peirce indeed makes clear, Peter Abelard, the fourteenth century scholastics, and Descartes went about ascertaining facts in very different ways, so they attached different pragmatic meanings to the word "truth." To Abelard, the truth was "simply his particular stronghold," the opinion that he was prepared to defend against all comers (CP 5.406). In the fourteenth century, when the church had taken upon itself the regulation of opinion, truth "meant little more than the Catholic faith" (ibid.). To Descartes and his followers, finally, truth meant whatever was agreeable to reason.

Peirce's gloss on the history of the meaning of truth closely parallels his extended discussion of the evolution of methods of inquiry, in the companion article "The Fixation of Belief." If it is belief we want, the simplest and most economical way of satisfying our desire is simply to go right on believing whatever we already do believe, employing the method of *tenacity* (CP 5.377–78). Where this method most conspicuously fails is in resolving disagreements between tenacious individuals with opposite beliefs. Why should a method of belief-formation be expected to resolve interpersonal disagreements? Because the very existence of beliefs that contradict mine suffices to shake my confidence in my beliefs, in the absence of any special reason to regard my beliefs as superior. So, the very nature of the failure of the method of tenacity suggests the remedy, to wit, to let some supraindividual authority, such as the state or the church, decree what everybody is to believe, and to preserve and protect the decreed beliefs by such means as tarring and feathering dissenters; this is the method of *authority* (CP 5.379). No state, however, can possibly legislate opinion on *all* questions that arise. On innumerable questions individuals still have to form their own opinions, and they will have no other way of doing it than thinking for themselves. Thus the method of authority, by default, generates its successor, the method of believing whatever is agreeable to reason — the a priori method (CP 5.382–83). This method, in turn, is liable to the same type of failure as tenacity: it is insufficiently effective in creating agreement. Once again, a collective authority is called in, but this time it is a new and different type of authority: the authority of collective, dialogic reasoning about publicly affirmed experiences. This, of course, is the scientific method, which differs from its three predecessors in being "self-corrective," that is, its failures call for no other remedy than the continued application of the scientific method itself (CP 5.384).

The steps in this evolutionary process — which bears some affinities to the historical movement Hegel brings his readers through in his *Phenomenology of Spirit*[23] — are not arbitrarily chosen. Peirce is showing us a progression from individual irrationality, through collective irrationality and individual rationality, to the collective rationality in which the process culminates. Then, in "How to Make Our Ideas Clear," he shows us how each of these habits of belief-formation gives its own pragmatic meaning to the concept of truth, irrespective of any change in the formal definition of the word "truth." The tenacious Abelard, who equated the truth with the opinion which he was prepared to defend against all comers; the fourteenth century scholastics, who proved their conclusions by citing chapter and verse from their authorities; the rationalist Descartes, who was prepared to accept all and only the logical consequences of self-evident premises — these thinkers all agreed that truth is correspondence to facts. But the function played by the concept of truth in our thinking is determined by our habits of going about ascertaining facts, and different habits can determine widely different understandings of the concept of truth.

The conclusion is not, however, that anything goes; nor does the relativity — more precisely, the practice-dependency — of meaning license the radical relativism embraced by the latter-day pragmatist Richard Rorty.[24] In Peirce's evolutionary story sketched above, it is not just that our methods of forming beliefs determine our concept of truth; there is also something about the nature of belief itself that motivates the development of our methods of belief-formation. A belief is essentially a belief *about* something, and in order for a method of belief-formation to have a chance at lasting success, it must allow that something the belief is about to play a role in determining the content of our belief. In Peirce's words:

> To satisfy our doubts ... it is necessary that a method should be found by which our beliefs may be determined by nothing human, but by some external permanency — by something upon which our thinking has no effect. ... The feeling which gives rise to any method of fixing belief is a dissatisfaction at two repugnant propositions. But here already is a vague concession that there is some *one* thing which a proposition should represent. (CP 5.384)

Elsewhere Peirce has made the same point with respect to assertion. Peirce distinguished between the analysis of the meaning of a proposition and the analysis of an act of assertion; as an "easily dissected" example of the latter, one in which "the assertive element is magnified," he instanced the act of making an affidavit, where "a man goes before a notary or magistrate and takes such action that if what he says is not true, evil consequences will be visited upon him" (CP 5.30). In general: "[To] *assert* a proposition is to make oneself responsible for it, without any definite forfeit, it is true, but with a forfeit no smaller for being unnamed" (CP 5.543). Peirce's analysis here is recognizably a specification of the "illocutionary act" of assertion (in J. L. Austin's terminology), that is, the act I perform *eo ipso* when making an assertion.[25] In this analysis, it is part of the meaning of the concept of assertion that any assertion may be falsified if the facts turn out otherwise than stated. Every assertion is essentially an assertion *about* something, and that something constrains what I may legitimately assert. An assertion may well be so vague that the speaker is unable immediately to specify its falsifying conditions. But whenever a statement is so structured — either by its semantics or by the pragmatics of the context of utterance — that the possibility of falsification is clearly excluded, no assertion will have been made.

In sum, all rational discourse is constrained by that which the discourse is about, even though there is no way of stepping outside the boundaries of discourse to characterize this "something" unambiguously. So far Peirce. Whether rational discourse is in fact thus constrained remains a central issue of contention in present-day pragmatism. Rorty's position, already alluded to, is that "there is only the dialogue" — there is nothing outside the dialogue for the dialogue to be about. Consistently with this view — however incredibly from any other perspective — Rorty has concluded that Peirce was no pragmatist at all.[26] Conversely, Hilary Putnam has struck a recognizably Peircean note in his reply to Rorty: "The very fact that we speak of our different conceptions as different conceptions of *rationality* posits a *Grenzbegriff*, a limit-concept of the ideal truth." [27] In the debate over what sort of pragmatism it is possible to adopt today, Peirce's doctrine will evidently remain an unavoidable point of reference for some time to come.

Notes

1. See Carolyn Elsele, *Studies in the Scientific and Mathematical Philosophy of Charles S. Peirce*, ed. R. M. Martin (Mouton: Hague, 1979).

2. See Max H. Fisch & Jackson L. Cope, "Peirce at the Johns Hopkins University," In *Studies in the Philosophy of Charles Sanders Peirce*, eds. P. P. Wiener & F. H. Young (Cambridge: Harvard Univ., 1952), pp. 277–311.

3. References to Peirce's *Collected Papers*, eds. for vols. 1–6, Charles Hartshorne & Paul Weiss, ed. for vols. 7–8, Arthur Burks (Cambridge: Belknap, 1931, 1958) are given parenthetically in the text, following the convention of referencing by volume and paragraph number: thus, "CP 1.3" refers to volume 1, paragraph 3.

4. Umberto Eco, *A Theory of Semiotics* (Bloomington: Indiana Univ., 1979), passim. It is no accident that this recognition has been the work of an Italian scholar; Italy is the only European country with an indigenous pragmatist tradition, going back to Peirce's contemporaries G. Papini, M. Calderoni, and G. Vailati. On the Italian Pragmatist tradition, see H.S. Thayer, *Meaning and Action: A Critical History of Pragmatism*, ed. (Indianapolis: Hackett, 1981), pp. 324–46.

5. John Locke, *An Essay Concerning Human Understanding*, ed. A.S. Pringle-Pattison (Oxford: Clarendon, 1924), pp. 370–71. On Peirce's Lockean antecedents, as well as Locke's scholastic antecedents in semiotic, see John Deely, *Introducing Semiotic* (Bloomington: Indiana Univ., 1982).

6. This aphorism, along with a sketch of its Peircean lineage, is found in David Lodge's novel *Small World* (Harmondsworth: Penguin, 1985), pp. 25, 28.

7. Resemblance is of course itself a complex relation; for one thing, it is always resemblance in some one respect. Arguing that resemblance is as complex a relation as signification, Eco has proposed eliminating iconicity from the trichotomy of signs. See his *Theory of Semiotics*, pp. 191–217.

8. A number of the classic contributions to this discussion — e.g., by Keith Donnellan, Saul Kripke, and Hilary Putnam — are conveniently collected in *Naming, Necessity, and Natural Kinds*, ed. Stephen P. Schwartz (Ithaca: Cornell Univ., 1977).

9. Charles S. Morris, *Foundations of the Theory of Signs* (Chicago: Chicago Univ., 1938), p. 6.

10. Rudolph Carnap, *Foundations of Logic and Mathematics* (Chicago: Chicago Univ., 1939), p. 4.

11. For a good, detailed discussion, see Bruce Altshuler, "Peirce's Theory of Truth and his Early Idealism," *Transactions of the Charles S. Peirce Society*, 16 (1980), pp. 118–40.

12. Israel Scheffler, *Four Pragmatists: A Critical Introduction to Peirce, James, Mead, and Dewey* (New York: Humanities, 1974), pp. 56–57.

13. For example, Ernest Nagel writes: "Peirce's own formulation of the pragmatic maxim leaves much to be desired in the way of explicitness and clarity; and more recent formulations, such as those by Professor Carnap and others, have the same general intent but superior precision" (*Sovereign Reason*, Glencoe: Free Press, 1954, p. 43). For a detailed discussion of this interpretation, see my *The Road of Inquiry: Charles Peirce's Pragmatic Realism* (New York: Columbia Univ., 1981), chaps. 3 and 4.

14. A. J. Ayer, *The Origins of Pragmatism* (London: Macmillan, 1968), pp. 85–86.

15. Karl R. Popper, *The Logic of Scientific Discovery* (London: Routledge & Kegan Paul, 1959), pp. 112–13.

16. See Ludwig Wittgenstein, *Philosophical Investigations* (London: Macmillan, 1953); J. L. Austin, *How to Do Things with Words* (Oxford: Oxford Univ., 1965). On the Peirce-Wittgenstein link, see Charles S. Hardwick, "Peirce's Influence on Some British Philosophers: A Guess at the Riddle," in *Studies in Peirce's Semiotic*, eds. K. L. Ketner & J. M. Ransdell (Lubbock: Institute for Studies in Pragmatism, 1979), pp. 25–30, and Thayer, *Meaning and Action*, pp. 79n, 304–13. The thumbnail sketch of pragmatism in the following pages is based on my article "Pragmatism and the Closed Society," which is used here with the kind permission of the editor of *Philosophy and Social Criticism*.

17. Hjalmar Wennerberg, *The Pragmatism of C. S. Peirce* (Lund: C. W. K. Gleerup, 1962), p. 147; W. B. Gallie, *Peirce and Pragmatism* (New York: Dover, 1965), p. 127.

18. Peirce wrote: "There are three things to which we can never hope to attain by reasoning, namely, absolute certainty, absolute exactitude, absolute universality" (CP 1.141).

19. Gallie, *Peirce and Pragmatism*, p. 136–37.

20. *Semiotic and Significs: The Correspondence between Charles S. Peirce and Victoria Lady Welby*, ed. Charles S. Hardwick (Bloomington: Indiana Univ., 1976), p. 11.

21. Bertrand Russell, "The Philosophy of Logical Atomism," in *Logic and Knowledge: Essays 1901–1950*, ed. R.C. Marsh (New York: Macmillan, 1956), p. 195.

22. See Thayer, *Meaning and Action*, pp. 118 ff. Also see my "Peirce's Conception of Truth: A Framework for Naturalistic Epistemology?" in *Naturalistic Epistemology: A Symposium of Two Decades*, ed. A. Shimony & D. Nails (Dordrecht: Reidel, 1987), pp. 73–90.

23. In a lecture from 1898, Peirce refers to Hegel's emphasis on "the marvellous self-correcting property of Reason" (CP 5.579). Like Hegel, also, Peirce professed himself to be an objective idealist; thus, in "The Architecture of Theories," he states: "The one intelligible theory of the universe is that of objective idealism ..." (CP 6.25). How much deeper the similarities go is

debatable; the particular idealist doctrine referred to in the above quote is that of Schelling, not Hegel, see CP 6.102, 6.605. Peirce's own attitude toward Hegel was at best ambivalent, see CP 5.436.

24. Richard Rorty, "Pragmatism, Relativism and Irrationalism," *Proceedings and Addresses of the American Philosophical Association*, 53 (1980), pp. 719–38.

25. Austin, pp. 98–99.

26. Rorty, p. 720.

27. Hilary Putnam, *Reason, Truth, and History* (Cambridge: Cambridge Univ., 1981), p. 216.

3

Richard Rorty
Philosophy Without Foundations

John Trimbur and Mara Holt

Richard Rorty is arguably the most influential spokesperson for what is currently known as the new pragmatism. According to Rorty's colleague-critic Richard Bernstein, "Not since James and Dewey have we had such a devastating critique of professional philosophy"[1] — a critique based on Rorty's thoroughgoing skepticism about the efforts of philosophers to guide inquiry from a standpoint above or outside practice.

Trained at Yale in the Anglo-American tradition of analytic philosophy, Rorty's early work is concerned with the problems that defined academic philosophy in the postwar period, particularly epistemology and philosophy of language. Rorty's first book, *The Linguistic Turn* (1967), is a collection of major statements on the philosophy of language by leading thinkers in the analytic tradition. In his lengthy introduction, Rorty reveals both his early affiliation to analytic philosophy and his growing skepticism about its research program of dissolving philosophical issues into the question of language. More recently, in *Philosophy and the Mirror of Nature* (1979), in the essays collected in *Consequences of Pragmatism* (1982), and in *Contingency, Irony, and Solidarity* (1989), Rorty has distanced himself decisively from the preoccupations of analytic philosophy, becoming in effect a philosophical apostate who defected from the tradition that shaped his early work.

In many respects, Rorty's career parallels those of the men he considers the three most important twentieth-century philosophers, Wittgenstein, Heidegger, and Dewey. Rorty's comment on the intellectual trajectory of these three philosophers seems equally valid as autobiography:

> Each of these three came to see his earlier work as self-deceptive, as an attempt to retain a certain conception of philosophy after the notions needed to flesh out that conception (the seventeenth-century notions of knowledge and mind) had been discarded. Each of the three, in his later work, broke free of the Kantian conception of philosophy as foundational and spent his time warning us against those very temptations to which he himself had once succumbed.[2]

In *Philosophy and the Mirror of Nature*, the work that most fully defines Rorty's contribution to current philosophical thought, Rorty follows the linguistic turn in analytic philosophy in a distinctly post-positivist direction — away from the goal of a secure foundation of knowledge and toward what Rorty calls "epistemological behaviorism." Rorty maintains that notions such as "knowledge" and "mind" are seventeenth-century inventions that can be traced to the historically specific discourses of philosophers such as Descartes and Locke, not enduring problems that form the inherent subject matter of philosophy. For Rorty, representations of knowledge, mind, truth, and rationality result from a figurative language that has held philosophers captive, a set of unacknowledged metaphors that picture the mind as a glassy essence equipped with a mental mirror to reflect reality and an inner eye to contemplate these reflections. According to Rorty, mirror imagery and perceptual metaphors have dominated Western philosophy for the past three hundred years: the figure of the mind as a glassy essence joins together rationalist and empiricist conceptions of philosophical reason in unsuspected ways. "It is," Rorty says, "as if the *tabula rasa* were perpetually under the gaze of an unblinking Eye of the Mind — nothing, as Descartes said, being nearer to the mind than itself" (PMN 143). Lockean empiricism, as much as Cartesian method, takes as its starting point the study of essential mental processes located in the inner space of the mind.

In contrast to the seventeenth-century turn inward to ground knowledge in the nature of the knowing subject, Rorty's epistemological behaviorism holds that there "are no essences in the area. There is no wholesale, epistemological way to direct, criticize, or underwrite the course of inquiry. ... It is the vocabulary of practice rather than of theory ... in which someone can say something useful about the truth."[3] Like William James and John Dewey, Rorty does not wish to abandon the usefulness of notions such as "knowledge" and "truth." He is arguing rather that we do not have to understand them in the terms provided by seventeenth-century mirror imagery — as accurate representation and correspondence to reality. Instead, Rorty says, we might think of knowledge and truth as matters of social practice, not of philosophical method. For pragmatists, the "true," as James describes it, is the "name of whatever proves itself to be good in the way of belief" (CP xxv). Following James and Dewey, Rorty sees the epistemological tradition in Western philosophy as a misguided attempt to base knowledge and truth on something more permanent and secure than the current ongoing deliberations about what we believe to be true.

At the same time, Rorty updates the pragmatist position by joining an appreciation of poststructuralist currents in continental philosophy with the pragmatism of James and Dewey. Rorty relates the anti-metaphysical hermeneutics of Nietzsche and Heidegger, Derrida and Foucault — which he sees as an attempt to get away from the notion of an enduring transcendental subject — to Dewey's vision of philosophy "without method," a kind of culture criticism without the baggage of the epistemological tradition. For pragmatists and poststructuralists alike, Rorty says, philosophy amounts to a style of writing, a literary genre and language practice that philosophers have repressed in their desperate attempts to keep their methods theoretically pure. According to Rorty, there is no discipline or method capable of transcending its own discourse, no way of getting beneath language to the thought it expresses, nothing to free us from the contingency of our vocabularies.

Rorty, however, appears to be uncomfortable with the antihumanism that pervades continental philosophy. He says, for example, that Dewey and Foucault make the same criticisms of the epistemological tradition but "put ... a different spin on it" — not just the difference in tone between "an ingenuous Anglo-Saxon" and a "self-dramatizing Continental" but, more important, a difference over "what we may hope" (CP 204–5). One of Rorty's telling projects is to translate the deconstructive impulse in continental philosophy into the idiom of American pragmatism, but he finds in thinkers such as Foucault and Jean-Francois Lyotard an "extraordinary *dryness*," an avant-gardist reluctance to say "'we' long enough to identify with the culture of the generation to which they belong." In contrast, Rorty wishes to endorse Dewey's "untheoretical sense of social solidarity."[4] There is a buoyant optimism that accents Rorty's work and that distinguishes him from the continental thinkers he admires. In Rorty's writings, we hear the inflection of a distinctly American voice in the liberal tradition, ranging its way through the intellectual free-for-all of postmodern critical theory.

What emerges from this overview of Rorty's career and preoccupations is the portrait of a philosopher who has increasingly come to resist the claims of professional philosophy. Like Dewey, Rorty wants to speak as a citizen and a secular intellectual, to practice a kind of culture criticism that dismantles the boundaries between literature, science, and philosophy. Rorty is a prolific essayist, and his work is as likely to turn up in the *New Republic* or the *London Review of Books* as in the *Review of Metaphysics* or the *Journal of Philosophy*. Rorty has left the solitude of the philosopher's study to enter the history of the contemporary, the postmodern world of blurred disciplinary lines and incommensurable discourses. Like Dewey, Rorty has set aside the eternal problems of the philosophers to write for his times.

This characterization of Rorty, of course, only raises a series of questions we will need to address: what kind of writer is Rorty trying to be? what is his rhetorical stance toward mainstream philosophy? what kind of discourse does he want to promote? This chapter suggests some answers to these questions and draws out some implications from Rorty's writings for the study of discourse.

Rorty and the Self-Image of Philosophy

In the introduction to *Philosophy and the Mirror of Nature*, Rorty says that the "traditional Cartesian-Kantian pattern" in Western philosophy amounts to an "attempt to escape from history" (PMN 9). By their own accounts, philosophers have traditionally located their professional concerns above the fray of everyday life, away from the contingencies of contemporary culture, in the deeper, more basic problems philosophy takes as its special mission to explore. Philosophers, Rorty says, "usually think of their discipline as one which discusses perennial, eternal problems—problems which arise as soon as one reflects" (PMN 3). By identifying philosophy with the activity of reflection itself, philosophers think of the "enduring problems" of their discipline—the relationship betweem mind and body, the nature of the knowing subject, the act of representation, the quality of the good and the beautiful—as ones that transcend any particular philosophical discourse, method, or school of thought. These problems are traditionally considered to be coterminous with the domain of reason, uncontaminated by the language used to describe them, by ideology or the accidents of history.

This self-image of philosophy, Rorty argues, takes shape in the modern period with Kant's effort to define philosophy as a foundational discipline. For Kant, philosophy is distinct from science, demarcated by its special task of establishing a theory of knowledge upon which science and other forms of inquiry may rest. While the empirical disciplines can produce knowledge, it is given to philosophy alone to ask what makes knowledge possible in the first place, to adjudicate knowledge claims, to act as a tribunal of reason with the other disciplines under its jurisdiction.

As Rorty says, without the notion of a theory of knowledge, "it is hard to imagine what 'philosophy' could have been in the age of modern science" (PMN 132). Once physics displaced metaphysics as the prevailing description of how the universe is put together, philosophy's claim to study the highest, most universal, and least material things was gravely shaken. In Rorty's account, however, Kant managed to transform the old notion of philosophy—"metaphysics as the 'queen of the sciences'" (PMN 132)—into the notion of philosophy-as-epistemology, a foundational discipline devoted to the "most basic" problems of how we know and what constitutes knowledge. By positing a priori categories of mental activity, Kantian epistemology makes it possible for philosophy to claim not that it has access to "higher" truths but more important that it possesses special knowledge of the workings of reason, of the empirical disciplines, and of human culture in general. By elaborating a theory of knowledge imposed by the nature of the knowing subject, philosophy in the Kantian tradition set itself up as an autonomous, nonempirical discipline capable of bringing all knowledge claims under its surveillance.

Rorty's career as a philosopher, as we have already suggested, represents a telling break with the traditional mission of defining philosophy as a foundational discipline, outside history in the realm of pure reason. We might describe Rorty's project as an attempt *not* to let philosophy escape from history, *not* to see philosophy as providing the grounds of reason and knowledge. Rorty counterposes to the foundationalism of Kantian philosophy what he calls an "edifying tradition" comprising such exemplary thinkers as Wittgenstein, Heidegger, and Dewey. The "common message" of this edifying tradition, Rorty says, "is a historicist one" (PMN 9). For edifying thinkers, philosophy needs to be redefined—not as the search for universal principles but as the search for historical understanding. In effect, the goal of Rorty's edifying thinkers is strategic: they want to divert philosophy from its quest for certainty and a secure foundation of knowledge, to rechannel its energies into the hermeneutic circle, where nothing is settled but where philosophy can be, as Hegel put it, the activity of historical self-consciousness, "its own time apprehended in thought."

Pragmatism and Narrative Philosophy

For Rorty's edifying thinkers, the problem of modern philosophy is not that philosophers disagree about method but that mainstream philosophy holds on to the possibility that such a method may in fact finally be discovered. According to Rorty, the antidote to such "objectionable self confidence" is history, or what he calls "narrative philosophy."[5] Narrative philosophy, in Rorty's view, offers an alternative to traditional argumentative philosophy. It asks us to see the discourse of philosophy not as a matter of proving and disproving propositions but rather "as a

matter of telling stories: stories about why we talk as we do and how
we might avoid continuing to talk that way."[6] From this historicist
perspective, there are no "enduring problems" nor is there an inherent
subject matter that defines philosophy's starting point or the scope of
its discipline. Instead, philosophy as we know it results from the
circulation of narratives, the accounts of projects and purposes that
have professionalized philosophy as an academic speciality. What we
wind up with, as Wittgenstein, Heidegger, and Dewey have reminded
us, are the vocabularies of a time and a place, the customary behaviors
of a particular intellectual subculture, the self-image of a profession.

Rorty's historicism in effect dissolves the boundary between philosophy and rhetoric. Rorty shifts the terms from a search for method
to a strategy of historicization. He urges us to look at philosophical
discourse as language-in-action — not a privileged perspective that
holds out the hope of finally moving from speculation to science but
simply the stories philosophers tell each other. In this sense, Rorty
denies the possibility of setting philosophy on firm ground, of revol-
utionizing its practices so that we can start out afresh with renewed
rigor and precision, without the cumbersome and misleading accounts
of past philosophers. All we can do, Rorty says, is to redescribe the
old descriptions in the hope that we can come up with something
useful for the present.

To historicize philosophy in this way, Rorty's edifying thinkers
maintain, means we will no longer possess a universal measure by
which to judge knowledge claims and the accuracy with which they
represent reality. Instead we will have genealogies of philosophy, new
accounts of old debates, more stories to tell and retell. To recognize
that philosophy is no more and no less than its own narratives is to
recognize that we will always get the past we deserve — not a final
definitive version of philosophical problems and issues but the version
our present situations calls up. We will have what was there all along —
ourselves, our common activities, our attempts to cope with reality.
And we will be no worse off in our judgments. It is just that our
judgments will no longer be concerned with what is true and accurate according to some extrahistorical criteria. Instead our judgments
will concern what is most useful to us, given our current historical
circumstances.

Not surprisingly, Rorty's pragmatism has opened his work to
charges of relativism — that Rorty's deconstruction of philosophy-as-
epistemology leaves nothing behind to help us decide whether one
belief on a topic is better than another. Rorty himself is quite aware of
the costs of his nonfoundationalism: "to suggest that there is *no* ...
common ground," Rorty says, "seems to endanger rationality. To
question the need for commensuration seems the first step toward a

return of 'all against all'" (PMN 317). But the real issue, Rorty says, is not the disturbing prospect of lapsing back into a Hobbesian world of intellectual anarchy. According to Rorty, no one "except for the occasional cooperative freshman ... says that two incompatible opinions on an important topic are equally good. The philosophers who get *called* 'relativists' are those who say that the grounds for choosing between such opinions are less algorithmic than had been thought" (CP 166). Pragmatists such as James and Dewey, Rorty says, are indeed "metaphysical relativists" in the sense that "they think there is no way to choose, and no point in choosing between incompatible philosophical theories of the typical Platonic or Kantian type." But they think the choice is pointless because they believe that such theories are "attempts to ground some element of our practices on something external to these practices" (CP 167).

If we abandon the traditional philosophical project of grounding our practices on first principles, pragmatists such as James and Dewey reassure us, we will still have heated debates about alternative cosmologies, political agendas, and ethical positions. The change Rorty recommends is that when "an alternative is proposed, we debate it, not in terms of categories or principles but in terms of the various concrete advantages and disadvantages it has" (CP 168). To do so recognizes that the real issue raised by the charge of relativism "is not between people who think one view is as good as another and those who don't," Rorty says. "It is between those who think our culture, or purpose, or intuitions cannot be supported except conversationally, and people who still hope for other sorts of support" (CP 167). For Rorty, there is no "outside" tribunal of judgment available to us, but there is nonetheless a network of narratives that provide the practical basis for making judgments in particular situations.

Hermeneutics and the Edifying Tradition

For Rorty's edifying thinkers, the traditional philosophical enterprise of establishing transcendental support for our practices is not so much wrong as misdirected. Rorty's edifying thinkers are not interested in refuting the epistemological tradition or replacing it with systems of their own making. Instead they want to sidestep such "basic problems" altogether in order to remind us that "investigations of the foundations of knowledge ... may be simply apologetics, attempts to eternalize a certain contemporary language game, social practice, or self-image" (PMN 9–10). According to Rorty, to be an edifying thinker means being "therapeutic rather than constructive" (PMN 5). The aim of edifying thinkers is "to help their readers, or society as a whole, break free from outworn vocabularies and attitudes, rather than to provide grounding for the intuitions and customs of the present" (PMN 12).

Wittgenstein, Heidegger, and Dewey each in his way polemicized against the visual metaphors in Western philosophy that picture the mind as a mirror of nature and knowledge as accurate representation. The point of their polemics, however, is not to give a better picture of what makes up the mind and knowledge. The point for Rorty's edifying thinkers is that philosophy has been blind to its own metaphors, to the fact, as Rorty puts it, that it "is pictures rather than propositions, metaphors rather than statements, which determine most of our philosophical convictions" (PMN 12). What edifying thinkers want to do is demystify these captivating pictures, to denaturalize what philosophy-as-epistemology has taken for granted by disclosing the figurative properties of philosophical discourse.

The characteristic gesture of Rorty's edifying thinkers, then, is a deconstructive one — and implicitly an argument about language. According to Rorty, philosophy-as-epistemology repeatedly swerves into a figurative language to legitimate its discourse and practices. Whether philosophical discourse relies on Cartesian perceptions, Lockean sense impressions, or the constitutive powers Kant ascribed to the knowing subject, philosophy-as-epistemology has been held in the thrall of the same underlying visual metaphors, governed by the same underlying task of "inspecting, repairing, and polishing the mirror" (PMN 12) of the mind in order to get more accurate representations. The attempt of analytic philosophy to foreground language as its departure point, Rorty says, is simply "one more variant of Kantian philosophy ... marked principally by thinking of representation as linguistic rather than mental" (PMN 8). Instead of thinking about how to match the word and the world together in accurate correspondences, Rorty says, we need to change the way we think about language. We should talk about language as neither a privileged object of inquiry nor a transparent medium of representation that can bring us into privileged relationship to reality. Rather we should think of language as an endlessly circulating discourse that can bring us into relationship to other speakers, other metaphors, other discourses.

For Rorty, the deconstructive urge to set language loose in endless disseminations thwarts the traditional philosophical quest for a "final vocabulary," a permanent neutral framework capable of adjudicating all knowledge claims. Rorty ties his deconstruction of the visual metaphors in philosophy-as-epistemology to a critique of the search for universal commensuration:

> The notion that our chief task is to mirror accurately, in our own Glassy Essence, the universe around us is the complement of the notion, common to Democritus and Descartes, that the universe is made up of very simple, clearly and distinctly knowable things, knowledge of whose essences provides the master vocabulary which permits commensuration of all discourses. (PMN 357)

According to Rorty, his edifying thinkers are united by their desire to abandon the quest for a master vocabulary and universal grounds of commensuration. They share the "hope that the cultural space left by the demise of epistemology will not be filled" (PMN 315). When Rorty talks about the hermeneutics of the edifying tradition, he is not describing a "successor subject" to epistemology but rather is expressing the resistance he shares with Wittgenstein, Heidegger, and Dewey to the assumption that we can, or even should aspire to, reach agreement on what constitutes the common basis of rationality.

For Rorty, the history of Western philosophy has been a series of attempts to impose a norm of discourse upon speakers. Despite differences in philosophical assumptions, mainstream systematic philosophers have been obsessed with commensuration, with the goal of establishing a single overarching framework of proper philosophical inquiry that would permit all competing claims to be "brought under a set of rules which tell us how rational agreement can be reached and what would settle the issue on every point" (PMN 316). Hermeneutics, as Rorty understands it, represents a struggle against the desire for commensuration, an ongoing subversion of all philosophical claims to a reigning univocal discourse.

The aim of Rorty's edifying thinkers, then, is not to correct the mistakes of past philosophers. Instead, they wish to speak from the margins of normal philosophical discourse, to be reactive, peripheral, subversive, and satirical, to poke fun at "the very notion of having a view, while avoiding having a view about having views" (PMN 371). By declining to play the role traditionally assigned to philosophy-as-epistemology — "to find a proper set of terms into which all contributions should be translated if agreement is to become possible" (PMN 318) — Rorty's edifying thinkers wish to situate themselves as intermediaries between incommensurable discourses, trying on the vocabularies of various discourses rather than translating them into the terms of a generally agreed upon master vocabulary. For Rorty's edifying thinkers, hermeneutics is simply a willingness to refrain from philosophy-as-epistemology in order to see the "relations between various discourses as those of strands in a possible conversation, a conversation which presupposes no disciplinary matrix which unites the speakers, but where the hope of agreement is never lost as long as the conversation lasts" (PMN 318). The difference between the system building impulse of mainstream philosophy and the hermeneutics of the edifying tradition, as Rorty describes it, amounts to the difference between "an *universitas* — a group united by mutual interests in achieving a common end" and "a *societas* — persons whose paths through life have fallen together, united by civility rather than by a common ground" (PMN 318).

Much of the time, Rorty speaks of the hermeneutics of the edifying tradition as purely oppositional, a kind of deconstructive stance toward mainstream philosophy. In this sense, edifying discourse is parasitic on normal or systematic discourse and to talk of edifying thinkers as having definite views is not so much wrong as in poor taste. As Rorty says, "It puts them in a position which they don't want to be in, and in which they look ridiculous" (PMN 372). Instead of normalizing hermeneutics into the terms of mainstream philosophy, Rorty says, we need to recognize that hermeneutics is engaged in a complex negative dialectic with philosophy-as-epistemology. "We will be epistemological," Rorty says, "where we understand perfectly well what is happening but want to codify it in order to extend, or strengthen, or teach, or 'ground' it. We must be hermeneutic where we do not understand what is happening but we are honest enough to admit it" (PMN 321).

In this regard, hermeneutics is related to epistemology in the same way that what Rorty calls "abnormal discourse" is related to normal discourse. Normal discourse takes place when there is a consensus about what problems need to be investigated and what counts as a good explanation or a telling criticism. Following Thomas Kuhn's notion of "normal science," Rorty says we get normal discourse "not because we have discovered something about 'the nature of human knowledge' but simply because when a practice was continued long enough the conventions which make it possible ... are relatively easy to isolate" (PMN 321). Abnormal discourse, by contrast, takes place when consensus breaks down, when anomalies challenge the reigning paradigms of inquiry, at moments of cultural crisis when the conventional wisdom gets called into question—when, as Rorty says, "someone joins in the discourse who is ignorant of these conventions or sets them aside" (PMN 320). Abnormal discourse makes chaos out of what is taken for granted and tries to muddle its way through to some new understanding of how things hang together. Abnormal discourse is not meant to be commensurable with the dominant discourse, paradigms, and disciplinary matrices of its time. Rather it expresses suspicion about the self-confidence and complacency of normal discourse and systematic inquiry. It seeks "to take us out of our old selves by the power of strangeness, to aid us in becoming new beings" (PMN 360). For this reason, Rorty says, edifying discourse "is *supposed* to be abnormal," to stand in a negative, oppositional stance toward normal discourse.

According to Rorty, abnormal discourse consists of an openness to the strange and unfamiliar. But if the edifying thinkers "dread their vocabularies should ever be institutionalized," there is nonetheless a sense in Rorty's work that the hermeneutics of the edifying tradition is more than the negative complement to epistemology. At times, Rorty seems to suggest that hermeneutics is not just a deconstructive struggle against final vocabularies and universal commensuration but that it represents a positive model of discourse in its own right. This is what Rorty calls "conversation."

Philosophy as Conversation

According to Rorty, we can think of knowledge in two ways. We can think of it as the result of a confrontation between the knowing subject and the object of inquiry, or we can think of it as the result of a conversation among knowing subjects. In the first case, Rorty says, we will be operating on the basis of the visual metaphors that have dominated philosophy-as-epistemology: we will think, that is, "of having our beliefs determined by being brought face-to-face with the object of belief" (PMN 163), and knowledge will be a matter of perfecting the quasi-visual faculties so that we can better match the mind's reflected images of reality with "true" reality. We will be certain about the accuracy of our representations when we "find, within the Mirror, a specially privileged class of representations so compelling that their accuracy cannot be doubted" (PMN 163). When this happens, we will have reached the foundations of knowledge, where, as Rorty says, "argument would be not just silly but impossible, for anyone gripped by the object in the required way will be *unable* to doubt or to see an alternative" (PMN 159).

If we think of knowledge in the second way, however, our "certainty," Rorty says, "will be a matter of conversation between persons rather than a matter of interaction with non-human reality" (PMN 157). Rorty's deconstruction of the visual metaphors and mirror imagery in Western philosophy seeks to clear the ground to talk about discourse as a social practice, not a confrontation with external reality. Once we discard the metaphor of the mind as a Mirror of Nature, we can "see people saying things, better or worse things, without seeing them as externalizing inner representations" (PMN 371). Once we "understand speech not as the externalization of inner representations, but as not a representation at all," Rorty says, we will then be able to see "sentences as connected with other sentences rather than with the world" (PMN 371–72). We will thereby no longer need to think of knowledge as accuracy of representation. Instead we will be able to think of it as the result of the continuing conversations by which we justify our beliefs, not as a causal explanation of those beliefs. And in this sense, we will have learned the lesson Rorty's edifying thinkers wish us to learn: we will be able to suppress what they see as the "philosophical urge," the desire "to say that assertions and actions must not only cohere with other assertions and actions but 'correspond' to something apart from what people are saying and doing" (PMN 179). We will have arrived, that is, at a propositional view of knowledge, not a perceptual or representational one. For Rorty, philosophy then can become what Michael Oakeshott calls the "conversation of mankind."

In Rortyean conversation, there is no compulsion to end the flow of speech, no final arguments to settle things and seal us off against what Rorty calls "the potentially infinite regress of propositions-brought-forward-in-defense-of-other-propositions" (PMN 159). It may be silly or counterproductive to keep talking once most people agree, but there are no grounds outside the conversation itself according to which we can decide. The agreements we reach are not subject to the authorization of an external touchstone of knowledge or truth. When we say something is "true" or "objective," we are, Rorty says, simply paying ourselves a compliment for assenting to statements to which there are currently no plausible alternatives or counterexplanations, no pressing need to call into question. There are no "metaphysical comforts" in Rortyean conversation, no "transcendental backups," no epistemological grounds to guarantee success. As Rorty says, "we do not know what 'success' would mean except simply 'continuance'" (CP 172).

To give up accuracy of representation as the touchstone of knowledge can be unsettling because it disqualifies traditional habits of thought that picture a legitimatizing source of knowledge outside ourselves and our discourses. The irreducibility of Rortyean conversation may in fact elicit a kind of linguistic claustrophobia. To imagine human culture and the quest for knowledge as a conversation between persons instead of a confrontation with reality may appear to lock us in a "prison house of language," a hermeneutic circle that offers no release, no standpoint to get outside our discursive practices in order to show how things really are. According to Rorty, however, the feeling of contingency and entrapment is a problem only for those who wish for somewhere else to be, somewhere outside the conversation that discourse can help us get to but that transcends and remains impervious to our talk about it.

For Rorty, this desire to get beyond the socially constructed world of discourse is one of the founding illusions of Western philosophy-as-epistemology. From Rorty's perspective, discourse cannot be the vehicle of escape because it is ubiquitous, the very environment "in which we live and move," the ongoing conversation about our communal purposes. Consequently, the task we face is that of learning to live in a world without foundations, in a world of ungrounded, floating discourses, where conversation is its own sufficient aim and justification.

Rorty acknowledges that to think of our cultural and intellectual traditions and practices as *simply* conversation — to see "all criteria as no more than temporary resting-places, constructed by a community to facilitate its inquiry" — may appear to be "morally humiliating" (CP xlii). Once we abandon traditional notions of rationality, objectivity, method, and truth, Rorty notes, there will be "nothing deep down inside us except what we have put there ourselves, no criterion that we have not created in the course of creating a practice, no standard of rationality that is not an appeal to such a criterion, no rigorous argumentation that is not obedience to our own conventions" (CP xlii). But if this "thought is hard to live with," Rorty says, it need not be reason for fatalism or despair. It may just as well be reason for moral responsibility.

According to Rorty, of his edifying thinkers, it is Dewey who sees more clearly that the "move 'beyond method' gives mankind an opportunity to grow up, to be free to make itself, rather than seeking direction from some imagined outside source" (CP 204). Along Deweyean lines, Rorty's notion of conversation represents something more than a metaphor left behind once we have deconstructed the epistemological claims of mainstream philosophical discourse. It also provides a vocabulary to talk about "unjustifiable hope and an ungrounded but vital sense of human solidarity" (CP 208). And in this sense, Rortyean conversation represents not the intellectual anarchy of incommensurable discourses but a reaffirmation of civility and moral agency.

Post-Philosophical Culture

For Rorty, the notion of conversation anticipates what he calls a "post-Philosophical culture." "This would be a culture," Rorty says, "in which neither the priests nor the physicists nor the poets nor the Party were thought of as more 'rational,' or more 'scientific,' or 'deeper' than one another. No particular portion of culture would be singled out as exemplifying (or signally failing to exemplify) the condition to which the rest aspired" (CP xxxviii). In Rorty's post-Philosophical culture, philosophy would still be around but we would understand that it was simply another style of writing — a set of vocabularies — not a method to apply or a special class of problems to be solved. We would think of philosophy, as Wilfrid Sellars describes it, as "an attempt to see how things, in the broadest possible sense of the term, hang together, in the broadest possible sense of the term" (CP xiv). Rorty's picture of a post-Philosophical culture gives us the "philosopher who has abandoned pretensions to Philosophy" (CP xl), a figure who resembles Rorty himself, whose "attempts to see how things hang together" look more like culture criticism than professional philosophy. Instead of "the Philosopher who could explain why and how certain areas of culture engaged a special relation to reality," there would be "all-purpose intellectuals who were ready to offer a view on pretty much anything" (CP xxxiv).

And this is indeed what Rorty intends for his post-Philosophical culture, to rerepresent not merely the role of the philosopher but more broadly the role of the secular intellectual in a culture without foundations. Just as the Enlightenment transcended the language of religion, Rorty's vision of a post-Philosophical culture offers a way to transcend the language of philosophy, to abandon the hope that "deep down beneath all the texts, there is something which is not just one more text but that to which various texts are trying to be 'adequate'" (CP xxxvii). In Rorty's post-Philosophical culture, secular intellectuals will be "polypragmatic," "informed dilettantes," not cultural guardians. They will range through the postmodern world of intertextuality much as Rorty himself aspires to do, comparing and contrasting texts, playing them off against each other "to produce new and better ways of talking and acting—not better by reference to a previously known standard but just better in the sense that they come to *seem* clearly better than their predecessors" (CP xvii). The role of secular intellectuals, as Rorty sees it, will be far removed from the role of nineteenth-century sages such as Carlyle and Arnold or twentieth-century custodians of liberal humanism such as F. R. Leavis or Lionel Trilling. Like Hermes, the patron of hermeneutics, the secular intellectuals of a post-Philosophical culture will be tricksters of blurred boundaries, plural meanings, and inexhaustible difference. Their role will be to stop the conversation from normalizing itself.

The goal of Rorty's post-Philosophical culture in this respect is to keep the conversation going by opening up new discursive spaces where speech can take place without reference to disciplinary lines, where an intellectual free-for-all keeps the talk circulating without privileged authorities telling us when we have arrived at the truth or a knowledge of the human condition. Rortyean conversation as the model of a post-Philosophical culture offers a spectacle of incommensurable discourses, a plurality of ways of speaking tied together by nothing beyond the speakers' mutual commitment to keep talking.

Rorty's Critics and Postmodern Bourgeois Liberalism

Rorty's notion of a post-Philosophical culture represents one of the most ambitious and far-reaching projects in postmodernist thought, and there can be little question that Rorty has become one of the most influential thinkers on the current intellectual scene. It should not be surprising, therefore, that Rorty's work has generated a wide range of response, some of it sympathetic and some of it not. As Rorty himself notes, his work tends to get "two kinds of criticism: one from my fellow philosophers suggesting that I want to put an end to philosophy, and one from the political left saying that I'm, in effect, defending the status quo."[7] To the first charge, Rorty replies that "philosophy just wasn't the kind of thing you could ever end, but it has quite often changed the way in which it was written and the topics to which it attended, and that you could think that a good deal of contemporary philosophy was becoming boring and repetitious without wanting to put an end to philosophy as a subject."[8] In this section we will focus on the second line of criticism and those aspects of Rorty's work the political left has found troubling, namely Rorty's attempt to generalize conversation into the political arena and his advocacy of what he calls "postmodernist bourgeois liberalism." The controversies surrounding Rorty's avowed liberalism carry telling implications not only for his politics but also for his view of discourse.

According to sympathetic critic and fellow neopragmatist Richard Bernstein, Rorty's efforts to link liberalism to the ungrounded solidarity of conversation reveals a central tension in Rorty's edifying philosophy between its deconstructive stance toward mainstream systematic philosophy and the "profound practical-moral vision [that] animates his work."[9] For all of Rorty's warnings against making hermeneutics the successor to epistemology, Bernstein argues, Rorty does seem to want to persuade us to replace epistemology with hermeneutics, argumentation with narrative, systematic inquiry with conversation. And by the same token, while Rorty insists that the conversation is ungrounded, he nonetheless does seem to imply that nonfoundationalism is more ethical, democratic, and morally responsible than philosophy-as-epistemology precisely because, at least as an ideal, philosophy-as-conversation privileges no particular discipline or part of human culture. Rather it permits the talk to flow of its own accord, without transcendental principles or cultural overseers to determine who may speak and what may be said. For Bernstein, the tension between Rorty's negative hermeneutics and the utopian impulses of Rortyean conversation remains unresolved, a problem that puts Rorty perpetually on the verge of falling into the very foundationalism he wishes to avoid.

The tension Bernstein identifies can be found, moreover, in Rorty's account of "postmodernist bourgeois liberalism." Postmodernism, Rorty says, following Lyotard, should be thought of as an attitude not a doctrine, the manifestation of "a distrust of metanarratives." Story telling on the grand scale, metanarratives are totalizing tales "which describe or predict the activities of such entities as the noumenal self or the Absolute Spirit or the Proletariat"; they are "stories which purport to justify loyalty to, or breaks with, certain contemporary communities."[10] According to Rorty, what distinguishes postmodernist bourgeois liberals from other sorts of liberals is the fact that they think we don't need recourse to such *grands recits*, the metanarratives of universal reason and natural rights, to sustain the liberal ideals of human dignity, democratic practice, and procedural justice. Rather than complimenting such ideals, as thinkers such as Jürgen Habermas do, Rorty says, "by reference to the 'elements of reason' contained in them, it would be better just to compliment those untheoretical sorts of narrative discourse which make up the political speech of the Western democracies."[11] To get rid of metanarratives, Rorty says, is to see that "legitimacy resides where it always has, in first-order narratives,"[12] in the stories we tell each other that hold our culture together, the accounts of communal purposes and past heroes and heroines, the exemplary tales of who we are and who we should be. For this reason, Rorty says, the task of the postmodernist bourgeois liberal is "is to convince society that loyalty to itself is morality enough."[13] Instead of trying to ground liberal institutions and practices — what Rorty calls the "hopes of the North Atlantic bourgeoisie" — on first principles, it "would be better," Rorty says, "to be frankly ethnocentric."[14]

Rorty's frankness here is as revealing as it is meant to be disarming. It is revealing because it catches Rorty balanced precariously between the postmodernist disbelief in the metanarratives that underwrite political legitimacy, on the one hand, and his hope of revitalizing liberalism and its institutions, on the other. A number of Rorty's critics accept his view that we can maintain "liberal habits" without philosophical convictions but worry that his cheerfully ethnocentric project of "convincing our society that it need be responsible only to its own traditions"[15] implicitly posits a source of cultural and political legitimacy in the conversation of the West and the circulation of its "first-order narratives, the accounts we give of our collective self-image. Clifford Geertz, for example, says that Rorty's disarmingly frank ethnocentrism amounts to a new variant of cultural narcissism, "a relax-and-enjoy-it approach to one's imprisonment in one's own cultural tradition" that has become "increasingly celebrated in recent social thought."[16]

According to Geertz, this easy celebration of one's cultural affiliations results from a "chronic misapplication" of the historicist notion "that meaning is socially constructed."[17] The new ethnocentrism, Geertz argues, inverts Wittgenstein's aphorism "the limits of my language are the limits of my world" to read "the limits of my world are the limits of my language." This inversion, Geertz argues, impoverishes Wittgenstein's sense that our structures of feeling and habits of thought are rooted in forms of life by making such forms of life — the human communities we necessarily live in — into "semantic monads."[18] The new ethnocentrism divides the world into communities of "us" and of "them" connected only by the occasional overlap between what Rorty calls the "rich North American bourgeois" communities, on one side, and those communities we "need to talk with ... to carry on whatever conversation between nations may still be possible,"[19] on the other.

In Geertz's view, Rorty's ethnocentrism fails to recognize that cultural diversity, alien customs, and the troubling moral asymmetries that invariably result "arise not merely at the boundaries of our society ... but ... at the boundaries of ourselves"[20] in the increasingly polyglot, multiethnic, and culturally diverse societies we inhabit in an era of global disruption. "Like nostalgia," Geertz says, "diversity isn't what it used to be."[21] Therefore, to divide the world into "perspicacious we-s with whom we can empathize" and "enigmatical they-s, with whom we cannot"[22] is to repress or ignore the contacts between peoples and cultures that the modern world has made unavoidable, at home, in the course of everyday life.

The difference here between Rorty and Geertz turns on their respective relationships to "otherness." For his part, Rorty urges us to

> think about cultural diversity on a world scale the way our ancestors in the seventeenth and eighteenth centuries thought about religious diversity on an Atlantic scale: as something to be simply *ignored* for purposes of designing political institutions.[23]

Rorty's response to cultural diversity and "otherness" is framed in a language of tolerance that, for Geertz, obscures real differences and unequal relations of power. The tolerant speaker — whether Rorty or, more broadly, the Western "we" — feels safely in control and therefore can afford to be compassionate, protective, and ultimately patronizing; the "other" remains at a comfortable distance, separated socially and geographically, whether at home or abroad. For Geertz, on the other hand, the Western "we" is no longer so securely in control and therefore needs to negotiate, to explore the "character of the space" between cultures. By contrast, the new ethnocentrism Rorty has fallen into takes the gaps produced by cultural diversity as givens, the result of the "sovereignty of the familiar," a position that cuts us off from a "working contact with a variant subjectivity"[24] and thus turns us back on ourselves, our culture, our traditions. The "we" we are becomes self-explanatory, removed from the "possibility of quite literally, and quite thoroughly, changing our minds."[25] Geertz's critique of Rorty's "frank" ethnocentrism points out some of the limits of Rortyean loyalty-to-itself as the justification of postmodern bourgeois liberalism: it relieves us of the pressure to change.

Feminists and left-wing critics similarly question Rorty's uncomplicated notion of "we." Dorothy Leland notes that Rorty "ignores ...

historically situated points of view, such as those of women, for which [Rorty's] sense of solidarity and identification is at best elusive and at worst non-existent."[26] For his critics, the problem Rorty overlooks is how speakers get into the conversation in the first place—how the "we" Rorty keeps referring to gets constituted, who allots the opportunity to speak, and who arbitrates the terms of discussion. Rorty worries about the tendency of discourse to normalize itself and to block the flow of conversation by posing as a "canonical vocabulary," but he never quite faces the ways in which the conversation is perpetually materializing itself in institutional forms that empower and disempower speakers. As Frank Lentricchia says, if "we put 'society' back into Rorty's analysis, we will quickly see that the conversation is not and has never been as free as he might wish; that the conversation of culture has been involved as a moving force in the inauguration, maintenance, and perpetuation of society."[27]

For this reason, Rorty's left-wing critics are skeptical of the way Rortyean conversation legitimates itself through its very performances. For Christopher Norris, the political "upshot" of Rortyean conversation amounts to "foreswearing the idea of social improvement through rational critique and relying instead on the free circulation of communal values and myths."[28] The problem, as Norris sees it, is that such "thinking transcribes readily enough into the present condition of Western 'liberal' democracy, where the appearance of open, pluralistic debate ... disguises the monopolistic interests of power."[29] Without a critique of the relations of power that organize the conversation, Rortyean conversation as the pluralistic ideal of postmodernist bourgeois liberalism can all-too-easily slide into a self-justifying account of business as usual, an ungrounded accomodation to the status quo.

To interrupt the conversation, as Rorty's left-wing critics wish to do—to interrogate it, for instance, as Habermas suggests, in the name of undistorted communication—is, for Rorty, to "go transcendental and offer principles." Stuck where we always must be—inside the conversation, within our own cultural traditions—the pragmatist, Rorty says, "must remain ethnocentric and offer examples" (CP 173). Rather than attempting to ground the conversation, as Habermas does, in a counterfactual "ideal speech situation," as an aspiration for communication without coercion or systematic distortion, Rorty says all we can do is argue from cases, tell stories to justify our liberal institutions and practices.

Whether Rorty's reply to his critics is persuasive will depend to a large degree on one's own analysis of the present condition of liberal democracy. If one agrees with Rorty that the "ideals of the Enlightenment not only are our most precious cultural heritage but are in danger of disappearance as totalitarian states swallow up more and more of humanity" (CP 202), then one presumably would want to defend and reaffirm an endangered liberal consensus against attacks from both the right and the left. Rorty's postmodernist bourgeois liberalism in this light can be regarded as an update of the Cold War liberalism of the fifties, with the postmodernist "disbelief in metanarratives" offering a more current and fashionable account of the "end of ideology" — the postwar disillusion of American intellectuals with Marxism and their subsequent celebration of the unique success of America's pluralistic democracy. If, on the other hand, one believes there *is* something wrong with liberal democracy, Rorty's warning that the left-wing search for "authentic criticism" can only "separate the intellectuals from the moral consensus of the nation"[30] will appear to be what Rebecca Comay calls a kind of "gentle blackmail"[31] — a shakedown that poses the choice of either joining the conversation as it is presently constituted or admitting to one's unfashionable essentialism in seeking a standpoint of criticism outside the conversation. For Rorty, the alienation from mainstream culture that has marked American intellectuals and shaped their desire for social and political reconstruction during periods of ferment such as the thirties and the sixties has turned into a liability, a self-deceptive marginalization into irrelevant vanguardism. Conversation, as Rorty poses it, is a deal no good postmodernist can refuse.

As Rorty himself might say, there are no grounds to decide, no principles to which we can appeal, no ahistorical backups to make things clear. What's at stake are competing narratives, alternative views of how we read history and of how our accounts of the liberal tradition form our relationship to and inscribe our motives in contemporary social, cultural, and political practice. According to Rorty's account, "we should be more willing than we are to celebrate bourgeois capitalist society as the best polity actualized so far, while regretting that it is irrelevant to most of the problems of most of the population of the planet" (CP 210, n. 16). An alternative view will hold that Rorty is telling the story wrong — that it doesn't take universalist notions of natural right, metanarratives of emancipation, or an avant-garde intelligentsia to see the contradictions in bourgeois liberalism, the gaps between its ideals and practices, between its proclaimed egalitarianism and the inequalities it legitimates. As Jonathan Arac writes, "For so long as bourgeois capitalist society dominates workers over most of the planet, so long as the defense of bourgeois capitalist society requires threatening the whole planet with nuclear destruction, and so long as that society continues to dominate women, however good it may be, it is hardly irrelevant to the problems of the overwhelming majority who do not enjoy its benefits. 'Postmodern bourgeois liberalism' does not hold the privilege of enclosure within a single community."[32]

The telling issue here is not a theoretical one of justifying democratic aspirations but a practical one of determining how these aspirations are likely to be realized. For Rorty, the postmodernist bourgeois liberal recognizes that we "have to work out from the networks we are, from the communities with which we presently identify."[33] A detheoreticized sense of community is all we can hope for and all we need to reaffirm an ungrounded solidarity with the legacy of the Enlightenment, its liberal traditions, institutions, practices, and discourses. In contrast, from a democratic socialist perspective, the ideals of the Enlightenment are not so much in need of reaffirmation as they remain unfinished business. As Raymond Williams puts it, "the democratic revolution is still in a very early stage."[34] The task confronting democratic socialists, therefore, is that of expanding and extending the democratic ideals of liberalism, not by falling back on theory but by radicalizing practice to reanimate the Enlightenment struggle for an empowering civic discourse, for new public spheres of opinion and influence, for a rerepresentation of political agency and democratic participation.

Several of Rorty's critics complain of Rorty's indifference to the historical and social practices that inform his work. "Rorty is helpful in deflating philosophy's claims," says Paul Rabinow, "but he stops exactly at the point of taking seriously his own insight: to wit, thought is nothing more and nothing less than a historically locatable set of practices."[35] Leland notes that Rorty uses the word "contingency" to mean vocabularies *disconnected* from universal truths; it might be more useful, she contends, to think of the contingency of vocabularies as *connected* to lived social practices.[36] Cornel West accuses Rorty of retreating into the methods of the analytic tradition he has broken with and stopping short of attending to the social practices that underwrite his claims. A problem with Rorty, West says, is that he offers historicism without history. He has written a history of philosophy without discussing the historical and cultural contexts within which notions such as "objectivity" and "transcendence" have arisen. While Rorty's work has been groundbreaking in helping us see how ocular metaphors have dominated philosophical discourse, at the same time Rorty offers, in his words, "no particular reason why this ocular metaphor seized the imagination of the founders of Western thought" (PMN 372). According to West, Rorty's history "fervently attacks epistemological privilege but remains relatively silent about political, economic, racial, and sexual privilege,"[37] as though epistemological privilege has no consequences or connection to lived historical experience.

Rorty's critique of professional philosophy — of its technical training and devotion to "cases" and argumentation — represents a valiant effort to reinvigorate the public philosophy of James and Dewey and to reclaim a public sphere of democratic discourse where public intellectuals can address public issues in a public language. Rorty's struggle against the academicization of knowledge is in many respects an exemplary one. But, according to his critics, Rorty's untheoretical sense of community finally founders within the self-imposed constraints of his solidarity with the liberal tradition. The loyalty-to-itself that Rorty relies on to justify his vision of postmodernist bourgeois liberalism eliminates not only the possibility of "authentic criticism," but also the need to project a practical program of social reconstruction.

As Bernstein puts it, Rortyean conversation "becomes extremely thin when conceived of as a 'metaphilosophical' position."[38] And in this sense, Bernstein argues, Rorty parts company with Dewey's program of American pragmatism as an engaged practice. For Dewey, pluralistic conversation as a model of freely circulating democratic discourse requires not only the "leisure and libraries" Rorty sees as necessary to continue the conversation "as the sparks fly upward." It will require, Dewey says, "actual and concrete liberty of opportunity and action . . . equalization of the political and economic conditions under which individuals are alone free in fact, not in some *metaphysical* way."[39] While Rorty acknowledges that the dangers to conversation come primarily not "from science or naturalistic philosophy" but "from scarcity of food and from the secret police" (PMN 389), his version of liberalism keeps slipping into accounts of "free and leisured conversation," talk about talk endlessly rebegetting and redescribing itself. Dewey's liberalism, on the other hand, was an activist one, passionately concerned with what Dewey called the "problems of men" — with radicalizing its own practices to use social power not "to ameliorate the evil consequences of the existing system . . . [but] to change the system."[40] As Bernstein says, "Whatever our final judgment of Dewey's success or failure in dealing with . . . the 'problems of men,' Dewey constantly struggled with questions Rorty never quite faces."[41] In Dewey's life and works, we can see that the democratic aspirations of American pragmatism require not only the reemergence of public intellectuals from their academic cloisters but, more important, that a truly democratic discourse must be a popular one, suffusing all social spheres, activating and enabling the population to take part in an ongoing conversation about our collective purposes, needs, and hopes.

Conclusion

In this chapter we have examined Richard Rorty's attack on philosophical foundationalism and his proposal for an alternative metaphor of conversation. Rorty's critique of the epistemological tradition challenges not only the prevailing metanarratives in philosophical discourse, but all potentially totalizing schemata. This challenge has influenced a host of scholars across the disciplines, including literary theory, psychology, sociology, anthropology, and rhetoric, among others. Rorty's work has provided them with intellectual tools and rhetorical strategies to question the metanarratives in their own disciplines. Indeed, it seems reasonable to suggest that Rorty has had a deeper and more vital impact on a wide range of academic fields than any other contemporary American philosopher. Even his critics admit the power of his analysis. Despite his shortcomings, Cornel West contends, Rorty has provided the "most adversarial position in American academic philosophy since the fervent antiprofessionalism of William James,[42] and in the process has developed a project "pregnant with rich possibilities" that have yet to be adequately explored. The most promising possibility for West is the use of Rorty's neopragmatism as a "springboard for a more engaged, even subversive philosophical perspective."[43] For West, Rorty's project is open to radicalization because it encourages a wide-ranging critical attitude toward metanarratives in general, and in doing so "creates new discursive space" in which intellectuals at the margins and oppressed people can challenge the "tenuous self-images and provisional vocabularies which have had and do have hegemonic status in past and present societies."[44] The message to be drawn from Rorty's edifying philosophy, West suggests, is one of protest against final vocabularies and univocal discourses. For Rorty, the point of conversation is to continue the dialogue of civil society, to practice the democratic virtues of civility and solidarity by agreeing to keep on talking. While Rorty perhaps identifies the conversation too closely with the "first-order narratives" of the West, his work nonetheless provides a vision of a public sphere of freely circulating discourse which can serve as a measuring rod by which to assess our present and future discursive practices.

Primary and Secondary Sources

By all accounts, the centerpiece of Rorty's work is *Philosophy and the Mirror of Nature*, published by Princeton University Press in 1979. This is a demanding work, especially for readers unfamiliar with analytic philosophy. Perhaps the best way to read it, as Kenneth A. Bruffee suggests, is to start with the Introduction, pages 3–13, and then skip ahead to Part 3: Philosophy, pages 313–94. By doing so, nonspecialist readers can take in Rorty's overall argument before encountering the technical problems Rorty works his way through in Parts 1 and 2.

More accessible to general readers are the essays from 1972 to 1980 collected in *Consequences of Pragmatism*, published by University of Minnesota Press in 1982. These essays are less technical and more explicit than *Philosophy and the Mirror of Nature* in developing Rorty's views on pragmatism and the relation of James and Dewey to current continental thinkers such as Derrida and Foucault. These essays will be particularly interesting to readers conversant with contemporary literary and critical theory. "The Introduction: Pragmatism and Philosophy" sketches Rorty's view of a post-Philosophical culture.

Of his more recent work, two essays that elaborate Rorty's politics and his engagement with the problem of postmodernism are especially interesting: "Postmodernist Bourgeois Liberalism" appeared in *Journal of Philosophy* in October 1983, and "Habermas and Lyotard on Postmodernity" is included in *Habermas and Modernity*, edited by Richard Bernstein on MIT Press in 1985.

Rorty's most recent book, *Contingency, Irony, and Solidarity*, was published by Cambridge University Press in 1989, as we were finishing this chapter. Here Rorty draws out some of the implications of the "general turn against theory and toward narrative"[45] on the current critical scene, arguing that literature and not philosophy is in the best position to promote the sense of human solidarity he believes is essential to a liberal culture. *Contingency, Irony, and Solidarity* is noteworthy, among other reasons, for the new strategy Rorty deploys to treat the tension between his deconstructive impulses and his normative vision: he erects a barrier between them, between the distancing ironies of postmodernist theory and the quest for solidarity and social justice. Rorty holds that the "ironist" theories of thinkers such as Hegel, Nietzsche, Derrida, and Foucault — theories based on an ironic perception of one's own contingency — are "invaluable in our attempt to form a private self-image but pretty much useless when it comes to politics."[46] Rorty's argument that we should therefore drop the attempt to develop a theory that reconciles the private and the public — the "equally valid, yet forever incommensurable" demands of self-creation, on the one hand, and of justice and solidarity, on the other — is likely to be quite controversial. Nancy Fraser, for example, says the public/private dichotomy Rorty relies on in his recent work is problematical because it negates the possibility of social and collective self-creation.[47] Social movements of the last hundred years, Fraser argues, have taught us to politicize everything — public and private, from language to housework — and to see self-creation as a fundamentally political act by which the oppressed and excluded have forged new self-images, new idioms, and new forms of historical agency. To privatize theory, as Rorty wishes us to do, Fraser claims, makes theory inconsequential and practice atheoretical. The separation of public and private spheres amounts to a rewriting of the potentially radical discourses of postmodernism that renders them individual and apolitical, isolated from the world of practical politics.

Because Rorty's most important work is so recent, there is not, properly speaking, a developed secondary literature of explication. Instead, Rorty's work is treated by such diverse figures as Richard Bernstein, Clifford Geertz, Christopher Norris, and Frank Lentricchia in the course of current intellectual controversy and debate. Reference to their engagements with Rorty can be found in this chapter. Kenneth A. Bruffee has developed the implications of Rorty's work for liberal education in a series of articles, including "The Structure of Knowledge and the Future of Liberal Education," *Liberal Education* 67 (Fall 1981); "Liberal Education and the Social Justification of Belief," *Liberal Education* 68 (Summer 1982); and "Collaborative Learning and the 'Conversation of Mankind,'" *College English* 46 (1984). Rorty's views on education can be found in "Hermeneutics, General Studies, and Teaching," *Synergos: Selected Papers from the Synergos Seminars* vol. 2 (Fairfax, Va.: George Mason Univ., 1982); and in his review of Allen Bloom's *Closing of the American Mind* in the *New Republic*, April 4, 1988.

Notes

1. *Philosophical Profiles: Essays in a Pragmatic Mode* (Cambridge: Polity, 1986), p. 21.

2. *Philosophy and the Mirror of Nature* (Princeton: Princeton Univ., 1979), p. 5. Hereafter PMN.

3. *Consequences of Pragmatism* (Minneapolis: Univ. of Minnesota, 1982), p. 162. Hereafter CP.

4. "Habermas and Lyotard on Postmodernity," in *Habermas and Modernity*, ed. Richard J. Bernstein (Cambridge: MIT, 1985), p. 172.

5. "Philosophy without Principles," in *Against Theory: Literary Studies and the New Pragmatism*, ed. W. J. T. Mitchell (Chicago: Univ. of Chicago, 1985), pp. 132–48.

6. Ibid., pp. 134–35.

7. "Social Construction: An Interview with Richard Rorty," *Journal of Advanced Composition*, 8 (1989), p. 9.

8. Ibid.

9. *Philosophical Profiles*, p. 204.

10. "Postmodernist Bourgeois Liberalism," *Journal of Philosophy*, 87 (1983), p. 585.

11. "Habermas and Lyotard," p. 165–66.

12. Ibid., p. 164.

13. "Postmodernist Bourgeois Liberalism," p. 585.

14. "Habermas and Lyotard," p. 166.

15. "Postmodernist Bourgeois Liberalism," p. 585.

16. "Uses of Diversity," *Michigan Review*, 25 (1986), p. 108.

17. Ibid., p. 112.

18. Ibid., p. 113.

19. "Postmodernist Bourgeois Liberalism," p. 588.

20. "Uses of Diversity," p. 112.

21. Ibid., p. 114.

22. Ibid., p. 112.

23. "On Ethnocentrism: A Reply to Clifford Geertz," *Michigan Review*, 25 (1986), p. 533.

24. "Uses of Diversity," p. 114.

25. Ibid.

26. "Rorty on the Moral Concern of Philosophy: A Critique from a Feminist Point of View," *Praxis International*, 8 (1988), p. 280.

27. *Criticism and Social Change* (Chicago: Univ. of Chicago, 1983), p. 16.

28. "Philosophy as a Kind of Narrative: Rorty on Postmodern Liberal Culture," *Enclitic*, 7:2 (1983), p. 34.

29. Ibid.

30. "Postmodernist Bourgeois Liberalism," p. 588.

31. "Interrupting the Conversation: Notes on Rorty," *Telos*, 69 (1986), p. 467.

32. "Introduction," in *Postmodernism and Politics*, ed. Jonathan Arac (Minneapolis: Univ. of Minnesota, 1986), p. xxxvi.

33. "Postmodernist Bourgeois Liberalism," p. 589.

34. *The Long Revolution* (New York: Columbia Univ., 1961), p. 13.

35. "Representations Are Social Facts: Modernity and Post-Modernity in Anthropology," in *Writing Culture: The Poetics and Politics of Ethnography*, eds. James Clifford and George E. Marcus (Berkeley: Univ. of California, 1986), p. 239.

36. "Rorty on Moral Concerns," p. 281.

37. "The Politics of American Neo-Pragmatism," *Post-Analytic Philosophy*, eds. John Rajchman and Cornel West (New York: Columbia Univ., 1985), p. 269.

38. *Profiles*, p. 48.

39. *Problems of Men* (New York: Philosophical Library, 1946), p. 132.

40. Ibid.

41. *Profiles*, p. 48.

42. "Politics of American Neo-Pragmatism," p. 266.

43. Ibid.

44. Ibid., pp. 270–71.

45. *Contingency, Irony, and Solidarity* (Cambridge: Cambridge Univ., 1989), p. xvi.

46. Ibid., p. 83.

47. "Solidarity or Singularity: Richard Rorty between Romanticism and Technocracy," *Praxis International*, 8 (1988), pp. 257–72.

The Frankfurt School

Introduction

Chip Sills

The phrase "critical theory" has become identified for many with the work of the Frankfurt School. Founded originally in the 1920s by a group of left-wing Jewish intellectuals, the tactful designation Institute for Social Research was chosen over the more provocative original title, Institute for Marxism.[1] Over the decades of its existence, the Institute (now usually referred to as the Frankfurt School) included a remarkable number of influential thinkers who have made contributions in Marxist theory, sociology, metapsychology, culture critique, philosophy, and aesthetic theory. At one time or another, Erich Fromm, Herbert Marcuse, Theodor Adorno, Max Horkheimer, Leo Lowenthal, Franz Neumann, Walter Benjamin, and Jürgen Habermas were associated with the Institute.

The Frankfurt School's primary contributions to contemporary discourse revolve around the notion of "critical theory." In a famous essay first published in 1937, Max Horkheimer, perhaps the most dynamic and influential of the early Institute participants, outlined the proposed differences between "traditional" and "critical" theory.[2] Building on the Marxist notion of the intellectual as an alienated product of the division of labor and the Kantian notion of a critique of reason, Horkheimer criticized existing (positivist and neo-Kantian) notions of science as resting on a traditional notion of "theory" that saw itself as being abstractly separated from practice. Specifically, traditional theory considered its objects as already existing objectively, and disclaimed any important connection between the *production* of such objects and the theoretical activity that grasped them. This abstract relationship between theory and practice posited in theory itself was held to reflect the abstraction of capitalist production relations. Critical theory, on the other hand, does not consider existing social relations as providing an adequate model for theoretical activity. Rather, since social reality is itself in need of criticism, the modes of thought that uncritically reflect that reality are also in need of criticism. The *critique* of such modes of traditional theoretical effort transcends their limitations by taking its point of departure from an empirically nonexistent vantage point — the point of view of an emancipated socialized humanity. The parallels with Kant's critical procedure and Marx's socialist critique of capitalist society are patent. But Horkheimer was articulating a Marxism with a difference. In 1937, Marxism was identified for many with the vast tragic experiment in progress in the Soviet Union. The Frankfurt School attempted to hold aloft an emancipatory ideal in Marxism that even then (before much of the horror of Stalinist Russia was accepted as actual in leftist circles) was being compromised by the coarse and simplistic *Realpolitik* of Soviet Marxism. By elaborating a theoretical program intransigeantly opposed to mass bourgeois society, critical of positivism, in favor of a many-sided emancipatory effort (including an appropriation of the greatest achievements of bourgeois aesthetic and cultural elements, as opposed to the Russian emphasis on mass production), and unabashedly supportive of dialectical analysis, Horkheimer and the Frankfurt School staked out a difficult middle ground in the battle between communism and capitalism. While the more loyal communist movements tried to root themselves in the realities of the working-class struggle in capitalist society and ally themselves with Soviet directives in foreign policy, the Frankfurt School Marxists were suspicious of mass movements and independent of the specific line being advocated in Moscow. These elements remained definitive of the work of the School throughout its career. In marked contrast with the work of Georg Lukács and Ernst Bloch, whose dialectical adventures did not preclude a resigned collaboration with Communist regimes, the members of the Frankfurt School (even though a number were in fact members of the Communist Party) remained above activist politics. For the Frankfurt School, the "socialized humanity" that has served as the utopian vantage point of Marxist theory was definitely not the actual proletariat of the industrialized West, nor was it the bureaucratically regimented workers of the socialist bloc. This unwillingness to tie the Marxian project to any specific social agent is one of the defining characteristics of Frankfurt School Marxism, and distinguishes it from other Hegelian-Marxist tendencies like that of Lukács, who was able to combine a defense of Hegelian-Marxist dialectical and historicist analysis with an endorsement of the Leninist centralized party. The Frankfurt School was bitterly attacked from the left for its unwillingness to play the political game, but this same reticence may serve to make its legacy attractive in an era during which classical communist ideology has lost most of its appeal among

Western intellectuals. The work of the school might come to seem more and more as an example of antibourgeois critique unstained by the excesses of Leninist Marxism.

The work of the School is too vast and too varied to even begin to outline in this space. Since the work of Adorno and Habermas is dealt with in some detail in the following chapters, I will refer the reader to those chapters for fuller treatment. But some mention must be made of the work of the School in attempting to combine the insights of Marx and Freud, and for popularizing that unlikely blend of leftism and nihilism that Allan Bloom has dubbed the "Nietzscheanization of the Left."[3]

The rise of Nazism made it necessary for the school to physically relocate in the 1930s to New York, and provided the occasion for a number of studies of the phenomenon of fascism, most notably Neumann's *Behemoth*, Erich Fromm's *Escape From Freedom* and Adorno's work on the authoritarian personality.[4] The Frankfurt theorists' sensitivity to (and distaste for) mass cultural phenomena allowed them to construct an analysis of Nazism that combined the Marxist theory that fascism was a last-gasp version of finance capitalism with a psychoanalytically informed account of the social and cultural dynamics that tended to create the personalities most susceptible to fascist manipulation. At the same time, the stark realities of Nazism, Stalinism, and global war brought home to the Frankfurt theorists the lack of any genuinely utopian trend. This realization initiated a darkening mood, captured in the *Dialectic of Enlightenment*, originally published in 1944, where Horkheimer and Adorno returned to the Enlightenment roots of the Marxian project and found them ambiguous with regard to emancipation.[5] In the Enlightenment urge to explain everything, to reduce the chaos of existence to a pure transparency, the authors claimed to discern the remnants of a primal terror, and the seeds of the "pure immanence" of contemporary positivism. This "pure immanence" — the incapacity to even conceive otherness — is already the concept of "one-dimensionality" that will become so important in the work of Herbert Marcuse. There is a Nietzschean quality in Horkheimer and Adorno's critique: reality is opposed on the basis of its *ugliness*. This elitist stance is justified by a singular reading of history. While the Marxist historicist account is not immediately abandoned, it is wondered whether the historical opportunity for human emancipation has been forever lost. In this case, the whole becomes the untrue, and the only purpose for critique is to oppose the invincible progress of a wholly immanent society characterized by an authoritarian state and a mass culture that defines needs as only those the society can satisfy. This gloomy pessimism was somewhat attenuated in the work of Herbert Marcuse.

Marcuse was the member of the Frankfurt School who first achieved true notoriety, because of his popularity among members of the international New Left in the 1960s. His works *Reason and Revolution, Eros and Civilization,* and *One-Dimensional Man,* in particular, were widely read and discussed.[6] *Reason and Revolution* provided for many students their first sympathetic study of Hegel's thought; *Eros and Civilization* countered the Freudian pessimism about culture that had been echoed by Horkheimer and Adorno by postulating an instinctual dimension to political liberation; and *One-Dimensional Man* presented a powerful indictment of "advanced industrial society" (lumping together capitalist and communist varieties) as inexorably tending toward the closure of all genuine alternatives to itself. The critique of positivism is elaborated into a global critique of a society bent on preserving its "pure immanence." The irony of this characterization, coming from a Marxist, is remarkable. One need only recall Marx's ringing tribute to the radical innovative and dissolving power of bourgeois production relations to see how far the theory has progressed. Yet Marcuse's work has had an enduring influence, somewhat obscured in academic circles by the present-day interest in other Frankfurt School members. We would point to the following elements of Marcuse's work as having entered into the collective unconscious of contemporary social critique:

1. The interpretation of dialectics as the negation—not the comprehension—of the present.

2. The "great refusal" to go along with contemporary industrial society, which valorized a continuing contempt for capitalist society even when the older communist critique was losing its power.

3. The emphasis on "marginal" elements—the third-world national liberation struggles, the countercultural and lumpen-proletarian elements of youth, feminist, and ethnic rebellion as opposed to the traditional working-class movement—as presenting the only possibility for genuinely radical change. The contemporary academic fetishizing of the "marginal" becomes comprehensible within Marcuse's covering conception.

4. An explicit co-opting of the "aesthetic dimension" for the purposes of radical political and cultural critique. It had long been common for various elements of the cultural avant-garde to express solidarity with leftist goals; Marcuse (along with Adorno and Benjamin) provided an analysis that somehow managed to claim the elitist snobbery of the old culture as the birthright of the anticultural culture critics of the New Left.

5. The notion of "repressive tolerance", with its corollary argument that tolerance—including the freedom of speech—is appropriately

extended only towards "progressive" tendencies, but denied to the Right. Contemporary discourse in the mass media and in academia show signs of having imbibed some of this.

6. The very concept of one-dimensionality, which reduces to a phrase the whole radical tendency to simplify the vast complexity of contemporary society, in all its cultural, economic, and political multifariousness, as "the status quo," "the system," etc.[7]

"One-dimensionality" is indeed a rhetorically powerful conception, resonant with the general assault on positivism that we have in our General Introduction to this book named as a central motivation of the "rhetorical turn." It is an acute irony of contemporary history that the most patent recent reassertion of a transcending dimension to human affairs has been in the struggles of Eastern Europeans to assert their freedom by casting off their Communist systems. The irony comes about because the Frankfurt School critics, from Horkheimer to Habermas, have always concentrated the bulk of their scorn on the systems of the West, honoring the dubious leftist tradition that the Soviet experiment had to be seen in as sympathetic a light as possible. Whether this incongruous lack of critical capacity will undermine the future influence of the Frankfurt School theorists remains to be seen.

Notes

1. See Martin Jay, *The Dialectical Imagination* (Boston: Little, Brown, 1973), p. 8. Jay's work is a masterly sympathetic study, and contains a full bibliography. A useful bibliography and biographical notes about the principal Frankfurt School members are also readily available in the anthology edited by Andrew Arato and Eike Gebhardt, *The Essential Frankfurt School Reader* (New York: Continuum, 1985).

2. Max Horkheimer, "Traditional and Critical Theory," trans. Matthew J. O'Connell, in Horkheimer, *Critical Theory: Selected Essays* (New York: Herder and Herder, 1972), pp. 188–243.

3. Allan Bloom, *The Closing of the American Mind* (New York: Touchstone Books, 1987), pp. 217–26.

4. Franz Neumann, *Behemoth: the Structure and Practice of National Socialism* (New York: Oxford Univ., 1942); Erich Fromm, *Escape From Freedom* (New York: Farrar & Rinehart, 1942); Theodor Adorno, with Else Frenkel-Brunswik, Daniel J. Levinson and R. Nevitt Sanford, *The Authoritarian Personality* (New York: Harper & Row, 1950).

5. Theodor Adono and Max Horkheimer, *Dialectic of Enlightenment*, trans. John Cumming (New York: Herder and Herder, 1972).

6. Herbert Marcuse, *Reason and Revolution: Hegel and the Rise of Social Theory*, with new Preface "A Note on Dialectic" (Boston: Beacon, 1960); *Eros*

and Civilization: A Philosophical Inquiry Into Freud (Boston: Beacon, 1955); *One-Dimensional Man: Studies in the Ideology of Advanced Industrial Society* (Boston: Beacon, 1964).

7. See, for instance, Jeremy J. Shapiro's seminal article, "One-Dimensionality: The Universal Semiotic of Advanced Industrial Society," in Paul Breines, ed., *Critical Interruptions: New Left Perspectives on Herbert Marcuse* (New York: Herder and Herder, 1970), and Paul Piccone, General Introduction to Arato and Gebhardt, *Essential Frankfurt School Reader*.

4

Contra-Diction
Adorno's Philosophy of Discourse
Lambert Zuidervaart

The ironical motto of *Aesthetic Theory* provides an indirect epitaph for its author: "What is called philosophy of art usually lacks one of two things: either the philosophy or the art."[1] The epitaph is indirect, for it indicates a challenge that Adorno met throughout his life: neither philosophy nor art was lacking. This helps explain the paradoxical character of his philosophy of discourse.

He was born Theodor Ludwig Wiesengrund on September 11, 1903, in Frankfurt am Main.[2] Frankfurt was to be home for the first three and last two decades of his life. The intervening years, from 1934 to 1949, he resided in Oxford, New York City, and southern California. During this exile from Nazi Germany he adopted the name by which he is best known: Theodor W. Adorno. The middle initial stands for the surname of his father, Oskar Wiesengrund, a wealthy assimilated Jewish wine merchant. Adorno is the surname of his mother, Maria Calvelli-Adorno, a Catholic of Corsican and Genoese descent. The other member of the family was Maria's sister Agathe. Maria and Agathe gave young "Teddie" the love for music that would motivate much of his scholarly work.

Philosophy fed a voracious intellectual appetite during Adorno's formative years in the Weimar Republic. Weekly sessions on Kant's first *Critique* with Siegfried Kracauer began when Adorno was fifteen. Close readings of philosophical texts became a lifelong passion. Adorno earned his doctorate in philosophy in 1924 with a dissertation on the phenomenology of Edmund Husserl. By this time he had already made the acquaintance of two older men who were to be his closest collaborators—Max Horkheimer, whom he met in a seminar on Husserl in 1922, and Walter Benjamin, to whom Kracauer introduced Adorno in 1923.

During his university years Adorno read such unorthodox works as Lukács's *The Theory of the Novel* and Ernst Bloch's *Geist der Utopie*. These were to inspire his own radical approach to philosophical aesthetics.[3] Just as important for the development of Adorno's thought, however, was his intense involvement with "new music," in particular that of Arnold Schönberg. Adorno spent two of these years in Vienna as the composition student of Alban Berg and the piano student of Eduard Steuermann. From the 1920s come Schönbergian impulses that become conceptual tone rows, as it were, in Adorno's subsequent writings. Commenting on a manuscript eventually published as *Against Epistemology*, Susan Buck-Morss writes:

> It seems clear that Schönberg's revolution in music provided the inspiration for Adorno's own efforts in philosophy, the model for his major work on Husserl during the thirties. For just as Schönberg had overthrown tonality, the decaying form of bourgeois music, so Adorno's Husserl study attempted to overthrow idealism, the decaying form of bourgeois philosophy.[4]

Adorno took from his Vienna days a model for an "atonal philosophy"[5] whose style and concerns prefigure the antifoundational and deconstructive themes in more recent philosophies of discourse.

It would be a mistake, however, to read Adorno's writings as no more than a peculiar fusion of antiidealist philosophy and expressionist art. The catalyst for this fusion is a social critique derived from Georg Lukács's *History and Class Consciousness*, a seminal text of Western Marxism.[6] Although there has been considerable discussion in recent years about the label "Western Marxism,"[7] it is a useful term to indicate a political and academic tradition animated by a set of shared concerns and arising in central Europe during the 1920s. Motivated in part by loyal opposition to the Leninist model of party politics, and in part by the apparent failure of proletarian revolution and the rise of fascism, Marxists such as Lukács, Karl Korsch, and Antonio Gramsci attempted to reformulate the intellectual legacy of Karl Marx in order to understand dramatically new conditions. A key factor, which gradually became thematic, was a structural shift in capitalism that forestalled indefinitely its expected collapse and rendered Marx's theory of revolution partially obsolete. At the philosophical-historical level, the scientism and determinism of prominent theorists after Marx had to be confronted, and the importance of philosophy and other cultural forms had to be reexamined. For Western Marxists the "failure of the socialist revolution to spread outside Russia" was not simply what Anderson describes as the "cause and consequence of its corruption inside Russia."[8] The failure was also an indication of theoretical deficiencies in the classical tradition of Marxism.[9]

Adorno's social critique shares such concerns with the writings of other Western Marxists. He gradually elaborated his critique in dialogue with members of the Frankfurt Institute of Social Research, of which Horkheimer became director in 1930. Its earliest stirrings appear in Adorno's first *Habilitationsschrift*,[10] which defends Freudian psychoanalysis as a rational theory of the unconscious, while attacking irrationalist accounts of the unconscious as ideological supports for the status quo. Additional incentives came from Adorno's frequent trips to Berlin in the late 1920s to visit his future wife, Gretel Karplus, and a circle of politically leftist writers and artists including Bloch, Benjamin, Moholy-Nagy, Bertolt Brecht, Hanns Eisler, Lotte Lenya, and Kurt Weill. The role of art in transforming social consciousness was uppermost in their discussions.

Even more decisive, according to Buck-Morss, was a methodology Adorno derived from the introductory chapter of Walter Benjamin's *The Origin of German Tragic Drama*.[11] Adorno's methodology emphasizes a close, imaginative reading that exposes social conflicts by uncovering problems inherent in works of art, philosophical texts, or the phenomena of daily life. The critic elicits a sociohistorical truth that might not have been intended by the artist, philosopher, or agent. Such critical interpretation has political significance, even when it is not directly useful for political purposes.

Although Adorno's actual method differs from Benjamin's, a Benjaminian inspiration clearly surfaces in his writings in the early 1930s. These include two lectures given during Adorno's first, brief career on the Frankfurt philosophy faculty,[12] a programmatic essay on music sociology,[13] and *Kierkegaard: Construction of the Aesthetic*, Adorno's first book.[14] The latter was published on the day Hitler came to power in 1933. Soon afterwards Adorno, Horkheimer, and many other Jewish professors were dismissed from German universities. The Institute of Social Research moved to New York, where it became loosely affiliated with Columbia University. Adorno enrolled as an "advanced student" at Oxford University but frequently returned to Germany to visit Gretel Karplus, whom he married in 1937. Benjamin had already moved to Paris, where he lived until 1940, when he committed suicide at the Spanish border while fleeing the Nazis.

The social-critical program forged in the early 1930s would remain central to Adorno's work until his death in 1969. So would his passionate interest in philosophy and modern art, especially music. One can trace gradual shifts in the topics and tone of his writings, however, shifts that are connected to his social circumstances and his collaboration on various projects. For convenience we may speak of three phases in his mature writings.

The first phase (approximately 1933–1949) is marked by inter-disciplinary critiques of popular culture. In this phase Adorno published several pathbreaking essays on the music industry, most notably "On the Fetish-Character in Music and the Regression of Listening."[15] He also coauthored *Dialectic of Enlightenment*, with its crucial chapter on "The Culture Industry: Enlightenment as Mass Deception."[16] These writings display an increasingly Hegelian style, a self-conscious importing of Freudian categories, and a complex appropriation of Nietzsche and of conservative culture critics such as Oswald Spengler. Closely connected with these writings is Adorno's work on *The Authoritarian Personality*.[17] During his years in the United States Adorno was searching popular culture for the economic, political, psychological, and deeply historical sources of fascism, anti-Semitism, and the loss of a critical public consciousness.

The second phase (approximately 1949–1958) is marked by essayistic interventions in high culture. It begins with Adorno's and Horkheimer's return to Frankfurt in 1949 and the reopening of the Institute of Social Research in 1951. It ends around the time Adorno replaced Horkheimer as director of the Institute in 1958. Although written earlier, Adorno's first major publications in this phase can be read as attempts to provoke the superintendents of German high culture during postwar reconstruction. *Philosophy of Modern Music* challenges the official music scene; *Minima Moralia* expresses the bitter experiences of German exiles; *In Search of Wagner* decodes the ambiguous work of the Nazi's favorite composer.[18]

The clue to such a reading comes from "Cultural Criticism and Society," an article written in 1949 and published in 1951. Republished in 1955 as the lead essay in *Prisms*,[19] the article claims that "cultural criticism must become social physiognomy" because cultural phenomena have become increasingly integrated into the structure of capitalist society. Such integration does not spare the culture critic:

> The more total society becomes, the greater the reification of the mind and the more paradoxical its effort to escape reification on its own. Even the most extreme consciousness of doom threatens to degenerate into idle chatter. Cultural criticism finds itself faced with the final stage of the dialectic of culture and barbarism. To write poetry after Auschwitz is barbaric. And this corrodes even the knowledge of why it has become impossible to write poetry today.[20]

Many of Adorno's writings on the arts in the 1950s share this provocative combination of agonizing self-criticism and polemical exaggeration. The combination seems intended to interrupt "business as usual" and to recall the horrors that consumers of high culture would like to forget.

Two programmatic essays announce the concerns occupying the last decade of Adorno's life. The first is the Introduction to *Against Epistemology* (1956), in which Adorno insists on the need to historicize ontology and epistemology.[21] The second is "The Essay as Form," a self-conscious reflection on philosophical style that opens Adorno's first volume of literary criticism.[22] Together the two essays announce a turn toward philosophical consolidation. Although by this time Adorno was becoming a well-known radio guest and public lecturer, the focus of his scholarly work shifted toward sustained treatments of topics that had been central to his earlier writings. Besides numerous volumes of essays on music[23] and literature,[24] Adorno published monographs on Mahler and Berg,[25] a book on Hegel,[26] and collections of essays in sociology and aesthetics.[27]

He also entered numerous academic debates about education, university politics, and sociological methods, the most famous of which was the "positivism dispute" with Karl Popper.[28] Whereas Popper continued to cling to a modified version of the ideal of value-neutrality in academic work, Adorno clearly insisted on the claim that no social theory is politically neutral. His central claim is this:

> The idea of scientific truth cannot be split off from that of a true society. Only such a society would be free from contradiction and lack of contradiction. In a resigned manner, scientism commits such an idea to the mere forms of knowledge alone.
>
> By stressing its societal neutrality, scientism defends itself against the critique of the object and replaces it with the critique merely of logical inconsistencies.[29]

Despite miscommunication on both sides, the debate led to a clearer understanding of an issue that has since come to dominate university politics in English-speaking countries. It also provided considerable impetus for followers of Adorno such as Jürgen Habermas, Karl-Otto Apel, and Albrecht Wellmer, all of whom have worked to diminish miscommunication while sharing with Adorno the quest for a politically committed social theory. Adorno's central claim continues to have effect in their work.

Adorno's major writings of this decade were *Negative Dialectics*[30] and *Aesthetic Theory*. *Negative Dialectics* can be called a work of metaphilosophy: it presents philosophical reflections on philosophy, and it elaborates the categories and procedures employed in Adorno's previous writings about other philosophers. In a similar fashion *Aesthetic Theory* is a work of metaaesthetics. It presents philosophical reflections on philosophical aesthetics, and it elaborates the categories and procedures employed in Adorno's previous writings on the arts. Each book provides a summation, not only of Adorno's own writings but also of the philosophy of the Frankfurt School.

In light of Adorno's life and work, in view of his passion for art and philosophy and his uncompromising criticisms of contemporary society, it is nearly impossible to read *Aesthetic Theory* without a sense of tragedy. Caught up in the endless wranglings of university politics, and under attack from some of his own militant students, Adorno died of a heart attack in August 1969, one month short of his sixty-sixth birthday, and one rewriting away from completing his *summa aesthetica*. The incomplete manuscript was published in 1970, the first of twenty-three volumes in Adorno's *Gesammelte Schriften*. *Aesthetic Theory* has become the last testament, as it were, of a truly remarkable man: a Hegelian Marxist who took distance from both Hegel and Marx; an assimilated German Jew who wrote some of his most seminal works in American exile; a polished modern musician who subjected music to ideology critique; an imaginative and rigorous philosopher who was better known for his work in the social sciences.

Recent conferences on Adorno attest to the continuing importance of his work.[31] It is not clear, however, exactly how Adorno's life and work are to be located in the traditions to which they belong. His writings occupy a historical "force field," according to Martin Jay. The field includes "Western Marxism, aesthetic modernism, mandarin cultural despair, and Jewish self-identification, as well as the more anticipatory pull of deconstructionism."[32] No one force dominates Adorno's work. The forces exist in creative tension. In *Aesthetic Theory* they become explosive.

Indeed, a survey of the secondary literature would bring to mind Habermas's remark that "Adorno has left philosophy with a chaotic landscape."[33] Adorno's writings lend themselves to divergent appropriations. Yet it is precisely the unresolved tensions in Adorno's thought that make it interesting for philosophers of discourse. Our interest is not only what Adorno says about discourse but also how he says it. The most important topics to be considered are ones of style, logic, and method.

Parataxis

Commentators often describe the difficulties of Adorno's writings. Martin Jay begins by frankly admitting that Adorno "would have been appalled" at an attempt "to render his thought painlessly accessible to a wide audience."[34] In a similar vein, Fredric Jameson asks:

> What serious justification can be made for an attempt to summarize, simplify, make more accessible a work which insists relentlessly on the need for modern art and thought to be difficult, to guard their truth and freshness by the austere demands they make on the powers of concentration of their participants, by their refusal of all habitual response in their attempt to reawaken numb thinking and deadened perception to a raw, wholly unfamiliar real world?[35]

Such descriptions help introduce readers to the subject matter at hand, which can hardly be considered easily comprehensible. There is no ready detour around the peculiar style of Adorno's most important writings.

The most obvious obstacles for an English-language reader are matters of translation. Such obstacles are reported in the first of Adorno's German books to appear in English. The title of the translator's preface tells the story: "Translating the Untranslatable." Samuel Weber says the concreteness of Adorno's style has little in common with the immediacy expected of contemporary English. Instead Adorno's concreteness has to do with "the density with which thought and articulation permeate each other." This "density" comes from pregnant words such as *Geist, Sache, Erkenntnis, Begriff*, and *Aufhebung* for which English lacks equally meaningful terms. Also, in contrast to the dynamic potential of German sentence structure, contemporary English grammar "taboos long sentences as clumsy" and seeks "brevity and simplicity at all costs."[36] It seems, then, that the problems of interpreting Adorno's writing resemble those facing any English-language student of German philosophy.

Yet there may be a special reason why only two translators have tackled more than one work by Adorno. Apart from frequent allusions to various authors and events, the main reason for hesitation probably lies in Adorno's unusual stylistic strategies. Adorno himself discusses these strategies and his reasons for employing them. Indeed, Gillian Rose asserts that "Adorno discussed his method and style in everything he wrote, often at the expense of discussing the ostensible subject of the piece."[37] Among the devices described by Rose are impersonal and passive constructions, parallactic formulations, chiasmatic structures, and ironic inversion. She suggests that all of these stylistic strategies reflect a concern "to achieve a style which will best intervene in society."[38] This concern arises from Adorno's conviction that we live in an "administered world" in which conflicts are papered over and suffering is repressed.

According to a frequently quoted passage from *Negative Dialectics*, true philosophy resists paraphrasing (ND 44/33−34). By itself, this statement is less striking than some commentators have thought. Its point is borne out whenever one tries to summarize Kant's *Critique of Pure Reason* or Heidegger's *Being and Time*. Adorno's next claim is more controversial. He says the fact that most philosophy can be paraphrased speaks against it. Whether most philosophy can be paraphrased is a moot point. The claim itself suggests something about Adorno's own writing, however. His writing deliberately resists easy consumption. The need for powerful expression weighs heavier on Adorno than the desire for direct communication. Martin Jay is probably right; Adorno would have been appalled at attempts to render his thought painlessly accessible.

No less important than resisting easy consumption, however, is Adorno's desire to achieve a fit between the form and content of his philosophy. This desire helps explain why his unusual strategies culminate in the thoroughly paratactical style of *Aesthetic Theory*. The editors quote Adorno as follows:

> My theorem that there is no philosophical "first thing" is coming back to haunt me. ... I cannot now proceed to construct a universe of reasoning in the usual orderly fashion. Instead I have to put together a whole from a series of partial complexes which are concentrically arranged and have the same weight and relevance. It is the constellation ... of these partial complexes which has to make sense. (AT 541/496)

The resulting text is neither a systematic treatise nor a collection of essays. At the same time it is neither haphazard nor disjointed. The text employs parataxis throughout: sentences, paragraphs, and entire chapters lie side by side without explicit coordination or subordination. Although this paratactical style defies traditional patterns of philosophical discourse, the movement from one sentence or paragraph or chapter to another seems carefully planned, and the topics of one chapter intersect those of other chapters. The text resembles a continually shifting kaleidoscope of topics and themes.

Adorno had definite philosophical reasons for writing in this manner, despite the problems it poses for both author and reader. His reasons are closely tied to his logic and method, which will be discussed later. The main reason has to do with the theorem he himself mentions. This theorem says that there is no first principle, no origin, no *arche* nor Archimedean point from which philosophy may proceed. Although the theorem operates in all Adorno's writings on philosophy after 1930, its first sustained elaboration occurs in his book on Husserl (1956). Thereafter one finds it continually reformulated, whether in programmatic articles such as "The Essay as Form" (1958), "Ohne Leitbild" (1960), "Why Philosophy?" (1962), and "Parataxis" (1964), or in his books on Hegel (1963) and *Negative Dialectics* (1966).[39] In addition to being a clue to understanding Adorno's own writing, his opposition to first principles gives an early announcement of the opposition to logocentrism and foundationalism that unites many pragmatist, poststructuralist, and feminist philosophies of discourse.

Adorno's book on Husserl makes clear that his theorem serves a metacritique of "idealist" epistemology. The ultimate target of this metacritique is Heideggerian ontology. By "idealism" Adorno means the affirmation of an identity between subject and object. This affirmation assigns constitutive priority to the epistemic subject. In Adorno's judgment, idealism has been the dominant philosophy in capitalist society since Descartes. It continues in Husserl's struggle against idealism and in Heidegger's attempt to return to a Being prior to the split between subject and object. Idealism is the modern form of "first philosophy," of philosophy that assigns primacy to one original principle, whether this be the epistemic subject or primordial Being.

Adorno makes two claims against first philosophy. The first, derived from Kant and Hegel, is that anything taken as first or original is already second or derivative simply by virtue of its being taken that way in a humanly constructed philosophy. We cannot jump out of our epistemological skin. The second claim, derived from Nietzsche and Marx, is that every principle or structure elevated above the flux of appearances is inescapably historical. It is inescapably historical both because the principle comes to be elevated within the push and pull of ongoing philosophical debate and because the act of elevating occurs within the social conflicts informing the philosophy in question. Both claims can be summarized as follows: "The first and immediate is always, as a concept, mediated and thus not the first."[40]

Because no first principle is first, and because every supposedly first principle is inescapably historical, Adorno refuses to proceed from any first principle. Because he insists that a philosophy's presentation must match its claims, Adorno continually searches for a style that does not suggest a hierarchical derivation from first principles. The paratactical style of *Aesthetic Theory* stands at the end of this search. The consistent employment of parataxis represents not only a deliberate attempt to jar and challenge the reader but also a stylistic strategy to oppose and avoid "first philosophy." Just as Schönberg undermined the tonal center without embracing chance as an organizational principle, so Adorno has found a way to defy traditional philosophical styles without becoming merely rhapsodic. Just as Schönberg's compositions call for new ways of listening, so Adornian texts demand a new way of reading, one which continually circles back upon itself.

Negative Dialectic

Adorno's opposition to first philosophy also affects the logic of his writings. By "logic" is meant not simply the patterns, principles, or categories of Adorno's arguments but rather all of these matters together with the substantive considerations behind them. "Negative dialectic," Adorno's own term, best indicates what we have in mind. Adorno's arguments are dialectical in the sense that they concentrate on unavoidable tensions between polar opposites whose opposition constitutes their unity and generates historical change. The dialectic is negative in the sense that it refuses to affirm any underlying identity or final synthesis of polar opposites, even though Adorno continually points to the possibility of reconciliation. The main oppositions occur between the particular and the universal and between culture in a narrow sense and society as a whole.

For Adorno, the tension between the universal and the particular occurs both in philosophy and in the phenomena that philosophers interpret.[41] Within philosophy a tension occurs between the need to employ universal concepts, on the one hand, and the desire to honor particular facts, on the other. The traditional ways to ease this tension have been through deduction or induction. Adorno thinks that neither approach does justice to conflicts among concepts, and that each overlooks important details. He sees dialectic as "an endeavour to overcome the rift between deduction and induction so prevalent in reified thought" (AT 510/471). Adorno's description of the essay as a genre summarizes the intentions of his dialectical discourse:

> It is not unlogical; rather it obeys logical criteria in so far as the totality of its sentences must fit together coherently. ... The essay neither makes deductions from a principle nor does it draw conclusions from coherent individual observations. It co−ordinates elements, rather than subordinating them; and only the essence of its content, not the manner of its presentation, is commensurable with logical criteria.[42]

Adorno's writings try to maintain a circular movement between universal concepts and particular facts without turning concepts into mere generalities, without treating facts as mere examples, and without covering up tensions between concepts and facts.

Substantive justification for a dialectical approach comes from the tension between universality and particularity within the phenomena to be interpreted. This is especially clear in *Aesthetic Theory*. According to Adorno, modern art has taken a "radically nominalistic position" (AT 521/480) that involves a widespread rejection of traditional forms and genres. The rejection touches even fundamental categories such as "art" and "the work of art." At the same time, however, modern art retains elements of universality. Anton Webern's compositions transform the traditional sonata form into miniature "nodal progressions" (AT 270/259−60). Indeed, "wherever art on its way to concreteness tries to eliminate the universal ... this negation preserves what it ostensibly eliminates" (AT 522/481). Artists and art critics cannot avoid using universal concepts such as "form" and "material," even though their meaning for modern art is far from clear (AT 507/468).

Thus modern art calls for a philosophy that respects the particularity of artistic phenomena but illuminates the universal elements within art itself. Dialectical aesthetics tries to raise art's "unconscious interaction" between universality and particularity "to the level of consciousness" (AT 270/259). It "deals with reciprocal relations between universal and particular where the universal is not imposed on the particular ... but emerges from the dynamic of particularities themselves" (AT 521/481). If the refusal to impose prescriptive universals places Adorno in opposition to deduction, the emphasis on reciprocal relations places him in opposition to inductive approaches. Dialectical logic is his alternative.

Adorno's dialectical approach calls into play the opposition between culture and society mentioned earlier. According to Adorno, quantitative exchange is the dominant principle in contemporary society. Deductivist and inductivist approaches tend to ratify this principle, whether by subsuming qualitatively different phenomena under a universal norm or by treating them as unrelated atoms. Like modern art, Adorno's aesthetics pursues a "utopia of the particular" (AT 521/480) that places both of them in conflict with traditional logic and "exchange society." Yet Adorno also insists that modern art and his own philosophy belong to the social totality against which they struggle. It would be utopian in a bad sense to act as if the utopia of the particular has already arrived. A major task for Adorno's aesthetics is to show exactly how modern art and his own philosophy participate in the very society they oppose.

The key to this demonstration is the claim that the dialectic is not simply a cultural matter. The ongoing opposition between the universal and the particular is not simply a matter of philosophical argument. Nor is it simply a tension within art. Instead it permeates all of advanced capitalist society. In the words of *Negative Dialectics*, the dialectic is neither a purely conceptual method nor simply a real process nor a mere mishmash of argument and subject matter:

> To proceed dialectically means to think in contradictions, for the sake of the contradiction once experienced in the thing [*Sache*], and against that contradiction. A contradiction in reality, [the dialectic] is a contradiction against reality. (ND 148/144−45)

When Adorno speaks of "contradictions," he is not simply referring to logical incongruities that could be cleared up by more careful thought. Instead the reference is to unavoidable conflicts occurring in a historical society and being brought to consciousness by philosophy and art. The latter oppose the society to which they belong. Indeed, within culture itself an unavoidable conflict occurs between Adorno's own philosophy and modern art. This conflict is supposed to make us conscious of sociohistorical contradictions.

There are two obvious objections to such a construal of the dialectic. One is that by applying the same category of "contradiction" to so many distinct matters, Adorno has emptied it of any precise meaning.

The other objection is that he is subsuming qualitatively different phenomena under a universal norm, contrary to his own intent. After all, is not dialectical philosophy supposed to be "the consistent consciousness of nonidentity"? (ND 17/5)

Such objections take us one step further into his understanding of negative dialectic. He does not deny that "contradiction" postulates an underlying identity between philosophical concepts and sociohistorical reality. These "are of the same contradictory essence" (ND 58/48). Yet he insists that such identity must not be considered complete and irrevocable. Instead all "contradictions" are to be thought of in view of their *possible* resolution. Philosophical concepts, sociohistorical reality, and their common "essence" are all revocable. Dialectical logic is not the final word: "In view of the concrete possibility of utopia, dialectics is the ontology of the wrong state of things. A right state of things would be free of dialectics: neither a system nor a contradiction" (ND 22/11).

The emphasis on possible resolution sometimes prompts Adorno to suspend dialectical logic. These temporary suspensions are philosophical attempts to acknowledge the presence and possibility of what escapes the net of logic. Adorno attributes such attempts to the impact of Walter Benjamin, who has bequeathed "the obligation to think dialectically and undialectically at the same time" (MM, sec. 98, 171/152). Dialectical logic must sometimes be suspended on behalf of the "nonidentical." There is a need to unite spontaneous experience and critical argumentation, even when experience threatens the consistency of an argument (ND 39−42/28−31).

Adorno's models for such thinking come from certain works of art. Their unification of spontaneity and rigor seems to refract the light of possible reconciliation upon a contradictory world.[43] When Adorno says "the paradoxes of aesthetics are those of its subject matter" (AT 113/107), however, he is telling only half the story. The other half is Adorno's own "utopia of knowledge." Adorno's philosophy seeks to give thoughtful expression to the particular without subsuming it under rigid categories. Unlike Wittgenstein, Adorno wants to say what cannot be said (ND 21/9−10 and 114−16/108−10). Unlike Heidegger, Adorno does not want this attempt to slide into nonphilosophical sayings. Despite artistic models, Adorno's thought does not purport to be artistic. It aims for the conceptual rigor of dialectical logic even while it suspends dialectical logic in order better to express what things would be like if freed of dialectic.

To think both dialectically and undialectically is a highly paradoxical endeavor. As a result, Adorno's "contradictions" come across as ones that may or may not turn out to be contradictory. The central paradox of texts such as *Aesthetic Theory* is that their argumentation seems to be both fundamentally contradictory and fundamentally paradoxical. Adorno's texts try to give shape to an overriding tension between real contradictions and possible reconciliation.

This central paradox puts critical interpreters in an awkward position. Normally a dialectical argument leaves one with two options. Either one can reject the formal and substantive premises of dialectical logic and determine which insights are worthwhile despite the rejected premises. Or one can accept the premises of dialectical logic and determine whether the argument is consistent with these premises and correct in its substance. Adorno pulls the rug from under either stance. To the hostile critic, Adorno can always say that his writings do not fully accept the premises of dialectical logic. To the sympathetic critic, Adorno can say that his arguments need not always be consistent with such premises. There is no graceful way to enter or leave Adorno's negative dialectic. Perhaps the best one can do is to grasp its substantive concerns, ask whether Adorno develops these concerns in a convincing manner, and consider what the central paradox does to Adorno's construal of his subject matter.

Critical Phenomenology

The methods of this construal can best be described as those of a "critical phenomenology" inspired by Hegel, Marx, and Nietzsche. By "methods" are meant the characteristic procedures of Adorno's research and of its presentation. In this sense Adorno's methods must be distinguished from his "methodology," his own reflections on proper procedures.

Some of these reflections suggest the absence of characteristic procedures in his philosophy. The essay on essays, for example, hints that Adorno's own work proceeds "methodically unmethodically."[44] Similarly, the "Draft Introduction" in *Aesthetic Theory* questions the legitimacy of stating a general methodology for work in aesthetics:

> A methodology in the ordinary sense of the term ... would fail to do justice to the relation between the aesthetic object and aesthetic thought. The only sound methodological imperative seems to be Goethe's: enter into works of art as you would into a chapel. ... Method is ... legitimated in its actual use, which is why it cannot be presupposed. (AT 530/489)

Yet such passages must be taken with a grain of salt. Not only might there be some characteristic procedures for "methodically unmethodical" work, but also Adorno himself recognizes that refusing to outline a general methodology "is to state some kind of methodology of one's own" (AT 530/489). Besides, to claim that methods are legitimated in their actual use is philosophically insufficient. The "legitimate" use of a method does not in itself provide a philosophical rationale for that method. One still must determine what makes for legitimacy or illegitimacy in the use of methods.

The primary reason for Adorno's qualified "antimethodism" is also the primary reason for describing his methods as phenomenological, namely his devotion to the object as an object of investigation. The "Draft Introduction" rejects abstract methodologies because they emphasize methods at the expense of the objects for which methods are devised. Adorno's own methodological reflections usually occur within specific investigations of particular objects. Whereas Edmund Husserl called philosophy "back to the things themselves" only to write general studies on how to get there, Adorno takes the call so seriously that his methods seem embedded in the things themselves.

This embeddedness renders problematic an attempt such as Susan Buck-Morss's to isolate "negative dialectic" as a "method" and then present it "in action." Negative dialectic was never a mere method for Adorno, nor were his methods ones which could simply be "applied" as if they were indifferent to the subject matter at hand. He would have objected to the claim that his originality "lay not in the ... substance of his theoretical arguments, but in the way he put them together." He would have found puzzling an approach that depicts his philosophy as primarily a method and then objects because his "method ... became total."[45]

Nevertheless there are good reasons for trying, as Buck-Morss does, to abstract Adorno's methods from his texts. Otherwise Adorno's own "methodological imperative" could force one to suppress methodological questions until a specific investigation has proved unconvincing. It would be hard to raise general questions about his methods. This difficulty is compounded in *Aesthetic Theory*, as it is in *Negative Dialectics*. Neither book is simply about specific objects of investigation. Each book also addresses pertinent categories and criteria for philosophical inquiry, especially ones that are prominent in Adorno's own previous writings. At the same time Adorno engages in substantive analyses, whether of Heidegger, Kant, and Hegel in *Negative Dialectics* or of selected philosophical positions and artistic phenomena in *Aesthetic Theory*. The text continually shifts across various levels of inquiry. Without some general understanding of Adorno's methods, readers quickly lose their way.

Some clues for orientation come from Adorno's own methodological comments. These help one reconstruct the intentions of his phenomenology. Whether his texts fulfill his intentions is another question. *Aesthetic Theory* is particularly instructive in this regard. Adorno envisions an aesthetics that combines "production-oriented experience and philosophical reflection" (AT 498/460). Contemporary aesthetics must be as close to the phenomena as the working artist is, but it must have the conceptual energy to go beyond them without relying on a preconceived system. How can such an aesthetics be achieved? Adorno points to three methodological principles: to interpret art from a contemporary perspective, to historicize aesthetic norms, and to construct conceptual constellations. All three principles provide guidelines for a program of "determinate negation" in aesthetics.

Adorno's program of determinate negation comes from the Introduction to Hegel's *Phenomenology of Spirit*. Adorno wants to carry out this program even more consistently than Hegel (Cf. MM 14−15/ 16; ME 12−15/3−6). Whether Adorno does is debatable. Less debatable, however, is the fact that he regards the "phenomenology of anti-spirit" (ND 349/356) — Marx's critique of capitalism — as a correction to Hegel's program. Moreover, Adorno thinks ideology has become all-pervasive and systemic in advanced capitalist society. Thus the context for Hegelian phenomenology has reversed itself. For Hegel, the true is the whole. Philosophy comprehends truth through determinate negation of partial truths. For Adorno, the current sociohistorical totality is the untrue. Philosophy criticizes society through determinate negation of cultural phenomena as partial untruths.[46] Every part of contemporary society, even philosophy, becomes an untrue part of the whole.

Determinate negation à la Adorno uncovers the untruth of various cultural phenomena, shows this untruth to be that of society as a whole, and helps the phenomena refer beyond themselves to their possible truth in a transformed society. As part of an untrue totality, philosophy cannot presume to have an absolute knowledge of the truth. Because all parts can refer to their possible truth, however, neither philosophy nor any other part is wholly untrue. Determinate negation is not simply negative criticism. Determinate negation remains what it was for Hegel, namely a process of disclosing truth. Truth itself is seen as a historical process rather than a fixed criterion for the correctness of propositions.

Besides the shift in context, Adorno's program evidences another departure from Hegel. Whereas various epistemological positions undergo immanent criticism in Hegel's *Phenomenology*, Adorno suggests that art history proceeds in a similar fashion. The history of art is a process of determinate negation, with one work "criticizing" another and thereby suggesting larger issues of truth and falsity (AT 59−60/52).

This view of art history gives rise to Adorno's first methodological principle, the only one explicitly labeled in this way:

> One methodological principle ... is to try to shed light on all art from
> the perspective of the most recent artistic phenomena. ... Just as,
> according to Valéry, the best features of the new correspond to an old
> need, so authentic modern works are criticisms of past ones. Aesthetics
> becomes normative by articulating these criticisms. ... This kind of
> aesthetics would be able to deliver what aesthetics so far has only
> promised. (AT 533/492)

The principle of interpreting art from a contemporary perspective
suggests both a retrospective and a prospective aesthetics. On the one
hand, Adorno's aesthetics has a retrospective character. The best way
to understand extant phenomena, whether recent or not, is from the
needs articulated when the best modern works establish themselves in
an objective "context of problems" (AT 532/491). On the other hand,
Adorno's aesthetics has a prospective edge. Because the old needs
remain, aesthetics must go beyond recent phenomena to consider what
art could become in a society where those needs would be met (AT
533/491). Aesthetics becomes normative by articulating the process of
determinate negation from a contemporary perspective, but authentic
modern works are not completely normative for Adorno's aesthetics.
They themselves fall under a prospective light when he asks what the
future holds for art, for society, and for currently definitive relationships
between art and society.

To concentrate on modern art is in effect to question the norms of
traditional aesthetics. From this comes Adorno's second principle,
namely to historicize aesthetic norms. Adorno says traditional norms
have become outdated and irrelevant. More appropriate norms cannot
be invented *de novo*, however: previous philosophies make possible
the very project of writing a contemporary philosophical aesthetics.
Instead we need to recapitulate in philosophy the sort of determinate
negation that characterizes the history of art:

> In an age of conflict between contemporary art and traditional aes-
> thetics, a pertinent philosophical theory of art is compelled to concep-
> tualize categories of perdition as categories of transition in determinate
> negation — to paraphrase a remark by Nietzsche. Modern aesthetics
> can take only one form, which is to foster the rational [*motivierte*]
> and concrete dissolution of conventional aesthetic categories. In so
> doing it releases a new truth content in these categories. (AT 507/
> 468)[47]

Much of *Aesthetic Theory* can be read as an attempt to release new and
relevant meanings from traditional norms such as "beauty," "expression," and "meaning."

Adorno's historicizing does not assume that traditional norms never had genuine validity. Nor does it imply that their validity is limited to the historical situations in which they arose. In both these negative ways Adorno differs from many historical relativists. He assumes that the norms of traditional aesthetics had genuine validity in their own day and can receive a new validity today. The principle of historicizing requires that traditional norms be tested and reformulated with an eye to the historical process that comes together in the current situation.

Adorno has three procedures, all closely related, for historicizing aesthetic norms: demonstrating their historical character, reconstructing philosophical debates, and confronting traditional concepts with the current situation. The first procedure is to show the transcience and variability of traditional norms, especially ones such as Plato's "beauty" that have been regarded as timeless universals. Adorno's second historicizing procedure is to pit various philosophical positions against each other in such a way that they exercise mutual correction. From these reconstructed debates emerges a new understanding of central notions within each position. Adorno employs such notions in their newly emergent meanings. The third procedure, already implicit in the first two, is to confront traditional norms with an "historicophilosophical analysis" (*geschichtsphilosophischen Analyse*) of the situation of modern art. This confrontation "relates the dynamics of art and [of] conceptualization to each other" (AT 530/489).

These three procedures result in a complex reading of modern art. Adorno is not simply trying to interpret modern art from within, even though closeness to the phenomena is a programmatic concern. He is also building a conceptual environment with materials taken from various disciplines and prepared by his own previous writings in philosophy and the social sciences. Indeed, the third methodological principle at work in *Aesthetic Theory* is to construct conceptual constellations.

As Buck-Morss shows, Adorno's inspiration for constructing constellations probably came from Walter Benjamin.[48] Yet Adorno's principle can also be considered a deliberate rewriting of a "central teaching" in Hegel's *Phenomenology of Spirit*.[49] According to Adorno, Hegel saw that the phenomena to be interpreted are mobile and internally mediated. When interpreting the phenomena, philosophers must keep their own concepts mobile and mediated. Adorno does not want to attribute the mobility and mediation of the phenomena to the conceptual work carried out by the philosopher. There is more to the phenomena than even the most flexible concepts can grasp. Against Hegel's glorification of the concept, Adorno has some sympathy with Husserlian phenomenology, which seeks to "intuit" the essence within particular phenomena.[50]

Unlike Husserl, however, Adorno thinks of essences as intrinsically social and historical. They characterize a certain society at a certain time, and they undergo development within society. In this respect Adorno's meaning is closer to Marx's concepts of "modes of production" and "objective tendencies" than either Hegel's or Husserl's concept of "essence." Adorno thinks of the essence within specific phenomena as a sedimented social prehistory and a possible social posthistory. Social history dwells both inside and outside a particular object. The object has become what it is within a larger sociohistorical process and in relationship to other objects, but this process and these relationships are intrinsic to the object's own identity.

The problem for such a conception is that historical phenomena resist conceptual definition, and that the concepts of specialized disciplines tend to suppress what is unique about particular objects. The constructing of conceptual constellations is a way of solving this problem. Adorno describes conceptual constellations as attempts to unlock the sociohistorical essence of particular phenomena without simply subsuming these under universal concepts. Conceptual constellations are also attempts to disclose what the phenomena could still become if the current direction of society were transformed, a disclosure that exceeds the scope of current concepts (ND 62–63/52–53 and 163–66/161–63). Only in relation to other concepts can a concept begin to approximate particular phenomena and their implicit social history. Constellations let concepts interrelate in such a way that both the sociohistorical essence of phenomena and their unique identities can emerge. A philosophical constellation provides conceptual mediations for mediations within the phenomena, but it refuses to equate conceptual and phenomenal mediations.

The conceptual constellations in *Aesthetic Theory* reflect Adorno's ambivalent attitudes toward Hegelian and Husserlian phenomenology. Hegel is praised for proposing the "programmatic idea" that "knowing is giving oneself over to a phenomenon rather than thinking about it from above" (AT 494/475), but his *Lectures on Fine Art* are criticized for imposing a "deductive system" on artistic phenomena (AT 524/484). Husserl is credited with proposing a fruitful method that is neither inductive nor deductive, but phenomenological aesthetics is criticized for coming up with an "essence of art" that "has little interpretive power" (AT 522/482). Instead of setting out on a wild goose chase for the original essence of art, Adorno proposes to think of artistic phenomena in "historical constellations": "No single isolated category captures the idea of art. Art is a syndrome in motion. Highly mediated in itself, art calls for intellectual mediation terminating in a concrete concept" (AT 523/482). Traditional attempts at defining art must be transformed into a dialectical phenomenology that delimits what art has come to be and suggests what art could become (AT 11–12/3).[51]

In *Aesthetic Theory* concepts once used to define art, such as imitation, semblance, and form, become part of a complex net in which Adorno tries to catch the dynamic structure of art without killing it. At the same time the sociohistorical content of these concepts becomes evident, and each concept takes on new meaning in the context of the others. Similar observations could be made about Adorno's approach to what analytic aestheticians might call "metacriticism": the discussion of concepts of art criticism such as intention and meaning in Chapter 8, the "thoughts on a theory of the art work" in Chapter 9, and the examination of art historiographical terms such as genre and style in Chapter 11.

Just as Adorno's paratactical style demands a circular reading, and just as negative dialectical logic requires a grasp of Adorno's substantive concerns, so too his phenomenological methods force readers to consult their own experience of phenomena in contemporary society. There is hardly any other way to check the results of his modernist, historicizing, and constructive approach. Given the methodological intentions of *Aesthetic Theory*, for example, it will not do simply to attack Adorno's apparent blindness toward non-Western art or even toward Western art from before the eighteenth century. Nor will it suffice to object that Adorno's own norms are not timeless universals or that his concepts are not clearly defined. One must test the fruitfulness of Adorno's methods for interpreting the phenomena in question.

The need to consult our own experience does not excuse arbitrary judgments, however. To function as a proving ground, our experience must be informed by philosophical reflections on contemporary phenomena, as Adorno himself recognizes (AT 513–20/473–79). At stake in our reading is neither simply the acceptability of Adorno's approach nor merely the correctness of specific assertions. At stake is what Adorno would call the "truth-content" of his texts and, by implication, the truth-content of our own reading.[52]

Perhaps a frustration with this interplay of experience and reflection helped prompt Habermas's remark that Adorno offers only "ad hoc determinate negation." To a system builder, Adorno's negative dialectic and critical phenomenology can seem long on brilliant aphorisms and short on substantive theories. Even more telling, however, is Habermas's claim that Adorno's critique of modern rationality entangles itself in a "performative contradiction." Habermas describes Adorno's critique of rationality as a "totalizing" critique: it is a critique of ideology that questions the basis of all ideology critique. According to Habermas, ideology critique normally tries to show that the theory being criticized conceals an inadmissible mixture of power and validity. In Horkheimer and Adorno's *Dialectic of Enlightenment*, however, "reason itself is suspected of the baneful confusion of power and validity claims, but still with the intent of enlightening." The authors try to show that the pervasive instrumentalizing of reason in modern society assimilates reason to power and destroys its critical force. This demonstration is paradoxical, however, because "it still has to make use of the critique that has been declared dead." Hence the critique of rationality does what it says cannot be done. Inherent in such a "total-izing critique" is a "performative contradiction," one that Adorno consistently tries to carry out in *Negative Dialectics* and *Aesthetic Theory*.[53]

According to the canons of logic, Habermas's objections are surely valid. There is an air of spontaneity and inconsistency about Adorno's writings even when they are most carefully crafted. But this is not merely due to failures in logic. Adorno acknowledges the age-old claims of rhetoric, and he puts these claims into practice in a way that few philosophers have matched. Because of the unusual persuasive power of his writing, even obvious contradictions can force one to ask whether they are more than logical inconsistencies. Given Adorno's suspicions about ordinary discourse and scientific language, one must admire the care with which he tries to avoid a different kind of performative contradiction: that between the saying and what gets said. The following passage illustrates such care, and it makes the central point:

> Rhetoric represents what philosophy cannot conceive except in language. Rhetoric lives on in the postulates of presentation, by which philosophy distinguishes itself from mere communication of matters already established and known. ... Dialectic — literally, language as the organon of thought — would be an attempt to rescue the rhetorical moment in a critical fashion: to bring about a mutual approximation between subject matter and expression, to the point where the difference fades. ... Mediating the rhetorical with the formal logical moment, dialectic tries to master the dilemma of either arbitrary opinion or unimportant accuracy. But dialectic leans toward content as something open, not predetermined by some frame-work. ... Knowledge that wants content wants utopia. ... The inextinguishable color comes from what does not exist. This is what thought serves, a piece of existence that, no matter how negative, extends to what does not exist. Only what is utterly distant would finally be near; philosophy is the prism that catches its colors. (ND 65–66/55–57; my translation)

To understand Adorno's philosophy of discourse, one must heed to the discourse of Adorno's philosophy. In his writings, as in his life, neither philosophy nor art is lacking.

Notes

1. Theodor W. Adorno, *Ästhetische Theorie, Gesammelte Schriften*, 7 (1970), 2d ed. (Frankfurt: Suhrkamp, 1972), p. 544; trans. as *Aesthetic Theory* by C. Lenhardt (London: Routledge & Kegan Paul, 1984), p. 498. Internal citations use the abbreviation AT and give the pagination of the second edition, followed by that of Lenhardt's translation, thus: AT 544/498. Modifications of the translation appear in parentheses within the passages cited.

2. My short biography relies mainly on the more complete accounts in Carlo Pettazzi, "Studien zu Leben und Werk Adornos bis 1938," in *Theodor W. Adorno*, ed. Heinz Ludwig Arnold (Munich: Edition Text & Kritik, 1977), pp. 22–43; Susan Buck-Morss, *The Origin of Negative Dialectics: Theodor W. Adorno, Walter Benjamin, and the Frankfurt Institute* (Hassocks, Sussex: Harvester, 1977), pp. 1–23; Eugene Lunn, *Marxism and Modernism: An Historical Study of Lukács, Brecht, Benjamin, and Adorno* (Berkeley: Univ. of California, 1982); and Martin Jay, *Adorno* (Cambridge, Mass.: Harvard Univ., 1984), pp. 24–55. See also Richard Wolin, *Walter Benjamin: An Aesthetic of Redemption* (New York: Columbia Univ., 1982).

3. Ernst Bloch, *Geist der Utopie* (Munich: Duncker & Humblot, 1918), 2d ed., rev. (Berlin: Paul Cassirer, 1923), reprinted (Frankfurt: Suhrkamp, 1964); various sections now in Ernst Bloch, *Man on His Own: Essays on the Philosophy of Religion*, trans. E. B. Ashton (New York: Herder and Herder, 1970), and in Ernst Bloch, *Essays on the Philosophy of Music*, trans. Peter Palmer, intro. David Drew (Cambridge: Cambridge Univ., 1985). Georg Lukács, *Die Theorie des Romans: Ein geschichtsphilosophischer Versuch über die Formen der grossen Epik* (Neuwied: Luchterhand, 1971); trans. as *The Theory of the Novel* by Anna Bostock (Cambridge, Mass.: MIT, 1971). Lukács's study first appeared in the journal *Zeitschrift für Ästhetik und Allgemeine Kunstwissenschaft* (1916). It was published as a book a few years later (Berlin: Paul Cassirer, 1920).

4. Buck-Morss, p. 15.

5. This apt description of Adorno's dialectical, antisystematic writings comes from Georg Picht, "Atonale Philosophie," in *Theodor W. Adorno zum Gedächtnis*, ed. Hermann Schweppenhäuser (Frankfurt: Suhrkamp, 1971), pp. 124–28.

6. *Geschichte und Klassenbewusstsein: Studien über marxistische Dialektik* (Berlin: Malik Verlag, 1923; Darmstadt/Neuwied: Sammlung Luchterhand, 1968); trans. as *History and Class Consciousness: Studies in Marxist Dialectics* by Rodney Livingstone (London: Merlin, 1971).

7. The most important books in this regard include Perry Anderson, *Considerations on Western Marxism* (London: NLB, 1976; Verso Edition, 1979), and *In the Tracks of Historical Materialism* (Chicago: Univ. of Chicago, 1984); Alvin W. Gouldner, *The Two Marxisms: Contradictions and Anomalies in the Development of Theory* (New York: Seabury, 1980); Russell Jacoby,

Dialectic of Defeat: Contours of Western Marxism (Cambridge: Cambridge Univ., 1981); and Martin Jay, *Marxism and Totality: The Adventures of a Concept from Lukács to Habermas* (Berkeley: Univ. of California, 1984). Useful anthologies include Dick Howard and Karl E. Klare, eds., *The Unknown Dimension: European Marxism Since Lenin* (New York: Basic, 1973); *Western Marxism: A Critical Reader*, ed. New Left Review (London: NLB, 1977); and *An Anthology of Western Marxism; from Lukács and Gramsci to Socialist Feminism*, ed. Roger S. Gottlieb (New York: Oxford Univ., 1988). A concise survey of the history of Marxism is given in David McLellan, *Marxism after Marx: an Introduction* (Boston: Houghton Mifflin, 1979).

8. Anderson, *Considerations*, p. 42. This assessment of the failure is partially corrected in Anderson's Afterword (pp. 109–21), which points to some weaknesses in classical Marxism.

9. Jay, *Marxism and Totality*, p. 7.

10. "Der Begriff des Unbewussten in der transcendentalen Seelenlehre" ("The Concept of the Unconscious in the Transcendental Theory of Mind"), written in Frankfurt 1926–1927, rejected by Adorno's mentor Hans Cornelius, and published posthumously in Adorno's *Gesammelte Schriften*, 1 (Frankfurt: Suhrkamp, 1973), pp. 79–322. Hereafter *Gesammelte Schriften* will be abbreviated as GS, thus: GS 1 (1973): 79–322.

11. Buck-Morss, pp. 20–23, 90–101, and passim. See Walter Benjamin, *Ursprung des deutschen Trauerspiels* (Berlin: Ernst Rowohlt, 1928), rev. ed. (Frankfurt: Suhrkamp, 1978); trans. as *The Origin of German Tragic Drama* by John Osborne (London: NLB, 1977). The book was begun in 1923 and submitted unsuccessfully as a *Habilitationsschrift* at the University in Frankfurt in 1925. The revised edition of 1978 contains the text of the critical edition of Benjamin's *Gesammelte Schriften*, 6 vols., ed. Rolf Tiedemann and Hermann Schweppenhäuser (Frankfurt: Suhrkamp, 1972–   ).

12. GS 1 ("Die Aktualität der Philosophie," 1931): 325–44, trans. as "The Actuality of Philosophy," *Telos*, 31 (Spring 1977), pp. 120–33; and GS 1 ("Die Idee der Naturgeschichte," 1932): 345–65, trans. as "The Idea of Natural History," *Telos*, 60 (Summer 1984), pp. 111–24. Although not published during Adorno's lifetime, both essays announce themes and concerns that were to remain central in his subsequent writings.

13. "Zur gesellschaftlichen Lage der Musik," *Zeitschrift für Sozialfor-schung*, 1 (1932): 103–24, 356–78; trans. as "On the Social Situation of Music," *Telos*, 35 (Spring 1978), pp. 128–64.

14. *Kierkegaard. Konstruktion des Ästhetischen* [Tübingen: J. C. B. Mohr (Paul Siebeck), 1933]; 2d and 3d eds. (Frankfurt: Suhrkamp, 1962, 1966); now in GS 2 (1979); *Kierkegaard: Construction of the Aesthetic*, trans., ed., and with a Foreword by Robert Hullot-Kentor (Minneapolis: Univ. of Minnesota, 1989). The book is a revision of Adorno's second *Habilitationsschrift*, which was sponsored by Paul Tillich and successfully defended in 1931.

15. "Über den Fetischcharakter in der Musik und die Regression des Hörens," *Zeitschrift für Sozialforschung*, 7 (1938): 321–55; revised version in *Dissonanzen. Musik in der verwalteten Welt* (Göttingen: Vandenhoeck &

Ruprecht, 1956); now in GS 14 (1973); 14–50. The revised version is translated as "On the Fetish-Character in Music and the Regression of Listening" in *The Essential Frankfurt School Reader*, ed. Andrew Arato and Eike Gebhardt, Introduction by Paul Piccone (New York: Urizen, 1978), pp. 270–99.

16. Max Horkheimer and Theodor W. Adorno, *Dialektik der Aufklärung. Philosophische Fragmente* (Amsterdam: Querido, 1947), 2d ed. (Frankfurt: S. Fischer, 1969); trans. John Cumming (New York: Seabury, 1972). The original manuscript was first published as a mimeograph in 1944. GS 3 (1981) contains the 1969 edition, supplemented by "Das Schema der Massenkultur" (GS 3: 299–335), which expands the chapter on the culture industry.

17. By T. W. Adorno, Else Frenkel-Brunswik, Daniel J. Levinson, R. Nevitt Sanford in collaboration with Betty Aron, Maria Hertz Levinson, and William Morrow (New York: Harper & Brothers, 1950). *The Authoritarian Personality* is the first volume in *Studies in Prejudice*, a series begun in 1944, sponsored by The American Jewish Committee, and edited by Max Horkheimer and Samuel H. Flowerman. Adorno's contributions to this massive and controversial volume are reprinted under the title *Studies in the Authoritarian Personality* in GS 9.1 (1975): 143–509.

18. *Philosophie der neuen Musik* [Tübingen: J. C. B. Mohr (Paul Siebeck), 1949]; subsequent editions in 1958, 1966, and 1972; 5th ed. in GS 12 (1975); trans. Anne G. Mitchell and Wesley V. Blomster as *Philosophy of Modern Music* (New York: Seabury, 1973). *Minima Moralia. Reflexionen aus dem beschädigten Leben* (Frankfurt: Suhrkamp, 1951), 2d ed. (1962), reprint (1969), now in GS 4 (1980); trans. E. F. N. Jephcott as *Minima Moralia: Reflections from Damaged Life* (London: NLB, 1974). *Versuch über Wagner* (Frankfurt: Suhrkamp, 1952), 2d ed. (Munich/Zurich: Droemer Knaur, 1964), now in GS 13 (1971): 7–148; trans. Rodney Livingstone as *In Search of Wagner* (London: NLB, 1981). Hereafter *Minima Moralia* is cited as MM from GS 4 and Jephcott's translation, thus: MM, sec. 98, 171/152.

19. *Prismen. Kulturkritik und Gesellschaft* (Frankfurt: Suhrkamp, 1955), subsequent editions in 1963 and 1969, now in GS 10.1 (1977): 9–287; trans. Samuel and Shierry Weber as *Prisms* (London: Neville Spearman, 1967; Cambridge, Mass.: MIT, 1981).

20. GS 10.1 (*Prismen*, "Kulturkritik und Gesellschaft," 1951): 30; trans. 34.

21. "Einleitung," in *Zur Metakritik der Erkenntnistheorie. Studien über Husserl und die phänomenologischen Antinomien* (Stuttgart: W. Kohlhammer, 1956), GS 5 (1970): 12–47; "Introduction," in *Against Epistemology: A Metacritique; Studies in Husserl and the Phenomenological Antinomies*, trans. Willis Domingo (Cambridge, Mass.: MIT, 1983), pp. 3–40. Hereafter cited as ME from GS 5 and Domingo's translation, thus: ME 12–47/3–40. For another translation of Adorno's introduction, see "Metacritique of Epistemology," *Telos*, 38 (Winter 1978–79), pp. 77–103.

22. "Der Essay als Form," in *Noten zur Literatur I* (Frankfurt: Suhrkamp, 1958), GS 11 (1974): 9–33; trans. as "The Essay as Form," *New German Critique*, 32 (Spring–Summer 1984), pp. 151–71. Gillian Rose summarizes

this essay in a chapter titled "The Search for Style." See pp. 14–15 in Rose, *The Melancholy Science: An Introduction to the Thought of Theodor W. Adorno* (London: Macmillan, 1978).

23. Collections on music include *Dissonanzen. Musik in der verwalteten Welt* (Göttingen: Vandenhoeck & Ruprecht, 1956) ("Dissonances: Music in the Administered World"); *Klangfiguren. Musikalische Schriften I* (1959) ("Tone Configurations: Musical Writings I"); *Einleitung in die Musiksoziologie. Zwölf theoretische Vorlesungen* (1962), trans. E. B. Ashton as *Introduction to the Sociology of Music* (New York: Seabury, 1976); *Der getreue Korrepetitor: Lehrschriften zur musikalischen Praxis* (Frankfurt: S. Fischer, 1963) ("The Loyal Musical Coach: Pedagogical Writings on Musical Praxis"); *Quasi una fantasia. Musikalische Schriften II* (1963); *Moments musicaux. Neu gedruckte Aufsätze 1928 bis 1962* (1964) ("Musical Moments: Newly Published Essays from 1928 to 1962"); *Impromptus. Zweite Folge neu gedruckter musikalischer Aufsätze* (1968); *Nervenpunkte der neuen Musik (Ausgewählt aus "Klangfiguren")* (Reinbek bei Hamburg: Rowohlt, 1969) ("Nerve Points of the New Music, Selected from *Tone Configurations*"). Books for which no publisher is listed were published by Suhrkamp. *Dissonanzen* and *Einleitung in die Musiksoziologie* are now contained in GS 14 (1973); *Der getreue Korrepetitor* in GS 15 (1976); *Klangfiguren* and *Quasi una fantasia* in GS 16 (1978); and *Moments musicaux* and *Impromptus* in GS 17 (1982).

24. *Noten zur Literatur* ("Notes on Literature") *I* (1958) *II* (1961), and *III* (1965). GS 11 (1974) contains all three volumes plus *Noten zur Literatur IV*, which was published posthumously.

25. *Mahler. Eine musikalische Physiognomik* ("Mahler: A Musical Physiognomy") (Frankfurt: Suhrkamp, 1960), now in GS 13 (1971): 149–319. *Berg. Der Meister des kleinsten Übergangs* ("Berg: The Master of the Smallest Transitions") (Vienna: Verlag Elisabeth Lafite; Österreichischer Bundesverlag, 1968), now in GS 13 (1971): 321–494.

26. *Drei Studien zu Hegel* ("Three Studies on Hegel") (Frankfurt: Suhrkamp, 1963), now in GS 5 (1970): 247–381.

27. *Eingriffe. Neun kritische Modelle* (1963) ("Interventions: Nine Critical Models"), now in GS 10.2 (1977): 455–594. *Ohne Leitbild. Parva Aesthetica* (1967, 1968) ("Without Guidelines: Parva Aesthetica"), now in GS 10.1 (1977): 289–453. *Stichworte. Kritische Modelle 2* (1969) ("Keywords: Critical Models 2"), now in GS 10.1 (1977): 595–782. All three books were published by Suhrkamp.

28. The main documents in this dispute are collected in *Der Positivismusstreit in der deutschen Soziologie* (Neuwied and Berlin: Hermann Luchterhand, 1969); trans. Glyn Adey and David Frisby as *The Positivist Dispute in German Sociology* (London: Heinemann, 1976). David Frisby's "Introduction to the English Translation" (pp. ix–xliv) gives a helpful survey of the debate.

29. GS 8 ("Einleitung zum *Positivismusstreit in der deutschen Soziologie*," 1969): 309; "Introduction," in *The Positivist Dispute in German Sociology*, p. 27.

30. *Negative Dialektik* (Frankfurt: Suhrkamp, 1966), 2d ed. (Suhrkamp,

1967), now in GS 6 (1973): 7–412; trans. E. B. Ashton as *Negative Dialectics* (New York: Seabury, 1973). Hereafter cited as ND from GS 6 and Ashton's translation, thus: ND 9/3. A closely related work is *Jargon der Eigentlichkeit. Zur deutschen Ideologie* (Frankfurt: Suhrkamp, 1964), now in GS 6 (1973): 413–526; trans. Knut Tarnowski and Frederic Will as *The Jargon of Authenticity* (London: Routledge & Kegan Paul, 1973).

31. Perhaps one should speak of a conference and a counterconference. The proceedings of the first, which was held in Frankfurt, are collected in *Adorno-Konferenz 1983*, ed. Ludwig von Friedeburg and Jürgen Habermas (Frankfurt: Suhrkamp, 1983). The proceedings of the second, which was held in Hamburg, are collected in *Hamburger Adorno-Symposion*, ed. Michael Löbig and Gerhard Schweppenhäuser (Lüneburg: Dietrich zu Klampen, 1984). Of particular interest in this second collection is the "Kritik der Frankfurter 'Adorno-Konferenz 1983'" (pp. 148–69) coauthored by Christoph Türcke, Claudia Kalász, and Hans-Ernst Schiller.

32. Jay, *Adorno*, p. 22.

33. Quoted by Thomas Baumeister, "Theodor W. Adorno—nach zehn Jahren," *Philosophische Rundschau*, 28 (1981): 1–26; the quote is from p. 25.

34. Jay, *Adorno*, p. 11.

35. Fredric Jameson, "T. W. Adorno; or, Historical Tropes," *Marxism and Form: Twentieth-Century Dialectical Theories of Literature* (Princeton: Princeton Univ., 1971), p. 3.

36. Weber, in *Prisms*, pp. 12–13.

37. Rose, p. 12.

38. Ibid., p. 25.

39. "Ohne Leitbild" originated as a radio address and was first published in *Neue Deutsche Hefte* (1960); it was republished as the lead essay in the collection *Ohne Leitbild. Parva Aesthetica* (1967, 1968); it is now in GS 10.1: 291–301. "Wozu noch Philosophie" also originated as a radio address; it was first published in *Merkur* in 1962; after being revised it became the lead essay in *Eingriffe. Neun kritische Modelle* (1963); now in GS 10.2: 459–73. "Parataxis. Zur späten Lyrik Hölderlins" was presented to the annual conference of the Hölderlin-Gesellschaft in June 1963; an expanded version was published in *Neue Rundschau* (1964); it was reprinted in *Noten zur Literatur*, III (1965), and is now in GS 11: 447–91.

40. ME 15–16/7. Similar formulations occur throughout the writings of Adorno's last decade.

41. In this connection see Matthias Tichy, *Theodor W. Adorno: Das Verhältnis von Allgemeinem und Besonderem in seiner Philosophie* (Bonn: Bouvier Verlag Herbert Grundmann, 1977).

42. GS 11 ("Der Essay als Form," 1958): 31–32; trans., 169–70.

43. Compare MM, sec. 153, 281/247 with ND 385–86/393 and 396–97/404–5.

44. GS 11 ("Der Essay als Form," 1958): 21; trans., 161.

45. Buck-Morss, pp. 186, 190. For similar reasons Adorno would have questioned Gillian Rose's claim that "the philosophical and sociological principles which structure his criticism of philosophy, sociology, music and literature are always the same" (*The Melancholy Science*, p. 10).

46. MM, sec. 29, 55/50: "The whole is the untrue." Hegel's dictum was "The True is the whole."

47. The translation "to conceptualize categories of perdition as categories of transition" does not capture the sense of Adorno's "die untergehenden Kategorien als übergehende zu denken." Perhaps a better translation would be "to conceptualize irrelevant categories as transitional categories"—i.e., as categories that participate in a necessary historical development and that can take on new meanings in the current situation.

48. Buck-Morss, pp. 90–110.

49. GS 5 (*Drei Studien zu Hegel*, "Skoteinos oder Wie zu lesen sei," 1963): 334.

50. For passages illustrating the mixture of Benjaminian, Hegelian, and Husserlian elements in Adorno's "phenomenology," see GS 1 ("Die Aktualität der Philosophie," 1931): 325–44, trans. as "The Actuality of Philosophy"; GS, 1 ("Thesen über die Sprache des Philosophen," 1931): 366–71; and ND 61–64/52–55 and 163–74/161–72. For cautious appreciations of Husserl and the "material phenomenology" of Hedwig Conrad-Martius and Max Scheler, see GS 5 (*Drei Studien zu Hegel*, "Skoteinos," 1963): 337–41, and ND 21–25/9–14.

51. One can say that Adorno has reached an antiessentialist conclusion like that of ordinary language philosophers, but for different reasons and with different implications. A classic and widely anthologized statement of the antiessentialist position is by Morris Weitz, "The Role of Theory in Aesthetics," *Journal of Aesthetics and Art Criticism* 15 (September 1956): 27–35. For refinements of Weitz's position, see his article on "Art as an Open Concept" in *Aesthetics: A Critical Anthology*, ed. George Dickie, Richard Sclafani, and Ronald Roblin, 2d ed. (New York: St. Martin's Press, 1989), pp. 152–59. The same anthology (pp. 653–55) contains a useful bibliography on the debate over defining art in English-language aesthetics since the 1950s.

52. I have attempted this sort of reading in a book manuscript titled *Adorno's Aesthetic Theory: The Redemption of Illusion* (Cambridge, Mass.: MIT, 1991).

53. Jürgen Habermas, "The Entwinement of Myth and Enlightenment: Max Horkheimer and Theodor Adorno," in *The Philosophical Discourse of Modernity: Twelve Lectures* (1985), trans. Frederick Lawrence (Cambridge, Mass.: MIT, 1987), pp. 106–30; the quotes are from p. 119. For an earlier version of this article, see "The Entwinement of Myth and Enlightenment: Re-Reading *Dialectic of Enlightenment*," *New German Critique*, 26 (Spring–Summer 1982), pp. 13–30.

5

Habermas
Enlightenment and the Philosophical Discourse of Modernity

David Ingram

There is perhaps no greater defender of the Enlightenment today than Jürgen Habermas. In an age racked by cynicism and doubt, he has consistently affirmed the power of rational discourse to ground consensus and secure emancipation. Indeed, of those figuring predominantly in current debates over the advantages and disadvantages of modernity, he alone continues to advocate universal truth as the *via regia* toward moral and cognitive progress.

Whence springs this obstinate commitment to reason? The small provincial town of Gummersbach where Habermas grew up would not have been very conducive to the formation of enlightened political consciousness under any circumstances, let alone those that prevailed during the dark years of Hitler's Third Reich.[1] Unaware of the Holocaust and living under an "impression of normality that afterwards proved to be an illusion," Habermas was recruited into the Hitler Youth and, at the tender age of fifteen, sent to the Western Front.

It was only after the war, in the wake of the revelation of Nazi atrocities, that Habermas began to discover himself. Cast into a situation of material deprivation and chaos, he turned to existentialism (Sartre), expressionism (Trakl and Benn), and German philosophy (most notably the phenomenology of Heidegger and the philosophical anthropology of Plessner and Gehlen). Without the benefit of any real exposure to Anglo-American literature or, for that matter, Marxism and Freudian psychology, these initial gropings toward enlightenment were bound to remain provincial. Yet by the time Habermas entered the University of Göttingen in 1949 he was already committed to pacifism and anti-nationalism.[2] Talk of Cold War and national rearmament caused him to fear that a "real break with the past had not been made." He soon realized that this break could only be achieved if the French and Anglo-American tradition of the Enlightenment, with its emphasis on civil and democratic rights, was assimilated into German culture.

Despite his deepening political awareness, Habermas felt that none of the bourgeois parties, including the German Social Democratic Party, offered much hope for securing the sort of radical break with the past that would be needed to found a rational consensus. Disillusioned with mass democracy, his political and philosophical "confessions" prior to 1953 were, in his words, "two universes which hardly touched one another" (Dews 76). Heidegger was still the main philosophical influence. However, the publication that year of *Introduction to Metaphysics* (1935), with its unapologetic retention of Nazi rhetoric, provoked a sharp response from him that was published in the *Frankfurter Allgemeine Zeitung*.[3]

Habermas's break with Heidegger was sealed the following year when he came across Karl Löwith's *From Hegel to Nietzsche* while completing his dissertation on Schelling.[4] Löwith's study led him to "discover" the humanistic writings of the young Marx and the Hegelian Marxism of Georg Lukács's *History and Class Consciousness* (1922). This was followed by a reading of Adorno and Horkheimer's masterpiece *Dialectic of Enlightenment* (1947). The latter's synthesis of Marx and Weber inspired Habermas's first major critique of technology and consumer society.[5] The awareness that the fragmentation and alienation besetting the modern age had social rather than metaphysical causes immediately drew him to the Institute for Social Research, which had recently returned to Frankfurt (1951) under the directorship of Max Horkheimer. From 1956 to 1959 Habermas worked as an assistant to Theodor Adorno—a mentor who, in the words of Richard Bernstein, "had the profoundest influence on Habermas ... despite or even because of (their) sharp temperamental and intellectual differences."[6] During this time he discovered Ernst Bloch, Walter Benjamin, Herbert Marcuse, and the seminal essays of the *Zeitschrift für Sozialforschung* published by the Institute during the 1930s and 1940s. He soon expanded his repertory to include Marxist economics (Dobb, Sweezy, and Baran) and social theory (Durkheim, Weber, and Parsons). However, the single most important event during this period was Marcuse's Freud lectures of 1956, which impressed upon him the lasting value of psychoanalysis for social theory (Dews 150).

As Adorno's assistant Habermas already demonstrated the propensity for systematic thinking and empirical research that would stay with him throughout his career. In this respect he showed himself to be perfectly in tune with the interdisciplinary synthesis of science and philosophy that had been the trademark of critical theory from Marx through the Frankfurt Institute of the 1930s. Unfortunately, it put him at odds with the prevailing climate of the Institute, which was then dominated by the heavily philosophical and dialectical — above all, antiscientific — outlook of Adorno's later thought. He nonetheless managed to continue his research, which was later published in *Student und Politik* (1961), *Strukturwandel der Öffentlichkeit* (1962), and *Theorie und Praxis* (1963).

The second of the above works soon catapulted him into national prominence as the intellectual guru of the new German student movement. So critical was Habermas of mass democracy and the technocratic manipulation of public opinion in serving the goals of steady economic growth that he was immediately branded a radical. His critique of social engineering and behavioral social science eventually culminated in a series of contributions to the *Positivismusstreit*, in which he and Adorno took on the "critical rationalism" of Karl Popper and other opponents of dialectical social science.[7] These early works display a preoccupation with rational discourse that eventually formed the cornerstone of his theory of communicative rationality.

Upon the recommendation of Karl Löwith and Hans-Georg Gadamer, Habermas was awarded a professorship of philosophy at Heidelberg (1961). After returning to Frankfurt to take over Horkheimer's chair of philosophy and sociology (1964–71), he became a powerful — if somewhat mercurial — force in student politics.[8] Before long his admittedly "bourgeois" penchant for rational discourse and responsible action clashed with the tactics and slogans of the student movement, which he felt were counterproductive toward achieving the democratization of the university.[9]

The 1960s marked a period of tremendous intellectual ferment for Habermas. Gadamer's *Truth and Method* (1960) led him to reconsider the moral foundations of social science and its relationship to language. His "intense involvement" with linguistic philosophy (Wittgenstein, Chomsky, and Searle) and analytic philosophy of science was further enhanced by his exposure to American pragmatism. Habermas's attempt to work out the implications of this encounter with respect to the German philosophical tradition culminated in his first magnum opus, *Knowledge and Human Interests* (1968). This project was abandoned shortly thereafter when, upon assuming the directorship of the Max Planck Institute (1971–1983), he set about reconstructing the "deep structures" underlying communicative competence in conjunction with insights drawn from developmental psychology.[10] Habermas's work in the 1980s has continued along the path marked out above. The *Theory of Communicative Action* (1981) — now regarded by many as the crowning achievement in an already distinguished career — argues that the alienation of modern life is related to disturbances in communication. This issue is also treated in *The Philosophical Discourse of Modernity* (1985), where Habermas notes that critics of modernity neglect the real cause of social malaise — not rationalization per se but its one-sided development under capitalism. As the leading German social thinker on the Left today, Habermas has continued to take an active interest in journalism and politics. His outspoken defense of peaceful civil disobedience on the part of antinuclear demonstrators and his support for the Green Party have earned him the enmity of many neoconservatives. Yet regardless of whether he is combating revisionist historians who bid the German people take leave of their Nazi past for the sake of recouping a strong nationalist identity, or defending the right of intellectuals to speak out on issues of common concern, Habermas remains a staunch defender of the Enlightenment and its ideal of rational democracy.[11]

Dialogue and Dialectic in Classical German Philosophy

Habermas's theory of discourse was originally worked out in confrontation with the epistemological theories of Kant, Hegel, and Marx. Today these thinkers still determine the direction, if not the content, of his thought. Yet twenty years ago they opened the door to an entirely new conceptualization of critical theory: *Knowledge and Human Interests*.

The genesis of this work can be traced back to the positivism debate of the early 1960s. Karl Popper and his followers held that epistemology should clarify the methods and logic of experimental science, for them the sole embodiment of knowledge. In doing so, they uncritically accepted a correspondence theory of truth that restricted knowledge to observable facts — what Habermas, following August Comte, calls *positivism*. Positivism is morally bankrupt, in Habermas's opinion. The peculiar association of science and philosophy that once fueled the Enlightenment's critique of religious ideology is virtually absent in it. By restricting knowledge to the discovery of technologically useful laws, positivism relegates all questions of right and wrong to the subjective sphere of opinion. Deprived of a rational basis for promoting critical moral enlightenment, social science is made over into a tool for passively implementing the unquestioned goals of the status quo. Science and technology, Habermas concludes — and here Marcuse's influence is strikingly apparent — have themselves become ideological.[12]

Knowledge and Human Interests seeks to overturn the positivistic exclusion of the moral from the cognitive. Its aim is to show that science cannot account for the conditions of its own possibility (i.e., the grounds underlying its own claim to objective validity). Such grounding, Habermas contends, can only be provided by philosophical reflection on practical *life interests*. Seen from an anthropological perspective, knowledge secures the self-preservation of the human species. This is evident in the case of technological science, but it is also true of scientific disciplines within the humanities, which have textual interpretation as their aim. According to Habermas, the maintenance of mutual understanding and communication fostered by these disciplines is basic to all knowledge. However, since true understanding can be secured only within a linguistic context free of ideological constraints, the conditions of possible knowledge point *beyond* an anthropological interest restricted to biological self-preservation. Knowledge at once presupposes *and* aspires to freedom and, as such, engages an interest in emancipation for its own sake. If biological self-preservation is sometimes forsaken in the name of freedom, it is because freedom itself has become a necessary (i.e., *transcendental*) condition for the attainment of a unified sense of self. In critical social science and philosophy, knowledge in the form of *reflection* secures the freedom necessary for knowledge of self, society, and nature. In doing so, it conditions the constitution of society and nature as unified realms of rational objectivity and intersubjectivity wherein more mundane pursuits of self-preservation first become possible. Habermas, therefore, concludes that epistemology can only be conducted as social critique that remains partisan on behalf of a democracy of rational (i.e., free, equal, and impartial) discourse.[13]

The argument of *Knowledge and Human Interests* is divided into three parts. The first part traces the progressive radicalization of epistemology from Kant through Marx. Kant had argued that one could not explain the necessary unity of objective experience by appealing exclusively to either brute sensation or analytic reasoning. Such unity was rather to be attributed to the mind's active (albeit largely unconscious) deployment of reason in synthesizing discrete sensations in causally ordered sequences of events. In Kant's opinion the notion that objective necessity is a *product* of the *spontaneous activity* of the mind rather than a fact existing indepedently of and prior to it has profound *practical* implications; for belief in the passivity of the knowing subject is closely connected to belief in the passivity of the acting subject. By assuming that causal necessity is something our minds impose on sense experience as a condition of objective knowledge and not something inhering in the "things themselves" we are able to think of the possibility of our own freedom and moral responsibility.

Kant's critique of objectivism was the single most important event fueling the emancipatory project of German idealism. His faith in the power of rational enlightenment to elevate humanity to the status of free, universal moral agency was later taken up by his successors, who identified this ideal with a society of total reciprocity, free of domination.

Despite its indebtedness to Kantian philosophy, critical theory, Habermas contends, must reject any taint of subjectivism. The objective idealism of Hegel and the historical materialism of Marx seem to him more congenial in this regard. To begin with, Hegel argued that reason is not properly conceived as an innate faculty inhabiting each person's soul in isolation from the objective sociohistorical contexts of labor and interaction. Whereas Kant understood the reciprocal interdependence of stable self-identity and rationally ordered world as an immediate mental reflex of the isolated subject, Hegel saw it as *self-externalizing* activity directed toward nature and society (KHI 7–24).

As is well known, Marx took his bearings from the "master-servant" dialectic of Hegel's *Phenomenology of Spirit* (1807). The latter demonstrates that rational identity and freedom are won only in the course of a long struggle involving the progressive mastery of nature and the elimination of social domination. Material labor is here conceived as the primary mode of self-expression and self-realization—a fact, Marx submits, which is otherwise forgotten in Hegel's privileging of pure reason (thought) as the always implicit substrate of reality. Habermas cites with approval Marx's Kantian retention of a "sensuous nature" existing "in itself," resistant to a purely idealistic (conceptual) reduction. However, he disagrees with Marx's assumption that labor is the sole vehicle of knowledge and self-realization. This assumption, he feels, led Marx to misconceive his critique of political economy as a quasi-predictive, instrumentally efficacious natural science. It therefore prevented him from working out the philosophical and methodological grounds of a critique of ideology oriented toward moral enlightenment. Indeed, in Habermas's opinion, it is precisely this fateful privileging of instrumental activity that is responsible for Marxism's later neglect of democratic culture and politics—a fact manifested in its bureaucratic empowerment of technological elites and totalitarian mind control (KHI 43–63).

If Marxism is to remain true to its original emancipatory goal of establishing a *democratic* association of producers in which the "alien" forces of the market, not to mention those of the state bureaucracy, are brought under rational, collective control, it must, Habermas submits, turn to a different kind of activity on which to ground itself. That activity is *communication*. At this juncture Habermas, like his predecessors in the Frankfurt School, turns to Hegel—but with a notable difference. Whereas they sought to retrieve the lost moment of emancipatory reflection in Hegel's mature writings on aesthetics, he seeks it in the early lectures of the Jena period (1803–06).[14] Only here, Habermas contends, did Hegel break out of the "monological" mold of a subject-based philosophy of consciousness to conceive the formation of "subjective spirit" in terms of intersubjective relations grounded in family, labor, *and* language.[15] On Hegel's reading of the moral relationship, individuals first achieve a sense of their own identity in loving one another. Individuation presupposes socialization; one recognizes oneself in the other through the establishment of a common moral identity based on reciprocal expectations—the mediation of particular and universal.

This is also a *dialogical* relationship. For Hegel, language is prior to labor and family in that it not only names and identifies objects but also functions as the bearer of a normative identity between subjects. This is amply borne out, Habermas claims, by Hegel's treatment of the struggle for recognition, which involves overcoming *distorted communication*. In an earlier fragment of the *Spirit of Christianity and Its Fate* (1797), this struggle was illustrated by the "causality of fate" associated with the guilt of the criminal; by violating the reciprocity of expectations and thus disrupting communication, the criminal experiences the self-alienated portion of his identity (the other) as external compulsion and "destiny" (guilt and punishment).

Appealing to Freud's analysis of neurosis as a "return of the repressed," Habermas uses Hegel's illustration of distorted communication as a cipher for understanding the mechanism underlying ideology. Ideology can be understood as a form of distorted communication and self-understanding whereby universal interests expressive of true reciprocity are repressed. On this reading, the mere appearance of reciprocity—the ideological veneer of universal validity that attaches to norms that in fact perpetuate class domination—cannot conceal the pathological symptoms of an unfree and alienated life: social disintegration and political strife. Habermas therefore concludes that emancipation cannot occur unless humanity is freed from *two* kinds of constraints: those emanating from *external* and *internal* nature. The former are overcome through labor (technology), the latter through communication.

It is Habermas's aim in the second and third parts of *Knowledge and Human Interests* to show that these two processes—the attainment of knowledge and the achievement of a rational democracy—converge within an epistemological reflection on scientific methodology. In Charles Peirce, the founder of American pragmatism, and in Wilhelm Dilthey, the leading exponent of hermeneutics at the turn of the century, knowledge is shown to have its basis in freedom as well as self-preservation. For these thinkers, reflection on the logic of causal explanation (in natural science) and textual interpretation (in historical and cultural science) reveals the life-preserving activities and interests underlying two types of knowledge: technically useful and morally binding knowledge.

Pierce shows how the production of a stable system of causal beliefs is a function of labor. The discovery of causal laws, he argues, only occurs in the course of instrumental interventions in nature. It is only by *actively* trying to bring about certain events through effecting changes in our environment that we isolate, by trial and error, real from apparent causes. Passive observation *alone* does not suffice to distinguish those observed regularities that represent noncausal connections (e.g., the rising of the sun being preceded regularly by the crowing of the rooster), from genuine causal connections. For Peirce, the kind of *experimental*, or trial and error, behavior necessary for the discovery of causal relations forms the basic *logic* underlying scientific inquiry.[16]

Especially significant for Habermas is the fact that causal knowledge acquires its *original meaning* and *validity* with respect to a *prescientific*, or methodologically unsophisticated, context of feedback-monitored, habitual behavior. Experimental methods correspond to more primitive behaviors that evolved in response to organic changes in the species. The need to adapt to changing conditions of scarcity, combined with the assumption of an upright posture, the development of opposable thumbs, and so forth, produced certain *reflex responses* to outer stimuli that took the form of instrumental interventions. Changing one's environment in order to satisfy one's wants — in short, *working* for one's livelihood — could only be successfully satisfied by learning to anticipate the typical effects of one's behavior. Yet such prediction remained unreliable prior to the discovery of a procedure for isolating true causes from apparent causes — a lack that was remedied by the discovery of the experimental method in the sixteenth century.

According to Habermas, scientific method transforms feedback-monitored behavior into a cumulative learning process by isolating causal chains under *controlled* conditions. Measuring procedures infuse instrumental actions with greater precision and intersubjective reliability. In Habermas's opinion, not only the *meaning* of descriptive statements and objective observations but also their *power to convince others*, i.e., their power to generate intersubjective agreement and thereby secure their own "truth," is grounded in the action framework of possible measuring operations (KHI 194–5). *Nature* as it is conceived by science — as a system of mathematically definable causal laws — is thus a product of human measuring activity. It is not an arbitrary construct, however. For it is rooted in a necessary, "anthropologically deep-seated" *technical interest* in securing and expanding control over *objectifiable* processes (KHI 91–139).

However, not only is nature constituted by the measuring activity of the subject, it is also *preinterpreted* by the conceptual categories of the scientific theory. "Facts" are descriptions that employ general concepts. The "truth" of the latter, Peirce would say, is a function of their pragmatic usefulness, not their correspondence with some uninterpreted "brute" sensation or reality. But what counts as useful is a question of what needs and interests ought to be satisfied. Consequently, the "truth" of concepts, and therewith the truth of scientific facts, is also a question of *value*.

Values imply prescriptions — purposes and ends that ought to be pursued. Generally, we justify our prescriptions by appealing to the commonly shared beliefs of our society. *Intersubjective agreement* here functions as a mark of validity. Nevertheless, we know that the collective judgment of a society might be distorted by ideology. Consequently, only a *general consensus* achieved through *rational communication* will suffice to validate a value judgment. Peirce himself believed that the validity of scientific method resided in its unique capacity to generate universal agreement regarding "true" beliefs. However, in that case the real meaning of truth would reside less in pragmatic adaptation than in *rational consensus*. Habermas himself points out that the notion of an ideal universal agreement that Peirce proposes as a substitute for the correspondence theory of truth cannot be understood in abstraction from the *community of scientists*.

A belief or theory may *produce* successful predictions, as in the case of Newtonian mechanics, and yet not be true, that is, rationally justifiable in the long run. Indeed, Thomas Kuhn's study of scientific revolutions, which Habermas cites, indicates that the most basic propositions of a scientific theory are worked out in advance of evidential confirmation. This happens in *conversations* between scientists about what counts as a pressing problem, how such a problem ought to be conceptualized, and so forth. Such propositions are *irreducible* to empirical predictions. For it is only when they are taken in combination with one another that they yield testable hypotheses. Consequently, their "truth" would have to be captured in terms of an *ideal consensus*. Thus true propositions are those which, according to Peirce, anyone would *agree to* in the long run, given sufficient time.

Discourse as Foundation for Science, Ethics, and Social Critique

The fact that scientific truth presupposes the existence of a *communicative community* leads Habermas to consider the action-interest framework in which intersubjective meaning and validity are constituted.

Here he appeals to Dilthey. According to Dilthey, the understanding of the past, or the interpretation of an ancient text, is an elaboration of the sort of retrospective self-interpretation that an individual continually engages in while reconstituting the continuity of his or her life history. To begin with, the generation and maintenance of a stable, personal identity involves assigning one's life experiences a meaning related to the intersubjectively recognized norms and concepts of a broader linguistic community. This is mainly accomplished by communicating with others, for example, by saying no to their commands, learning to see oneself in light of their descriptions of our behavior, etc.

It is here, Habermas notes, that everyday communication reveals an interpretative structure. The three classes of "life expressions" distinguished by Dilthey — verbal utterances, actions, and nonverbal expressions (gestures, body language, and the like) — "interpret" each other in a circular manner in the same way that words, sentences, paragraphs, and narratives do in the part/whole dialectic of textual interpretation. Linguistic understanding is (con)textual. The expression "I love you" can be understood seriously, facetiously, humorously, etc., depending on the occasion, the body language of the speaker, what he or she is trying to do, and so on. Even a simple utterance such as "Close the door" may be understood in different ways (as a command, a request, a wish). Likewise, aspects of reference (the door-object referred to) and address (the listener designated by the utterance) require actions and gestures to be clearly understood (KHI 140–86).

Dilthey's analysis of linguistic expression underscores the moment of textual interpretation in all communication and self-understanding. But in what sense does the reverse hold true? How are history and cultural anthropology — interpretative sciences par excellence — related to communication and self-understanding? It is here that Habermas turns to the *philosophical hermeneutics* of Hans-Georg Gadamer. Gadamer's hermeneutics attempts to show the interpretative structure underlying all experience. Most importantly, it demonstrates that even the most methodologically sophisticated forms of textual interpretation are based on a prescientific communicative competence

Dilthey, Gadamer argues, mistakenly identifies textual interpretation with reproduction of the private intentions of the author. He commits, in other words, an objectivistic fallacy by presuming that the meaning disclosed by "correct" interpretation is identical to (corresponds with) the meaning originally intended by the author. This fallacy, Gadamer believes, renders both understanding and *intersubjective* (transcultural and transhistorical) "truth" incomprehensible.

According to Gadamer, understanding serves to *bridge* the cultural horizons of interpreter and author by means of a *shared*, public language. Understanding of meaning is here conceived as a process of *reaching mutual understanding* between different cultural horizons. Gadamer sees the bridging of cultures as foundational for any *moral* relationship. Ultimately, the goal is to achieve a *universal*, cosmopolitan perspective in which the narrow boundaries of one's own native self-understanding are gradually *expanded*, or *opened up*, to include ever broader points of view. Such a process of moral *enlightenment*, of discovering and generating *commonalities* of interest linking oneself with others, can only occur through *communicative understanding*.[17]

The agreement between communicating horizons is clarified by Gadamer in terms of the *dialogical* dynamics of textual understanding. The objectivity of textual interpretation, like that of the moral point of view, is achieved by checking the distorting effects of one's prejudices. However, contrary to the objectifying methodology of analytic-empirical science, this is not accomplished by putting one's prejudices out of play. The attempt by Dilthey and others to cancel the influence of those values, preferences, and linguistic assumptions that form the tacit background of their own understanding by immediately identifying with the mind of the author is futile. These assumptions alone provide the familiar reference points, questions, and so on necessary for opening up a dimension of possible meaningfulness in the first place. Thus, textual meaning is not pregiven by the author's original intentions but is partially constituted by the subjectivity of the interpreter.[18]

Does this then mean that textual interpretation is an act of arbitrarily projecting one's own prejudices onto the text, reading into the text whatever one chooses to find there? If this were the case, then there would be no difference between correct and incorrect interpretation. It would also be hard to conceive how understanding could serve the function of moral enlightenment, that is, of discovering the moral truth embedded in cultural tradition — one's own as well as others.

It is only by conceiving textual interpretation along the model of simulated communication (dialogue) that objectivity and moral enlightenment can be accounted for. A text drawn from the past or a different culture can question our values by resisting *easy* translation into our familiar horizon of understanding, Conversely, by resisting *sustained* attempts at translation, the text may reveal those aspects of itself that are parochial and anachronistic. These are then *questioned* as to their validity in communicating a message that can be understood as true and reasonable by persons from other cultures. Thus, text and interpreter confront one another as participants in a Socratic dialogue — each *critically reflecting* its own horizon of understanding off the other, so to speak.

Moral knowledge and self-limitation, like objective interpretation and self-understanding, involve a process of *critical reflection* that can only be provoked and sustained in communication with self and others. As we have just seen, the competencies requisite for ordinary *communication* — openness toward the other as an autonomous being worthy of respect, the simultaneous assumption of speaker (questioner) and listener (respondent) roles, dialogic reciprocity, critical attitude toward self and other — are precisely those that are required in assuming the moral attitude.

In Habermas's opinion, the interdependency between communication, interpretation, and moral knowledge has decisive consequences for critical social science. Interpretative sociology, he claims, can only escape ethnocentrism when the interpreters adopt a communicative — and inherently critical — attitude with respect to their own prejudices as well as those of the agents whose actions they are trying to understand. "We" must critically assess what "they" count as good reasons for their action with reference to "our" own standards of rationality. Only then can we begin to discover the limits of our own *reason*.

The connection between textual interpretation and communication enables Habermas to ground the historical-hermeneutic sciences in a *moral-practical interest* in maintaining a free identity in solidarity with others, past and present. Here the action framework of *ordinary language* constitutes the necessary conditions for maintaining a form of life dependent on meaning. Yet implicit in the notion of a meaningful life, Habermas argues, is an ideal type of *rational communication*. Besides being oriented toward the renewal of cultural tradition and the preservation of norms, rational speakers are oriented toward their own freedom. Unlike the technical and practical interests, which are related directly to the preservation of life, the emancipatory interest, Habermas notes, only emerges in the course of cultural evolution as a *response* to economic and political *domination*. In particular, it indicates the fact that the renewal of cultural tradition and preservation of normative solidarity in everyday communication is unreliable due to ideological distortion. Knowledge is rendered suspect, and one's identity is victimized by an unfree, false consciousness.

It is Habermas's contention that the *ideological distortion* of communication and self-understanding by *power relations* that are as anonymous as they are diffuse must be criticized by transcending the participatory context of everyday language. For Habermas, ideology is analogous to neurosis in that it manifests itself as a form of delusion. In particular, one is deluded into thinking that the satisfaction of certain needs is necessary for the achievement of happiness when, in fact, just the opposite is true. Habermas is especially struck by the fact that both neurotic and ideologically compelled behavior exhibit a high degree of mechanical rigidity. This is to be explained by the fact that the real determinants of one's behavior operate below the threshold of rational, conscious deliberation.

Following Freud, Habermas suggests that these unconscious determinations of behavior be understood as suppressed motives. Suppression here operates by means of *linguistic censorship*. Communication with self and others is *distorted* by the confusion and truncation of meanings. For example, one is no longer permitted to speak of freedom in terms of communal reconciliation but only as a limited property right. Still, suppressed needs somehow manage to appear in social behavior — not as explicit demands for social liberation, but as *pathological symptoms*, patterns of discontent registered by feelings of alienation, meaninglessness, and lack of freedom (KHI 219–29).

Because the real meaning of such behavior cannot be rendered transparent in everyday communication (indeed, language itself functions to distort it), it must be *interpreted* and *diagnosed* by relating it to the subterranean force fields of the economic and political "system." For Habermas, it is the *therapist* who is in a privileged position to do this. Only the therapist *understands* both the emancipatory potential implicit in the economic development of society and the systemic causes motivating continued acceptance of forms of domination masquerading as substitute gratifications.

Psychoanalysis thus exemplies the third, *critical* type of science sought by Habermas. Psychoanalysis combines the explanatory methodology of natural science with the interpretative methodology of historical and cultural science. Like the latter, psychoanalysis aims at restoring the full text of a patient's life history. It does so by reincorporating repressed motives into the stream of consciousness. Once the neurotic understands that his behavior is a symbolic reenactment of a childhood scene involving the painful suppression of some need by parental authority, the compulsion to repeat the behavior is dissolved. Consequently, unlike textual interpretation, the understanding of neurotic and ideologically constrained behavior will involve tracing its source to some *objective*, that is, consciously *un*intended, *cause* related to the systemic dynamics of either personality or economy.

On the surface, at least, Habermas's suggestion that critical social theory be conceived along the lines of psychotherapy seems promising. However, it seems less so in practice. Is the relationship between social theorist and society really analogous to the clinical relationship between doctor and patient? The latter relationship is built upon a mutually accepted asymmetry. The patient accepts his or her lack of rationality in turning to the doctor for enlightenment. The moral authority of the social critic, by contrast, would not extend beyond those groups who, by and large, already agree with the critic on the substantive ills of society. These groups might then appeal to the social critic's insight in explaining the ideological behavior of other members of society.

The privileging of the social critic's point of view is problematic for another reason. As Gadamer pointed out, it tacitly encourages an elitist refusal to engage the "deluded" others in a critical debate on their terms. One renounces critical dialogue with others by *prejudging* their competence as *rational* speakers. Habermas claims that the validity of any set of agreed-on terms is questionable if it hasn't been freely and consciously produced by fully rational agents. But that would indicate that no language is above suspicion. Following through on this line of reasoning, critical theorists would seem to be justified in refusing to engage in any mutual give-and-take with those who hold opinions different from their own. But refusing to engage in such dialogue could only amount to a kind of moral obtuseness.

As we shall see, Habermas's more recent formulation of a discourse ethic acknowledges the importance of moral dialogue in which theorists and lay persons confront one another as equals.[19] Whether there are *preexisting* universalizable interests or whether such interests are the outcome of a dialogical process of personal growth and *transformation* can only be determined, Habermas insists, in public discourse. This ethic is less a concrete recipe for acting than an abstract justification for participatory democracy. As such it is critical of the kind of mass democracy that has taken shape in Western capitalism, in which participation is restricted to voting. Moreover, it is apparent from the *formal* conditions that Habermas attributes to rational discourse generally that mass democracy is quite undemocratic. For it functions to establish compromises, or balances of power, between competing interest groups in which wealthier, more educated, and more powerful persons have a decisive advantage.

The formal structures of *discourse* — a technical term referring to rational dialogue that has been freed from the constraints and pressures of everyday action — are worked out by Habermas in great detail. They articulate *pragmatic* conditions (the *ideal speech situation*) that stipulate that anyone capable of rational speech and action be allowed to participate, that all have an equal chance to initiate and continue communication, and that no one be prevented from enjoying the above-outlined rights in virtue of internal and external (political, economic, social, cultural, or educational) domination.[20]

From a procedural standpoint participants in discourse are predisposed toward reaching *consensus* on problematic claims to truth and moral rightness. Unlike judgments of taste, factual statements and moral prescriptions claim universal validity. In order for a social norm to be accepted voluntarily as morally binding (legitimate) all those affected by it would have to agree that the consequences of its institutionalization would work to each and everyone's advantage. Ideally, this would also require that each person's needs be critically evaluated in light of their potential to further the freedom and well-being of all. In turn, discussion regarding the validity of given needs would inevitably provoke questions regarding the language in which such needs are formulated: to what extent is *it* ideological?

The Philosophical Discourse of Modernity

It would not be exaggerating to say that the overriding concern of Habermas since 1980 has been the defense of reason and the Enlightenment against critics on both the Left and the Right. Those on the Right consist of two parties. First, there are the "old conservatives" who reject all aspects of modern society and seek a return to simpler, more traditional forms of life. Second, there are the "neoconservatives" such as Daniel Bell, Irving Kristol, and Norman Podhoretz in America, and Carl Schmidt, Arnold Gehlen, and Joachim Ritter in Germany, who defend modern economic and political institutions up to a point but reject various aspects of modern culture. In particular, they feel that the Enlightenment's emphasis on individual emancipation and democratic self-determination threatens social stability, and so they recommend a return to some variety of traditional authority (patriarchal family, religion, nationalism, etc.) as a substitute for rational morality.[21]

Habermas's breakdown of the left-wing opposition is a bit more complicated. First, there are the "young conservatives" of Nietzschean provenance who follow the path marked out by Bataille "via Foucault to Derrida." Their leftist credentials are displayed in their celebration of *aesthetic modernism*, that is, that single aspect of cultural modernity that produced "a decentered subjectivity, emancipated from the imperatives of work and usefulness." Their conservatism, Habermas believes, resides in their evocation of the preconscious and the archaic — "the will to power or sovereignty, Being or the dionysiac force of the poetical" — that prescinds from *publically* institutionalized forums of *communicative* rationality. Extolling imagination over reason, expression over communication, they reduce all questions of value to the subjective or, better, to the *presubjective* powers hidden in the archaeology of linguistic structures. Repudiating the universal validity of communicative rationality, they are as little capable of justifying their own critical stance as they are of distinguishing it from the reactionary celebration of the archaic found, for example, in the aestheticized politics of fascism.

Distinguished from this brand of antirational aestheticism is the aesthetic rationalism of first-generation critical theorists. Habermas contends that Horkheimer, Adorno, and Marcuse never abandoned the emancipatory goals of the Enlightenment, but merely relocated them in the unconscious imagination. Adorno and Horkheimer's masterpiece, *Dialectic of Enlightenment*, contains a genealogical critique of reason fashioned after those of Nietzsche and Freud in which the very *birth of consciousness* — the splitting of subject and object — is seen as an act of domination. Violence against the uncontrollable other and repression of self should promote emancipation from the blind forces of both inner and outer nature but instead achieves the very opposite:

a remythicization of reason (the return of the repressed). In an age in which scientific and technological rationality has colluded with the forces of capitalism in a total (and totalitarian) commodification and instrumentalization of language and culture, the only refuge left for emancipatory reason — and its goal of a noninstrumental reconciliation of autonomous nature and autonomous humanity — is, the authors submit, the aesthetic imagination.[22]

Habermas does not find this solution to be very promising. In what sense can an aesthetic imagination that is entirely preconceptual be described as rational? What implications could it conceivably have for the elimination of domination?[23] Marcuse's attempt to answer this question by alluding to the possibility of developing a nonobjectifying science and technology seems to imply, Habermas thinks, some kind of intersubjective, or communicative, relationship between nature and humanity. Such a relationship, Habermas insists, cannot ground a form of cognitive learning that is cumulative, rational, and inherently oriented toward instrumental objectification.[24]

Habermas claims that the only way out of the dialectic of the Enlightenment is to reconceptualize rationality in terms of communication. The *philosophy of consciousness* dating back to Descartes assumes the primacy of an isolated subject as the point of departure for grounding knowledge. This epistemological standpoint privileges a certain kind of relationship (that between subject and object) and thus a certain kind of rationality (instrumental) (TCA1 392–99). Even *Knowledge and Human Interests* did not entirely break out of this manner of framing the problem of critical theory, despite its progressive emphasis on communication. However, the transition from philosophy of consciousness to theory of communicative action only establishes the democratic norms underlying critical theory. It does not provide the systemic framework necessary for diagnosing social crises. The loss of meaning, freedom, and identity that critics of modernity interpret as outgrowths of rational culture are actually *symptoms of capitalist growth*. The cumulative effects of rationally calculated economic actions constitute a self-regulating *system* that *functions* independently of, and often contrary to, the rational will of the combined actors.

Habermas had already appreciated, in his monograph *Zur Logik der Sozialwissenschaften* (1967), the potential value for critical theory of Talcott Parsons's functionalist analysis of societies as self-regulating systems. He criticized Parsons, however, for neglecting contradictions within the economic and political system of advanced capitalism. Moreover, he noted that systems theory overlooks contradictions between the system as a whole and that aspect of society — the communicative lifeworld — responsible for free interaction. It was not until the 1970s, after he amalgamated systems theory with the genetic structuralism of

Piaget and Kohlberg, that Habermas was able to fuse systems theory with a logic of moral development, creating thereby a theory capable of elucidating these contradictions. *Legitimation Crisis* represented the first step in this direction. There Habermas argued that the welfare state manages economic contradictions at the expense of incurring "rationality deficits." Torn between contradictory "steering imperatives" — the allocation of revenues for sustaining economic growth and the compensation of the victims of such growth — the welfare state suppresses debate regarding the ultimate foundations of the system (private property) in order to maintain its legitimacy. The "depoliticization" of the public realm that the system encourages should "uncouple" the state from a communicatively structured lifeworld and thereby enable it to plan the economy free of demands for public accountability. But this has not happened (despite the apathy of "happy consumers"), since increased state intervention in education, health, and welfare tends to repoliticize the public.

Chronic legitimation crises thus appear unavoidable — a condition that is further compounded, Habermas believes, by the erosion of consumer and achievement ideologies. According to Habermas, this "motivation crisis" is but one of several cultural crises advanced capitalism must confront. These other crisis tendencies center around the *impoverishment of culture* and the *bureaucratization and commodification of everyday life*.[25] Impoverishment of culture manifests itself in a deterioration of aptitudes necessary for critically analyzing experience. Commodification and bureaucratization involve the substitution of legally organized spheres of economic-administrative activity for communicative interaction. Together these syndromes conspire to undermine the communicative conditions for appropriating culture, coordinating action, and fostering personal identity freely and rationally. The result is fragmentation and objectification of life.

Habermas contends that the loss of freedom, meaning, and identity plaguing modern society is caused by two parallel processes: the *splitting off of elite (specialized) subcultures* and the *inner colonization of a communicatively structured lifeworld by economic and political systems*. By encouraging passive acceptance of one overriding goal — managed economic growth — the welfare state fosters an equally passive acquiescence in the authority of administrative elites claiming technological expertise. To a certain extent, of course, the institutionalization of specialized fields of knowledge permits a more rational resolution of technical problems. However, the welfare state encourages the reduction of all political problems to the single technical problem of maintaining stable economic growth. Confronted with the technical intricacies of economic management, citizens are more than willing to let specialists do the thinking for them. Yet the cost is high. Citizens cease to regard themselves as guardians of moral ideals to which administrative elites must be held accountable. Consequently, they abdicate responsibility for critically generating an informed public opinion with regard to their own common good.

In order to understand how Habermas's critique of capitalism relates to communication one must turn to his theory of language, what he calls "universal pragmatics." This approach combines the structural linguistics of Chomsky, which aims at reconstructing universal competencies necessary for generating grammatically well-formed sentences, and the more empirically oriented speech-act theories of John Austin and John Searle. The result is a program designed to reconsruct the *pragmatic* conditions necessary for mastering the *performative* rules of *social interaction*, especially those revolving around *speaker* and *listener* roles.

According to Habermas, everyday speech — in contradistinction to poetic and literary language — contains a performative as well as an informational component. The informational component normally consists of a factual proposition (P), for example, "It is raining outside." The performative component consists of a first person verb phrase, for example, "I promise (know, assure, etc.) that P," in which the speaker proposes to take on certain future obligations in exchange for the listener's entering into social interaction with him. A speech act consists of both components. For example, "I know that it is raining outside," succeeds when the listener voluntarily accepts its truth, appropriateness, and sincerity. In return for this acceptance the speaker tacitly agrees to take on an obligation to make good the evidenciary backing behind the claim should the listener so request it.

Habermas's unique contribution to speech-act theory consists in his use of structural linguistics to show that every conceivable speech act raises, either implicitly or explicitly, four major validity claims: to truth, normative rightness, sincerity, and comprehensibility. These claims vary in emphasis depending on the kind of speech act under consideration. A factual assertion, for example, highlights a claim to truth, whereas a moral command highlights a claim to normative rightness. However, since all four claims are raised simultaneously in any speech act, one could in principle challenge the sincerity, normative appropriateness, or even comprehensibility of a factual assertion.[26]

It is Habermas's contention that rational speakers must be prepared to justify the truth, rightness, sincerity, and comprehensibility of their communications if so challenged. To the extent that they are *predisposed* to coordinate their actions communicatively — bearing in mind that unconstrained communication is a necessary condition for maintaining stable social and personal identity — *discourse* must always remain an immanent possibility for them. Consequently, unless circumstances warrant a departure from standard practice — the strategic use of power and manipulation are sometimes called for in adversarial relations — rational speakers will *tacitly* assume that the normative conditions specified by the ideal speech situation obtain, even if they in fact don't.

As an analysis of what rational speakers in Westernized societies tacitly assume, this conviction may not seem very controversial. However, as a claim about linguistic communication in general, it seems obviously false. No anthropologist would seriously entertain the notion that the sorts of mythic narratives and cultic practices around which aboriginal peoples conduct their lives are structurally differentiated into distinct cognitive, normative, and expressive components. To deflect the charge of ethnocentrism, Habermas has had to rely on a theory of social evolution. Such a theory is indispensable to social critique, Habermas insists, for without an evolutionary ranking of universal types of social organization it would be impossible to identify "progressive" developments in morality and law that act as "pacesetters" for *and* limits to economic and administrative growth.

Habermas contends that individual cognitive and moral development is intimately related to acquiring communicative competence. Pragmatism, he believes, has shown that spatial perception is primarily developed through the manipulation of objects. Yet he notes that the identification of things and their properties is linked to the propositional use of names and predicates.

The acquisition of communicative competence is also essential to moral development. Like Piaget and Kohlberg, Habermas divides moral development into three major stages: preconventional, conventional, and postconventional. Preconventional morality is primarily self-centered, and involves the moral assessment of actions solely in terms of their consequences for the judging ego. Yet despite its egocentric focus, this stage of morality presupposes the beginning of a kind of reciprocity which manifests itself in the form of an I'll-scratch-your-back-if-you'll-scratch-mine attitude. Reciprocity here involves a capacity to identify with two points of view: that of ego and alter. The ability to identify with the other in this way, however, is predicated on the ability to assume the reciprocal roles of speaker and listener roles.

The conventional stage of morality implicates communicative competence even more deeply. At this stage persons learn to issue commands that claim a validity transcending the satisfaction of personal interests. In issuing moral commands the speaker must not only identify with the second person listener role (alter) but must identify with the third person standpoint of a *generalized other*, representing the interests of the community, the nation, etc. Finally, at the postconventional level of morality persons learn to evaluate conventional norms in light of their universality for all rational beings, temporal and geographical boundaries notwithstanding. At this level communication involves the freedom to propose and reject, justify and criticize, validity claims *at ascending levels of generality* (TCA2 27–42).

Habermas claims that changes in language also effect social evolution in a manner that parallels moral-cognitive development in the individual. Individual development involves the progressive *differentiation* of cognitive, normative, and expressive attitudes as well as the progressive *decentering* of the ego. Something similar happens at the level of social evolution, in which (as Weber has shown) the unitary religious *worldviews* of premodern cultures are differentiated into objective, social, and subjective "worlds," and value spheres. Habermas dubs the mechanism by which this is accomplished the *linguistification of the sacred.*

The lack of cognitive and moral differentiation evident in mythic worldviews finds a correlate in ritualized modes of social interaction that permit little individual freedom. Even the metaphysical worldviews of more advanced traditional societies lack the differentiation requisite for critical reflection. Religious and metaphysical forms of speech conflate the informational, performative, and expressive uses of language so that it is difficult to determine whether an utterance is a factual assertion raising a claim to objective truth, a moral command raising a claim to intersubjective rightness, or an expression of feeling raising a claim to subjective sincerity. This confusion immunizes ideological justifications against rational critique. The possibility for *rational critique* and *progressive learning* first arises when communication evolves to the point of *grammatically differentiated speech* in which cognitive assertions, normative prescriptions, and subjective expressions are clearly distinguished from one another in accordance with the structural components of speech action. A higher stage is achieved when specialized domains of *discourse* (science, law and morality, and art) branch off from everyday communicative action.

Habermas follows Weber in describing social evolution as a process of *cultural* and *social rationalization*. From the standpoint of the participants engaged in modern life, the process appears as a rationalization of a communicatively integrated *lifeworld*. Rationalization here refers to the establishment of formally consistent modes of behavior incorporating an efficient calculation of means and ends (what Weber calls *purposive rational action*) in accordance with universal norms. It too is characterized by structural differentiation: learning processes centered around the cultural value spheres of truth, rightness, and aesthetic value are institutionalized in science, jurisprudence, and art. Nature is divested of its teleological meaning. Religious sentiments find secular embodiment in universal ethical and legal institutions (civil and democratic rights). The latter, in turn, permit individuals greater freedom to pursue private interests and criticize authority (TCA1 157–58).

To sum up: the process of social rationalization enables individuals to become increasingly autonomous with respect to culture and society. *Concrete contents* of life experience are gradually distinguished from *formal-universal* cognitive structures, normative principles, and personal competencies, and levels of *critical reflection* are progressively deepened (TCA2 140–52). This results in increased individual responsibility for bestowing meaning and value on the world one inhabits and *increased demand for democratic participation as a condition for bestowing legitimacy on social norms and institutions.*

The process of societal rationalization also involves what Habermas calls the "uncoupling of lifeworld and system." The rationalization of the lifeworld described above is characterized by the spread of formal-legal (contractual) relations that serve as the normative basis for market economy and bureaucratic state. Family and public realm (the "critical public" constituted by mass media, cultural exhibits, political gatherings, etc.) are primarily located in the lifeworld, where action is *intentionally* coordinated through communication. State and economy, by contrast, are located in self-regulating systems which are *functionally* integrated by wholly impersonal and anonymous *exchange relationships*. These relationships are mediated by *money* and *power*, which enable a purely strategic, noncommunicative form of interaction based on a calculation of rewards and punishments.

Habermas maintains that the distinction between lifeworld and system is essential to understanding the sorts of social pathologies which figure predominantly in current debates about modernity. At first glance, it does indeed appear as if the rationalization of the lifeworld is paradoxical: the formalization of communicative rationality through the medium of civil and constitutional law makes possible the growth of economic and administrative subsystems that threaten to turn back and "devour" the very lifeworld which lends them legitimacy. Administrative regulations threaten to strangle democratic initiative and create bureaucratic dependency while moral incentives get eclipsed by the unbridled pursuit of power, pleasure, and wealth.

Habermas has serious reservations about the unchecked growth of the system. Like Marx, he diagnoses the problem in terms of the *objective lawfulness* of forces that have escaped the rational control of social agents and now confront them as a *natural fate* to which they must submit. Although he thinks that some uncoupling of lifeworld and system is rational he feels that it has gone too far. The system must be made accountable to a democratized lifeworld. Nothing less than the ecological and geopolitical survival of the planet depends on it. Indeed the very identity of persons as free, morally accountable agents hangs in the balance as well. For this too depends on the cultivation of critical public opinion in associations permitting free debate. However, today's critics of the Enlightenment, nourished on the writings of Nietzsche, Heidegger, Foucault, and Derrida, attribute the extension of strategic modes of behavior to reason as such (TCA2 186). Their mistake, according to Habermas, consists in identifying reason with instrumental rationality, and value-commitment with pre-rational religious motivation. Yet this is not, he is quick to add, their only oversight. Besides neglecting the linguistification of the sacred reflected in communicative rationality, they also overlook the true cause of social disintegration — the colonization of the lifeworld by the system. The rationalization of the lifeworld establishes only the necessary conditions for a process of modernization that can either fail or succeed. Under the peculiar historical conditions which gave rise to a capitalist mode of modernization, rationalization could only proceed in a *one-sided*, or *selective* fashion, subordinating communicative to instrumental reason.

Without a notion of system to complement one's lived experience of alienation, one is unavoidably led to attribute the failings of modern society to rationalization. Conversely, without a notion of lifeworld one is bereft of any universal norm upon which to base one's social critique. According to Habermas, this is the difficulty that Foucault and other poststructuralists encounter. In bracketing the dimension of *subjective meaning* Foucault reduces the lifeworld to socially discrete and historically discontinuous functional systems, or discursive regimes, integrated by power relations. As valid as these descriptions may be, they alone cannot explain social pathology.[27] Once lifeworld is assimilated to system the peculiar *normative resistance* responsible for *social crises*, namely, the resistance of individuals oriented toward democratic self-determination, is suppressed. Hence one must beware of the "ideology" of a "stable system" which co-opts all forms of resistance in the form of technological efficiency, adaptation, etc. (TCA2 186).

Our all-too-perfunctory survey of Habermas's response to post-structuralism raises some serious doubts about the success of his own program. Habermas has always been concerned to make good Marxism's claim to unify theory and practice. Indeed, it is precisely poststructur-alism's failure to provide rationally justifiable reference points for action that disturbs him the most. Self-determination, Habermas tells us, presupposes an orientation toward *unconstrained intersubjectivity* and, therefore, *reciprocal identity* based on *universal norms*. The post-structuralist dissolution of a *self-determining and self-identical* sub-jectivity into a plurality of language games (Lyotard), a force-field of relations of power (Foucault), or an open system of *archewriting* wherein binary oppositions are continually relativized and referential loci dis-placed (Derrida), opens up a nihilistic void in which politics becomes meaningless.[28] Why be political if there is no ideal to be fought over, no subject to be emancipated?

Of course, thinkers as diverse as Lyotard and Rorty have tried to show how a *kind* of relativism is still compatible with political engagement — whether they have succeeded or not is debatable. More important, Habermas seems not to have fully understood the price that any modern culture has to pay for the luxury of emancipation. One need not go so far as Lyotard in dissolving subjectivity into linguistic pluralism to question whether the added responsibility and freedom that comes with rational autonomy (to the extent that it is possible) is most conducive to stable identity formation. Moreover, Habermas has not convincingly shown that the rationalization of law is entirely innocent in contributing to the hyperextension of system complexity.

But there remains a more serious problem. Habermas's overriding preoccupation with refuting relativism and defending the universal project of enlightenment seems to have taken him far afield from his original Marxian concern with emancipatory practice. Critical theory, he now insists, can venture only so far in proffering moral enlightenment. To the extent that it remains a scientific and philosophical enterprise critical theory must confine itself to the rational reconstruction of formal-universal structures, principles, and competencies. This means, however, that critical theory can no longer project concrete visions of utopia. Taking Habermas at his word, a critical theory guided by purely formal principles of justice cannot even criticize societies as totalities embodying conceptions of the good life — an extraordinary presumption if we bear in mind that social pathology manifests itself as a disequilibrium of rationality complexes affecting the *whole of society* (TCA2 383). What remains is the liberal and not too radical enterprise of grounding "the moral point of view" — a worthy project to be sure, but one that is of greater interest to academicians engaged in metaethical debates about relativism than to activists searching for political inspiration. Yet if anything is to be said in Habermas's favor it is surely this: foresaking of the bourgeois "ideology" of constitutional democracy and individual freedom by Marxists and fascists alike is a mistake that "we" in the West do not wish to see repeated again. For that reason alone the defense of pluralism touted by poststructuralists cannot do without a healthy appreciation of unconstrained communication, however modest its form.

Notes

1. The political climate in his family — his father was head of the local Bureau of Trade and Industry, his grandfather a minister and director of a local seminary — was, as he himself puts it, "marked by a bourgeois adaptation to a political situation with which one did not fully identify, but which one didn't seriously criticize either." See *Habermas: Autonomy and Solidarity.*

Interviews With Jürgen Habermas, ed. Peter Dews (London: Verso, 1986), p. 73.

2. From 1949–54 Habermas attended the Universities of Göttingen, Bonn, and Zurich, where he studied philosophy, history, psychology, German literature, and economics. The professors who influenced him the most (and under whom he later wrote his dissertation) were Erich Rothacker, a theoretician of the *Geistewissenschaften* who was schooled in the thought of Dilthey, and Oskar Becker, a former student of Husserl who specialized in mathematics and logic. With the sole exception of Theodor Litt, his professors were either ex-Nazis or survivors who had learned to adapt their professional responsibilities to the constraints imposed by the Party. See Dews, p. 196.

3. The details of Habermas's most recent critique of Heidegger are contained in *The Philosophical Discourse of Modernity*, pp. 131–60, and in the Foreword to the German translation of Victor Farias's detailed exposition of Heidegger's involvement with National Socialism, *Heidegger und der National-sozialismus* (Frankfurt: S. Fischer Verlag, 1989), pp. 11–37 (reprinted under the title "Work and Weltanschauung" in *Critical Inquiry*, 15 (Winter 1989).

4. J. Habermas, *Das Absolute und die Geschichte. Von der Zwiespältigkeit in Schellings Denken* (Univ. of Bonn, 1954).

5. See "Die Dialektik der Rationalisierung. Vom Pauperismus in Production und Konsum," *Merkur*, 1954.

6. Richard Bernstein, Introduction to *Habermas and Modernity*, ed. R. Bernstein (Cambridge, Mass.: MIT, 1985), p. 5.

7. The debate is contained in *The Positivist Dispute in German Sociology*, ed. T. Adorno, et. al. (New York: Harper and Row, 1976).

8. Along with his friend, Wolfgang Abendroth (under whose tutelage he would receive a second doctorate in political science), he helped found the Socialist League — a sort of "'old folks' section of the German SDS," as he later described it (Dews, p. 78).

9. Habermas's articles on student politics were published in *Protest-bewegung und Hochschulereform* (Frankfurt: Suhrkamp, 1968), some of which were reprinted in *Toward a Rational Society*, trans. J. Shapiro (Boston: Beacon, 1970).

10. Many of these essays were later published in *Communication and the Evolution of Society*, trans. and ed. T. McCarthy (Boston: Beacon, 1979).

11. Habermas's critique of revisionist historians Ernst Nolte and Andreas Hillgruber are contained in J. Habermas, *Eine Art Schadensabwicklung* (Frankfurt: Suhrkamp Verlag, 1987), pp. 115–58.

12. See J. Habermas, "Dogmatism, Reason, and Decision: On Theory and Praxis in Our Scientific Civilization," *Theory and Practice*, trans. J. Viertel (Boston: Beacon, 1973), pp. 253–82; "Technology and Science as 'Ideology'," *Toward A Rational Society*, trans. J. Shapiro (Boston: Beacon, 1970), pp. 81–122; and Herbert Marcuse, *One-Dimensional Man* (Boston: Beacon, 1964).

13. J. Habermas, *Knowledge and Human Interests*, trans. J. Shapiro (Boston: Beacon, 1971), pp. 3–5. Hereafter KHI.

14. J. Habermas, "Remarks on Hegel's Jena *Philosophy of Mind*," *Theory and Practice*, pp. 142–69.

15. Habermas argues (ibid., pp. 161–67) that as early as the *Phenomenology* labor and interaction begin to lose their status as principles of spiritual formation, i.e., as models of dialectical movement, and are reduced to "subordinate real conditions" (or mere stages) of a *dialectic of self-reflection*. In the Jena system the dialectical movement involves an emancipatory struggle between two subjects for mutual recognition, or the restoration of an unconstrained intersubjectivity (*reconciliation*) that has been sundered. Even the dialectic of labor, of externalization and appropriation, is assimilated to this moral dialectic, so that nature is seen "as a hidden subject in the role of the other." By contrast, in the *Phenomenology* and *Encyclopaedia* the dialectic involves *conscious, subjective appropriation of an implicitly self-externalized objectivity*. Here moral interaction is assimilated to the "labor" and *self-sacrifice* of a solitary "Absolute Spirit," or "Absolute Idea," working *itself* out as destiny.

16. Specifically, the logic of scientific inquiry consists of three types of instrumental activity: (1) *discovery* of causal laws via trial and error (*abduction*); (2) *explanation*, or inference of effects from antecedent (3) conditions and causal laws (*deduction*); and (4) *experimental confirmation* of laws (*induction*). These activities comprise a *methodologically* sophisticated set of *operations* which make possible the *cumulative* acquisition of causal knowledge in ways that are convincing for all persons.

17. See Hans-Georg Gadamer, *Truth and Method* (New York: Crossroad, 1975), pp. 274–341.

18. Ibid., pp. 192–274; Habermas, p. 182.

19. J. Habermas, *The Theory of Communicative Action. Volume Two. Lifeworld and System: A Critique of Functionalist Reason*, trans. T. McCarthy (Boston: Beacon, 1987), p. 164 – hereafter abbreviated TCA2; and "Questions and Counter-Questions," *Praxis International*, 4:3 (1984), p. 239.

20. J. Habermas, "Wahrheitstheorien," in *Vorstudien und Ergänzungen zur Theorie des kommunikativen Handelns* (Frankfurt: Suhrkamp, 1984), p. 178.

21. See J. Habermas, *Der Philosophische Diskurs der Moderne* (Frankfurt: Suhrkamp, 1985); translated by F. Lawrence as *The Philosophical Discourse of Modernity* (Cambridge, Mass.: MIT, 1987); and *Die Neue Unübersichtlichkeit: Kleine politische Schriften V* (Frankfurt: Suhrkamp, 1985).

22. See "The Entwinement of Myth and Enlightenment: Max Horkheimer and Theodor Adorno," in *The Philosophical Discourse of Modernity*.

23. This line of argumentation is developed at length in *The Theory of Communicative Action. Volume One: Reason and the Rationalization of Society*, trans. T. McCarthy (Boston: Beacon, 1984), pp. 366–99. Hereafter TCA1.

24. See "Technology and Science as Ideology", pp. 81–90.

25. J. Habermas, TCA2.

26. The details of Habermas's universal pragmatics are worked out in "What is Universal Pragmatics?" included in *Communication and the Evolution of Society*; and "Towards a Theory of Communicative Competence," and in TCA 273–337.

27. *The Philosophical Discourse of Modernity*, pp. 270–93.

28. Habermas criticizes Derrida's deconstruction of the philosophy/literary criticism distinction on the grounds that it subverts the unique function of each in mediating specialized discourses (science and literature) with the everyday lifeworld. In particular, he argues that philosophy can only fulfill its problem-solving function by remaining bound to procedures of rational argumentation. See *The Philosophical Discourse of Modernity*, pp. 185–200.

Russian Formalism, Prague Structuralism, and the Bakhtin Circle

Introduction

George H. Jensen

Because Bakhtin was such an original thinker, one of the more interesting ways to set his work in context is to discuss what he is not. While most of his contemporaries worked within the framework of Marxism, played roles in the short-lived movement of Russian Formalism, left Russia to contribute to the theory of the Prague structuralism, or were involved with some other -ism, Bakhtin stood apart. His thought was compatible with that of the members of his circle, yet it is unclear whether Voloshinov, Medvedev, and others in the Bakhtin Circle substantially contributed to its original ideas or even substantially authored some of the works that bear their names. Bakhtin stood apart, but he was not aloof. He developed his thought by entering into a dialogue with the important movements of his day, including Russian Formalism and Prague structuralism.

Russian Formalism — despite the attention it has drawn for its contributions to linguistics, literary criticism, and structuralism — has a murky history that is as difficult to follow as a poorly written detective novel. Thus, a brief chronological overview will make this short introduction to the movement's theory easier to follow.[1] Osip Brik is credited with founding the Petersburg Circle of Formalists in 1914, about the time that Bakhtin began to study at Petersburg University. The term Opoyaz (an acronym for the Russian equivalent of Society for the Study of Poetic Language) is used to refer to this original group and its theory. Although Bakhtin was not a member of the group, he undoubtedly knew of its work. P. N. Medvedev's *The Formal Method in Literary Scholarship* (1928) is regarded by many to be primarily his work. By 1915, a second circle was founded in Moscow under the leadership of Roman Jakobson. The two circles appear to have interacted fairly often, although the Moscow Circle lost much of its power after

Jakobson moved to Prague in 1920. There, Jakobson formed the Prague Circle, where most scholars believe that the later Formalism developed into structuralism. Here again, the name of Bakhtin, or at least another of his potential pseudonyms, appears. V. N. Voloshinov's *Marxism and the Philosophy of Language* (1929), reportedly penned substantially by Bakhtin, had some influence on the development of Jakobson's thought.[2]

Each of these circles held regular meetings during which one of the members, or a guest, would lecture. It is this oral genesis and transmission of theory that clouds some of the movement's history. To unravel the development of Formalism and its contributions to structuralism, one must determine who lectured to whom at what time and what was said, which is no easy task. Many of the lectures were lost or published only as summaries. Other important works, such as Mukarovsky's *The General Principles and Evolution of Modern Czech Verse* or Jakobson's *On Czech Verse*, simply do not translate.[3] The history of the movement is further complicated by its eventual diversification as more circles were formed and its theory evolved.

Unlike its later history, Russian Formalism as it emerged from 1914 to 1920 was remarkably cohesive. The nearly univocal manifesto of the Petersburg Circle, as stated in its first publication, *Collections on the Theory of Poetic Language* (1916), represented a reaction against the current state of literary criticism — a sorry assortment of biographical anecdotes, psychological platitudes, and sociological analyses — as well as an attempt to create a true discipline of literary analysis. In the words of Boris Eichenbaum, one of the early members of the group:

> Our Formalist movement was characterized by a new passion for scientific positivism — a rejection of philosophical assumptions, of psychological and aesthetic interpretations, etc. Art, considered apart from philosophical aesthetics and ideological theories, dictated its own position on things. We had to turn to facts and, abandoning general systems and problems, to begin "in the middle," with the facts which art forced upon us. Art demanded that we approach it closely; science, that we deal with the specific.[4]

The Formalists — who had watched Symbolists' criticism lose its power by being locked into the analysis of a single poetic feature, the image — did not want to be restricted by ideology or a rigid theory of poetics. Eichenbaum claims that the Formalists wanted to eschew, in accordance with the then-pervasive ideology of positivism, any preconceived ideas and linguistically analyze their object of study, the literary fact.

This claim of Eichenbaum and other Formalists to focus on "the literary fact" can, however, be misleading, for Formalist research often transcended the boundaries of specific literary works. The Formalists were not so much "factual" as "transfactual." Rather than interpret a specific work, they more frequently analyzed how formal elements functioned within the medium of poetic language. Roman Jakobson wrote in *Modern Russian Poetry* (1921) that the "object of the science of literature is not literature, but literariness — that is, that which makes a given work a work of literature."[5] Even in the early work of Formalists, the analysis of form is more the stuff of grand theory (closer to Saussure's *langue*) than the specificity of minute critical work (or *parole*). Too often, the stated agenda of Formalists (particularly as expressed by Eichenbaum) is taken as an accurate description of their actual agenda.[6] Thus, their contributions have sometimes been slighted.

It is the early work of the Formalists, their studies of poetic language, that is best understood. To move beyond traditional studies of meter, they relied on the work of two important linguists. The work of Jan Baudouin de Courtenayand on phonology came to them through Lev Scerba and perhaps D. K. Petrov, both of whom were Baudouin's students. By 1917, the ideas of Ferdinand de Saussure exerted an influence when Sergej Karcevskij returned from his studies in Geneva, shortly after *Course in General Linguistics* was published.

Equipped with the most recent advances in linguistics, the Opoyaz group set out to understand the nature of poetic language, how it was different from practical language, and how the elements of poetic language functioned within the system of a poem or within the broader system of poetic language. An element or technique could not actually be described as poetic in isolation; it must function as a poetic element within the system of poetic language. It is the Formalists' emphasis on function that places their movement in the realm of *parole* as well as *langue*. In its 1916 collection of essays, Leo Jakubinsky wrote:

> The phenomena of language must be classified from the point of view of the speaker's particular purpose as he forms his own linguistic pattern. If the pattern is formed for the purely practical purpose of communication, then we are dealing with a system of *practical language* (the language of thought) in which the linguistic pattern (sounds, morphological features, etc.) have no independent value and are merely a *means* of communication. But other linguistic systems, systems in which the practical purpose is in the background (although perhaps not entirely hidden) are conceivable; they exist, and their linguistic patterns acquire *independent value*.[7]

The early Formalists generally felt that poetic language was independent; it was a physical object, significant beyond the meaning of its words, that was felt rather than interpreted. As Victor Shklovsky wrote in "Art as Technique" (1917), "Art exists that one may recover the sensation of life; it exists to make one feel things, to make the stone *stoney*."[8] Although Medvedev and Bakhtin complimented the Formalists for working out a theory of poetics (a problem that Marxist critical theory had not yet tackled), they felt that their method was essentially flawed. They wrote: "It is not necessary to renounce normal vision, to renounce a wide ideological horizon, in order to examine the total specificity of art. The wider the horizon, the brighter and more distinct is the individuality of each concrete phenomenon."[9] The Formalists, Medvedev and Bakhtin felt, forfeited a view of the literary work from the ideological (meaning roughly the cultural or social) perspective in order to examine specificity, when the ideological perspective would have allowed for a more accurate analysis of specificity. Throughout his work Bakhtin posited that the way to understand the concrete and specific aspects of language was to understand it within a cultural or social context. Medvedev and Bakhtin also argued against the views of the early Formalists that language does express values, that poetic and practical language cannot be neatly separated, that no literary work is ever complete or self-contained, and that literature does not always change from internal forces.[10]

The Formalists' work on poetic language, which continued even after the movement branched out into other issues (Medvedev/Bakhtin claimed that the movement revolted against itself),[11] was highly influential and was cited extensively in Wellek (who addressed the Prague Circle in 1934 and 1937) and Warren's seminal *Theory of Literature*.[12] Although it cannot be adequately summarized here, the movement continued to develop exceptionally original approaches to metrics, but the Opoyaz's cohesive effort to unlock the secrets of poetic language soon split into a wide range of projects. Formalists were, by 1919, beginning to investigate plot and literary history and to some extent the impact of social factors on literature. The Prague Circle would push even further into what the Opoyaz group considered forbidden territory by investigating the particularly unfactual and unscientific area of aesthetics.

In *Literature and Its Theorists* (1984), Tzvetan Todorov argues that the Formalists' early agendum — their focus on poetic language exclusive of history, biography, aesthetics, etc., — is precisely what led them to their later more comprehensive agenda. He says:

> An attentive analysis of the "works themselves" — made possible by the hypothesis of literary specificity — shows Formalists that the specificity in question does not exist. More precisely, it exists only in historically and culturally circumscribed terms; it is not universal or eternal; by the same token to define it in terms of autotelism is untenable. Paradoxically, their Romantic presuppositions are precisely the source of the Formalists' anti-Romantic conclusions.[13]

As stated earlier, it is questionable how successfully the Formalists ever enacted the Opoyaz goal of "specificity," and their work became broader and more theoretical as it developed. When Shklovsky argued that poetry reeducated our senses, that it made stones feel stoney, he was virtually forced to move from the synchronic to the diachronic. What happens when our poets' techniques are stale and stones no longer feel stoney? The poet must develop new techniques, new functions of previous poetic elements, to awaken our senses once more to the touch of stones. When Propp, in the mid-1920s, investigated the synchronic form of fairy tales, he found that certain elements, about one hundred fifty of them, recur repeatedly but in slightly different ways and with different functions. One element is the hut where some agent furnishes the hero with a magical tool. Propp found that some variations of this element can be explained by a theory of literary evolution, but some cannot. For example, in a religious culture, the hut may become a church. The Formalists' shift from a synchronic analysis of the "literariness" of literature to literary evolution, aesthetics, and culture was, given their starting point, almost unavoidable.

It is this movement beyond the original Opoyaz theory that marked the work of the Prague Circle. Before Formalism was suppressed in Russia in 1930, the Prague Circle had already committed itself to continuing the expanded Formalists' agenda, largely through the collaboration of Jakobson and Tynjanov. On January 13, 1926, Jakobson delivered "The Concept of Sound Law" to his colleagues in Prague. On December 16, 1928, Tynjanov, visiting from Leningrad, delivered a lecture entitled "On the Problem of Literary Evolution." Later that year, the two collaborated on "Problems in Literary and Linguistic Research," which significantly contributed to the development of structuralism.[14] They wrote:

> The sharp opposition of synchronic (static) and diachronic cross sections has recently become a fruitful working hypothesis, both for linguistics and for the history of literature; this opposition reveals the nature of language (literature) as a system at each individual moment of its existence. At the present time, the achievements of the synchronic concept force us to reconsider the principles of diachrony as well. The idea of the mechanical agglomeration of material, having been replaced by the concept of system or structure in the realm of synchronic study, underwent a corresponding replacement in the realm of diachronic as well. The history of a system is in turn a system. Pure synchronism now proves to be an illusion: every synchronic system has its past and its future as inseparable structural elements of the system.[15]

In the work of Jakobson and Tynjanov are many of the basic tenets of Prague structuralism: there should be a fusion of the diachronic and the synchronic (which would later be worked out by Jakobson and Mukarovsky in the early 1930s); a literary work is a system; literature in general is a system of systems; literature contains a "limited series of actually existing structural types"; these types evolve in what is yet another dimension of structures; and any evolution in diachronic structures affects the entire system of synchronic structures.

In *Marxism and the Philosophy of Language*, Voloshinov and Bakhtin at times expressed affinities with structuralists. For example, they wrote: "The understanding of a sign is, after all, an act of reference between the sign apprehended and other, already known signs; in other words, understanding is a response to a sign within a sign."[16] It is understandable that Jakobson would like the book, for he certainly found familiar ideas there. But Voloshinov and Bakhtin felt that signs could not be studied apart from the ideological, that is, apart from the interaction of individuals within a cultural setting:

> This ideological chain stretches from individual consciousness to individual consciousness, connecting them together. Signs emerge, after all, only in the process of interaction between one individual consciousness and another. And the individual consciousness itself is filled with signs. Consciousness becomes consciousness only once it has been filled with ideological (semiotic) content, consequently, only in the process of social interaction.[17]

Later Bakhtin alone criticized structuralism for being too enclosed, limited, and decontextualized. The reality that the structuralists felt they were codifying was, in Bakhtin's view, lifeless. The structuralists dissected discourse; Bakhtin wanted to vivisect it. As he wrote in the process of criticizing structuralism: "Nothing is absolutely dead: every meaning will have its homecoming festival."[18]

Even though Bakhtin cannot be considered a Formalist — at least, in the restricted sense of the term — or a structuralist, he did not dismiss the movements, for this would not be dialogic. Rather, he established his affinities with them but also, through his utterances, clarified and marked his differences.

Notes

1. This brief history of the movement is drawn from Victor Erlich's *Russian Formalism: History-Doctrine* (New Haven: Yale Univ., 1965); Boris Eichenbaum's "The Theory of the 'Formal Method,'" in *Russian Formalist Criticism* (Lincoln: Univ. of Nebraska, 1965); Jan M. Broekman's *Structuralism: Moscow-Prague-Paris* (Boston: D. Reidel, 1974), and P. N. Medvedev and M. M. Bakhtin's *The Formal Method in Literary Scholarship: A Critical Introduction to Sociological Poetics* (Baltimore: Johns Hopkins Univ., 1928, 1978).

2. See Translator's Preface to *Marxism and the Philosophy of Language*, trans. Ladislav Matejka and I. R. Titunik (Cambridge: Harvard Univ., 1929, 1973), pp. vii–viii.

3. F. W. Galan, *Historic Structures: The Prague School Project, 1928–1946* (Austin: Univ. of Texas, 1985), p. 36.

4. Eichenbaum, p. 106.

5. Quoted in Tzvetan Todorov *Literature and Its Theorists: A Personal View of Twentieth-Century Criticism*, trans. Catherine Porter (Ithaca: Cornell Univ., 1984, 1987), p. 11.

6. Fredric Jameson wrote: "The Formalists were ultimately concerned with the way in which the individual work of art (or *parole*) was perceived differentially against the background of the literary system as a whole (or *langue*). The Structuralists, however, dissolving the individual unit back into the *langue* of which it is a partial articulation, set themselves the task of describing the organization of the total sign system." See *The Prison-House of Language: A Critical Account of Structuralism and Russian Formalism* (Princeton: Princeton Univ., 1972), p. 101. Jameson, as is typical of many critics, makes the historical movement from Formalism to structuralism more of a radical break than a natural evolution. Galan feels that this is because Jameson's study ignored the work of the Prague circle, which formed a link between the agenda of the Formalists and the Parisian structuralists (see *Historic Structures*, p. 2).

7. Quoted in Eichenbaum, p. 108.

8. In *Russian Formalist Criticism*, p. 12.

9. *The Formal Method in Literary Scholarship*, p. 72.

10. For a discussion of Bakhtin's criticism of Formalism, see Katerina Clark and Michael Holquist's *Mikhail Bakhtin* (Cambridge: Harvard Univ., 1984), pp. 186–96.

11. *The Formal Method in Literary Scholarship*, p. 75.

12. *Theory of Literature* (New York: Harvest, 1942), pp. 159, 170, 217, 235.

13. *Literature and Its Theorists*, p. 26.

14. Galan, pp. 9–10.

15. In *Readings in Russian Formalism*, p. 79.

16. *Marxism and the Philosophy of Language*, p. 11.

17. Ibid.

18. *Speech Genres and Other Late Essays*, trans. Vern W. McGee (Austin: Univ. of Texas, 1986), p. 170.

6

Mikhail Bakhtin:
Philosopher of Language

Charles I. Schuster

This essay offers itself less as an explanation of what Bakhtin means than as a reading — a dialogic, unfinalizable, reactive/proactive/ interactive response to the unfolding work of Bakhtin. Indeed, my purpose in writing this essay could never be to "explain" Bakhtin's theories; such a project is not feasible, given the Bakhtinian positions on discourse and dialogism. For Bakhtin, the act of explaining deadened the relationship between speaker and subject, in contrast to comprehending (or understanding), which maintained between them a living relationship. In "The Problem of the Text," an essay that is more a collection of Bakhtin's notebook jottings than finished work and that is included in *Speech Genres*, Bakhtin develops this fundamental distinction:

> To see and comprehend the author of a work means to see and comprehend another, alien consciousness and its world, that is, another subject ("Du"). With *explanation* there is only one consciousness, one subject; with *comprehension* there are two consciousnesses and two subjects. There can be no dialogic relationship with an object, and therefore explanation has no dialogic aspects (except formal, rhetorical ones). Understanding is always dialogic to some degree.[1]

The problem Bakhtin poses for an author attempting to write a prolegomena to his work is how *not* to explain him while "explaining" him, that is, how to create an understanding that maintains an awareness of the multiplicities of nuance, value, accent, and meaning that exist between "explainer," "explained," and "explainee."

Some additional cautions. Mikhail Bakhtin does not simply believe in heteroglossia, dialogism, carnival, novel, speech genres — his work is situated within them because they represent vital philosophical, theoretical tenets that, in his view, are constitutive of language. This fact alone sets Bakhtin apart from most theorists, from most writers and critics, who argue (for example) about aesthetics in distinctly non-aesthetic language, language that is devoid of the dialogizing power that characterizes contemporary novelistic language. Bakhtin stands counter to such thinking, so counter that he is at times baffling to read. He has been criticized for his loopy, associative style, his conceptual shiftiness, his tendency to think things through in prose. Ken Hirschkop can be taken as a representative voice among those who find Bakhtin maddening to read:

> The debate on Bakhtin is made yet more difficult by the nature of his writing: immensely varied stylistically and topically, but also — and more importantly, I believe — writing which strives for solutions it cannot quite articulate. It moves between alternative and contradictory formulations in a single essay and thus produces a set of concepts whose explanatory importance is matched by an unnerving tendency to slide from one formulation to the next with disturbing ease. Such ambiguities are not the sign of an open and sceptical mind, but neither are they mere inconsistencies which can be safely ignored. These internal contradictions dictate that argument over concepts like "dialogism" and "heteroglossia" cannot be settled by a definitive decision as to what they "really" mean; instead, we must discuss how to manage these complexities and contradictions, and to what ends.[2]

Hirschkop may be right in much of what he says, but for the wrong reasons. Bakhtin believes that language is alive, that listeners (and readers) must enter into the discourse of others, that words shift in meaning even when merely reiterated, that the process of thinking through metaphysical problems as a writer is privileged over producing a text that clarifies issues for a reader. Bakhtin is a celebrant of traveling, not destination. Moreover Bakhtin holds that all words, texts, discourses, languages are joined together in a "chain of speech communion" (SG 76), linked both to antecedent and anticipatory responses. This simple theory of mutual responsiveness invigorates all his thinking and leads him to collapse distinctions between ordinary and poetic discourses, technical and nontechnical forms of utterance. Clive Thomson explains it this way:

> For Bakhtin, meta-language is not an abstract code different in kind from the text that it supposedly accounts for. There is no basic difference between the discourse to be studied and the discourse used to study a discourse. ... The relationship between meta-language and the language (or texts) that it analyzes is always dialogical.[3]

The danger of muting the distinction between these discourses is the potential to conflate literature with criticism, a move that is already apparent within the academy. Bakhtin's point here is not that criticism is literature but rather that criticism must engage its objects of study dialogically, as part of an ongoing conversation in which all parties maintain roles as speaking subjects.

Bakhtin's resistance toward definition and explanation would be less of a problem did he not simultaneously demonstrate a preference for neologizing. In vain will one search Bakhtin's texts for definitions of "dialogism," "heteroglossia," "polyphony," "novel," "carnival," and the like; neither will the desperate reader find clear-cut definitions in this essay. Nor is this mere perversity. Bakhtin's method of inquiry is circular. He celebrates the loophole, the sideward glance, the various oppositional elements that create resonance in language. Bakhtin delights in flux; one of his favorite participles (in translation at least) is "unfolding," and it is not possible for meanings to unfold once they have been set into the rigid form of a definition, a point Clark and Holquist make clear in *Mikhail Bakhtin*:

> Bakhtin was an enemy of anything that had ceased to be in process, which was no longer open to correction, addition, or contribution from the outside. He was ambivalent about the status of writing as opposed to speech, and some of the subtlest of his own applications of his theories open up other written texts to the kind of give and take usually thought to obtain only between two people engaged in conversation.[4]

Instead of definition and explicitness, Bakhtin provides descriptive analyses, examples, a great deal of thinking through what he means when he extols Dostoevsky as polyphonic, or Menippean satire as an early form of carnival. Reading him is in a very real sense like overhearing a conversation; as eavesdropper, one must maintain concentration even as Bakhtin digresses, lowers his voice, loses his place, stares off into space and then reconsiders, rethinks, reformulates.

Because Bakhtin resists definition, categorization, and linear analysis, he hovers outside traditional Western epistemology as defined by the Aristotelian method. Aristotle's analytic methodology was dissective; it understood the world as comprising its composite parts. Discourse consists of the deliberate, epideictic, and judicial. Appeals are categorized in terms of ethos, pathos, and logos. Such a scientistic mode of inquiry assumes that we understand best by isolating phenomena, the way many linguists understand language by isolating a word from a phrase, a sentence from a discourse, the way cellular biologists understand life by the titration of protein molecules. Bakhtin is opposed to such taxonomizing, opposed to the kind of thinking that characterizes the Western intellectual tradition. For him, the world can only be understood, appreciated, celebrated in terms of relation. To isolate a word, an utterance, a text in Bakhtin's thinking was to destroy its very meaning and significance, like trying to study a flake of snow by placing it under a heat lamp. The result, for many readers, is a body of theoretical work that feels so folded in upon itself as to resist entry. As Clark and Holquist state, "What is difficult about Bakhtin is the demand that his way of thinking makes on our way of thinking, the demand to change the basic categories that most of us use to organize thought itself" (MB 6). The only solution is to immerse oneself in Bakhtinian texts and suspend that Aristotelian desire for clarification by means of definition and division.

Within the critical tradition, it might be best to label Bakhtin a Socratist (a neologism of my own). Bakhtin read the formalists, the structuralists, the German Romantics, the literary historians. He read and admired neo-Kantians like Hermann Cohen and Ernst Cassirer, the linguist Wilhelm von Humboldt, and many others. But his ideas about the world of the word take on an original and uncategorizable flavor — and they are focused on and focused through a celebration of the orality of discourse. His writing reflects this; Bakhtin's texts are forms of conversation, forms of engaging in dialogue. As he states in *Problems of Dostoevsky's Poetics*:

> The single adequate form for *verbally expressing* authentic human life is the *open-ended dialogue*. Life by its very nature is dialogic. To live means to participate in dialogue: to ask questions, to heed, to respond, to agree, and so forth. In this dialogue a person participates wholly and throughout his whole life: with his eyes, lips, hands, soul, spirit, with his whole body and deeds. He invests his entire self in discourse and this discourse enters into the dialogic fabric of human life, into the world symposium.[5]

This commitment to open-ended dialogue means that Bakhtin is often repetitive (but not redundant) as he rethinks his positions and that his texts require readers to position themselves as active participants engaged in open-ended dialogue.

Mikhail Bakhtin is, I believe, a Romantic theorist in the best sense of the word, a condition that gets him criticized for being soft, fuzzy, idealistic. He sees discourse as a vital force, something in some sense living that possesses energy and even consciousness. For Bakhtin, the word has multiplicities of meanings; it carries a semantic history and, though it exists in the present, it always anticipates the future. The word collapses time/space understandings. It takes on a life of its own, has affect, gives voice. Moreover, unlike most critics, Bakhtin does not seek to provide intellectual machinery whereby the reader can perform an analytic act with more efficiency and precision. On the contrary, Bakhtin slows the act of reading and interpretation, for one voice becomes many voices. In a post-Bakhtinian reading, the word resonates; its edges blur.

That a theorist who celebrates double-voicedness and trespassed borders where one's word becomes another's should himself be subject to considerable confusion about authorship is perhaps inevitable. The perplexing question of authorship may never be answered to everyone's satisfaction; regardless, it needs to be considered from the outset. The name "M. M. Bakhtin" appears on four major texts (translated into English): *Problems of Dostoevsky's Poetics*, *Rabelais and His World*, *The Dialogic Imagination*, and *Speech Genres and Other Late Essays*. These texts are indisputably Bakhtin's, as is another important early essay, "Toward a Philosophy of the Act," which is not yet translated into English. Several other texts, however, show strong Bakhtinian influence but have appeared under the names of other individuals who were associated with Bakhtin, specifically: V. N. Voloshinov (who met Bakhtin in 1918) and P. N. Medvedev (who met Bakhtin in 1920). These three men were friends, fellow intellectuals, and important figures in the intellectual renaissance that appeared in post-Czarist Russia in the 1920s. Voloshinov is the apparent author of several significant texts: "Discourse in Life and Discourse in Art," *Freudianism: A Critical Sketch*, and *Marxism and the Philosophy of Language*. The Medvedev text under question is *The Formal Method in Literary Scholarship*. (For dates and publishers, see Bibliographic Note.) Since the names of Voloshinov and Medvedev appear on these books, one might ask how anyone could claim that Bakhtin authored them.

The answer is complicated and probably never will be answered to everyone's satisfaction. During the past few years, scholarly camps have fortified themselves with various historical evidence—Holquist and Clark maintaining that Bakhtin wrote at least ninety percent of each work and Titunik, Emerson, and Morson arguing that Voloshinov and Medvedev were the primary authors of their own work. Holquist and Clark, for example, maintain that Bakhtin found it politically necessary to publish his work under the names of friends once he fell under the unflinching gaze of the Stalinist police state. They argue that all the works in question were "assembled" from Bakhtin's dense notebooks; that they represent a variety of perspectives on the same issue, namely language as a socially constituted and socially constituting medium (MB 148–50); that Bakhtin is known to have published his own work under the name of his friend Kanaev, thus creating a precedent; that Bakhtin would enjoy the joke, the carnivalistic act, of publishing his own words in someone else's mouth. Titunik, Morson, and Emerson marshal equally persuasive arguments in opposition, stating that Voloshinov was an intellectual heavyweight in his own right and would not allow his professional credibility and personal safety to be undermined in this way; that the Marxist thinking in Voloshinov's and Medvedev's work is different in tone and timbre

from anything Bakhtin wrote under his own name; that in the absence
of concrete proof, we must assume that the name on the book cover is
indeed the name of the author. Todorov tries to mediate, quoting V.
V. Ivanov, who states unequivocally that Bakhtin essentially wrote the
books in question, but also noting that Bakhtin never publicly
acknowledged authoring these texts. Ultimately Todorov adopts a
compromise of sorts:

> A conclusion seems unavoidable: it is unacceptable to simply erase
> Voloshinov's and Medvedev's names, and to thus go against Bakhtin's
> obvious desire not to assume the *publication* of these writings. But it
> is equally impossible not to take into account the unity of thought
> evidenced by the whole set of these works, a unity one could attribute
> in accordance with the various testimonies, to Bakhtin's influence.[6]

Todorov's solution is to add a slash and the name "Bakhtin" after the
names Voloshinov and Medvedev. My own solution in this essay is
simply to cite the works as published (although my usage is complicated
by the decision of Albert J. Wehrle, translator of *The Formal Method*,
to cite "P. N. Medvedev/M. M. Bakhtin" as author), but also freely to
interchange one name for another. This policy derives from my belief
that the Voloshinov texts in question are substantially influenced/
authored by Bakhtin as are significant portions of the Medvedev book.
The ideas expressed in the books by Bakhtin are so similar and fit so
well with the great proportion of ideas expressed by Voloshinov and
Medvedev that it seems unavoidable to conflate them. Moreover,
Bakhtinian theory itself argues for a fusion of self and other, multiple
transgressions of textual boundaries — or at the very least, a relaxation
of attention on whose mouth utters whose word. Bakhtin and Voloshinov
(and to a lesser extent Medvedev) authored and, at least in terms of
significant influence, coauthored texts; to consider them all under the
name of "Bakhtin" may do some harm to literary and textual historical
scholarship but ultimately allows us to make greater sense of the works
as a whole. As Albert J. Wehrle reminds us, the late 1920s was a time
of the collective and "only as a movement (a body of texts unified by
approach) could Bakhtin's ideas enter the ideological struggle on an
equal footing with other trends."[7] In this essay I will often follow the
lead of Wehrle and Ann Shukman, who characterize the group as the
Bakhtin school, Shukman describing the school as "a tightly knit group
of friends and intellectual equals who met regularly for intensive philosophical discussions ('strong tea and talk till dawn' as Voloshinov
recalled)."[8] With Bakhtin as the theoretical center, this group of individuals can be considered at the very least as the collective author of
texts on language, consciousness, and the notion of authorship.

The Life

It is always tempting with a thinker as original as Bakhtin to search for root causes, psychoanalytic insights that explain his philosophy of language. In the finest biographical treatment to date, *Mikhail Bakhtin*, Katerina Clark and Michael Holquist attempt to do just that, theorizing for example that Bakhtin's close emotional-intellectual relationship with his older brother Nikolai greatly influenced his theory of the dialogic. Rather than offer such psychoanalytic and speculative readings, insightful as they may be, I will instead present a brief and mostly "factual" biographical sketch, drawing largely from Clark and Holquist.

Bakhtin was born November 16, 1895, in Orel, a provincial town south of Moscow, and died on March 7, 1975, in Moscow of complications primarily from emphysema. Bakhtin might well have lived longer had he not been such an inveterate smoker: to work, he always had to have his cigarettes and his strong tea. The following story would be apocryphal were it not true: Bakhtin's manuscript, *The Novel of Education and Its Significance in the History of Realism* was destroyed when Soviet Writer, the publishing house, was blown up during the early months of the German invasion of the Soviet Union. Bakhtin had worked on this manuscript for at least two years; back home in Savelovo, possibly unaware that his manuscript had been destroyed, he used most of the original pages that he retained as cigarette paper. Only a fragment of the manuscript remains. Unlike most authors, it was not the written word that obsessed Bakhtin: it was *writing* the word. Once the work was done, Bakhtin was sufficiently ambitious to want to see it published but cavalier enough about it to sacrifice scholarship for the pleasures of tobacco and the driving necessity to sustain speculation. Toward the very end of his life, when he was being rediscovered by a new generation of Russian intellectuals, it was "only after the most strenuous arguments by Vadim Kozhinov and Sergej Bocharov that Bakhtin could be persuaded first of all to reveal the whereabouts of what unpublished manuscripts he had (in a rat-infested woodshed in Saransk) and then to permit them to be retranscribed for publication."[9]

Son of a bank official and descendant of untitled nobility that traced itself back to the fourteenth century, Mikhail Mikhailovich Bakhtin was one of five children. Other than his emotional and intellectual relationship with Nikolai, his older brother (born 1894), Bakhtin apparently developed only a tenuous relationship at best with his mother, father, and three younger sisters. Holquist and Clark claim that Bakhtin's relationship with Nikolai, who among other activities fought with the White Army, joined the French Foreign Legion, and became a Greek scholar at Birmingham University, "was the great defining aspect of Bakhtin's childhood and the most formative contact of his life" (MB 17). Certainly the two brothers developed along similar intellectual lines.

Until the age of nine, Bakhtin and his brother were privately educated by a German governess who provided them with extensive readings in European culture, particularly the Greeks and Romans, but "refracted through the medium of German" (MB 21). It is interesting to speculate here that one of the major influences on Bakhtin at this early, formative stage was Hegel, especially since we know that the boys read Hegel early. Whether Bakhtin's theories concerning the dialogic qualities of language owe a debt to Hegel's formulations of dialectic, contradiction, and the theory of the absolute cannot be stated with certainty; Bakhtin himself seldom refers to Hegel as a major source. Hegel's belief in synthesis is substantially different from Bakhtin's belief in dialogism. As Todorov states, "For Voloshinov/ Bakhtin there is no third, synthetic term as we find in Hegel, and this fact is revealing; for him, oppositions will always have an unsurmountable character" (MBDP 76). Julia Kristeva, on the other hand, argues for a more substantial influence:

> The notion of dialogism, which owed much to Hegel, must not be confused with Hegelian dialectics, based on a triad and thus on struggle and projection (movement of transcendence), which does not transgress the Aristotelian tradition founded on substance and causality. Dialogism replaces these concepts by absorbing them within the concept of relation. It does not strive towards transcendence but rather toward harmony, all the while implying an idea of rupture (of opposition and analogy) as a modality of transformation.[10]

From the scant available evidence, it seems likely that Hegel provided a metaphysical model of being in the world which Bakhtin then invested with his own voice and accent.

From the age of nine until fifteen, Bakhtin lived in Vilnius, the capital of Lithuania, a vibrant intellectual center which impressed Bakhtin with its magnificent, historic architecture and "colorful mix of languages, classes, and ethnic groups" (MB 22). Clark and Holquist argue that experiences such as living in Vilnius ("the Jerusalem of the North" [MB 22]) and being introduced early to a wide variety of literatures in a number of languages led Bakhtin toward certain of his fundamental attitudes concerning the endless variety of the word; certainly they would contribute to a carnivalized appreciation of life as difference.

Bakhtin attended Russian schools in Vilnius, but he and his brother additionally hired a private tutor to teach them Greek. In 1910, at the age of fifteen, Bakhtin moved to Odessa, where he finished gymnasium.

He entered Odessa University in 1913 but moved to Petrograd University at the beginning of his sophomore year, in part to join his brother. Clearly even in these early years, Bakhtin was fully engaged in an intellectual life: he read and argued about (with his brother and others) the French and Russian symbolists, German philosophy, Russian literature, the Greeks and Romans, futurist and Formalist thought, Kierkegaard, Buber. He was an active participant in the Petersburg Religious-Philosophic Society. Indeed, Clark and Holquist argue that Bakhtin was deeply committed to a philosophic version of Russian Orthodox theology that celebrated community "where each individual personality would flourish, there would be no absolute authorities, and yet all would have a sense of common bond—something like the Bakhtinian polyphony or heteroglossia translated into social terms" (MB 129). Of course this was also a time of extraordinary social and political upheaval: World War I was decimating Europe and the Russian Revolution broke the hold of the czarists just as Bakhtin was finishing his stay at the University. In 1918, in the midst of social upheaval, Bakhtin moved to the relative calm and safety of Nevel, where the well-known Bakhtin Circle first formed.

Like Bakhtin, all members of the Nevel Circle (or Bakhtin Circle as it later came to be called) were committed to fiercely debating a broad range of issues and ideas from art, music, and ideology to the history and future of Russia. They saw themselves as founding a school of philosophy, and their mission included education through public lectures and public service. The members included Valentin Nikolaevich Voloshinov, whose interests spanned philosophy and music; the charismatic Lev Vasilievich Pumpiansky, who became a professor in the Philological Faculty at Leningrad University; Maria Veniaminovna Yudina, who became one of the Soviet Union's most famous concert pianists; Matvei Isaevich Kagan, who possessed wide-ranging interests including mathematics, philosophy, the natural sciences, and economics; and later Pavel Nikolaevich Medvedev, a rising star in the Communist Party whose major commitment was to art and culture. By 1920, Bakhtin followed Pumpiansky to Vitebsk, a larger town, where the Bakhtin Circle reestablished itself. Within this community, Bakhtin and his colleagues engaged in concentrated and sustained discussions. Undoubtedly these dialogic exchanges led to a kind of intellectual collaboration that makes it all the harder to establish a conventional notion of single authorship, something Bakhtin himself did not strictly believe in. It is also clear that in terms of intellectual contributions and overall direction, Bakhtin emerged as the central figure within the circle; moreover, he engaged in public activities that typified his entire life: talks, lectures, weekly meetings focusing on books and ideas. During these years—indeed through much of his life—Bakhtin led a scholarly life with little official recognition and reward. He read, wrote, actively debated with friends and colleagues, and struggled to consolidate his ideas. In these early years in the 1920s, two other major events occurred: he met Elena Aleksandrovna Okolovich, his landlady's daughter, whom he married in 1921; and in 1923, he began to suffer acutely from osteomyelitis, a disease that would afflict him all his life and eventually would lead to the amputation of his right leg. Bakhtin's marriage to Elena was the great, sustaining relationship of his life. Elena's devotion to Bakhtin enabled him to continue his scholarly work under the most daunting domestic circumstances of poverty and privation.

In 1924, Bakhtin moved to Leningrad, preceded by most of his friends. During these years Voloshinov published "Discourse in Life and Discourse in Art" (1926), *Freudianism* (1927), and *Marxism and the Philosophy of Language* (1929), all of which have been attributed wholly or in part to Bakhtin. Medvedev published several articles as well as *The Formal Method in Literary Study* (1928; revised 1934), a book also attributed wholly or in part to Bakhtin. In the 1920s, Bakhtin himself first began to author important work on literature and aesthetics, although little of it now remains. A pattern was already being established: Bakhtin would write an essay and have it accepted only to see the academic journal disappear or his manuscript be destroyed or political censors halt publication. One success he did achieve was the publication in 1929 of *Problems of Dostoevsky's Creative Works*, a work attributed indisputably to Bakhtin. Unfortunately, the Soviet Union turned sharply to the Right during the 1920s; as rigidity set in, Bakhtin fell victim to the Stalinist purges of intellectuals (as did most of his friends). In 1929, at a time when his career should have been assured, he was accused of crimes such as having his name on a list of anticommunists published in Paris as well as "corrupting the young" (MB 142). Ultimately, through the intercession of friends, he was given a moderate sentence: six years of exile in Kustanai, Kazakhstan, where the average winter temperature was −64 degrees Fahrenheit.

For the next thirty-nine years, Bakhtin lived essentially a life of exile, moving from Kustanai to Saransk to Savelovo and back to Saransk. It is also fair to say, however, that he not only survived but in an intellectual sense at least, flourished. His wife saw to his physical needs, preparing simple meals, brewing tea, buying his tobacco, doing his typing. The two of them lived the kind of plain life that destroyed many of Bakhtin's fellow exiles but suited his own needs for privacy, solitude, reflection. In addition, Bakhtin's "ability to survive was due in part to his equanimity, his sense of humor, and his capacity for accepting gracefully any interlocutor" (MB 254). During this time Bakhtin authored major works: "Discourse in the Novel" (1934−35),

"Forms of Time and Chronotope in the Novel" (1937–38), *The Novel of Education and Its Significance in the History of Realism* (1936–38), *Rabelais and His World* (1940; pub. 1965), "The Problem of Speech Genres" (1953–54), and a revised edition of the Dostoevsky book entitled *Problems of Dostoevsky's Poetics* (1963), as well as other essays and prefaces.

This is not to say that Bakhtin isolated himself from the major events between 1930 and 1969. Although initially banned from teaching the young in Kustanai, Bakhtin was asked to teach bookkeeping to farmers and worked as a bookkeeper himself. His wife also worked as salesperson, bookkeeper, cashier. He moved fairly often, endured the Stalinist purges in the 1930s, and lost his right leg to osteomyelitis in February 1938. At one point during this time he would have starved without gifts of food from friends.

Between 1938 and Russia's entry into World War II in 1941, Bakhtin engaged in an intellectual life more fully, lecturing on the novel and beginning an assocation with the Gorky Institute of World Literature. Indeed, had the war not occurred, Bakhtin might have achieved considerable eminence earlier: in 1940 his manuscript on the novel of education was to be published and he was completing his doctoral dissertation on Rabelais for the Gorky Institute. The war interrupted such activities but governmental need allowed Bakhtin to work professionally. He taught German and Russian in local schools in Savelovo, which improved his economic situation but left him little time for his own scholarship. In 1945, the war over, Bakhtin returned to the Pedagogical Institute in Saransk, where he had taught briefly before the war, and assumed the position of chair of the Department of General Literature and subsequently Chairman of the Department of Russian and Foreign Literature in the Pedagogical Institute's successor, Ogarev University of Mordovia, in 1958. He remained in Saransk until 1961, apparently devoting himself primarily to his brilliant teaching and administrative work. Life in Saransk was difficult. As Clark and Holquist describe it:

> The town had an acute shortage of accommodations, and the only place that could be found to house Bakhtin was a disused jail. Even this jail was in such a bad state of repair that it was considered unfit for use, but Bakhtin, who had a soft spot for rogues, not only moved in but made friends with a thief who lived in the basement.(MB 322)

It seems altogether appropriate that the professor who celebrated carnival, himself a political "criminal," would live unofficially behind bars.

In 1947, Bakhtin attempted a defense of his dissertation on Rabelais, but the political climate in postwar Russia again shifted dramatically to the Right. There was a great deal of nervous temporizing among the faculty at the Gorky Institute who were under attack by government authorities for liberalist tendencies; ultimately, Bakhtin was denied a doctor's degree but granted a candidate's degree in June, 1952 — twelve years after completing the dissertation. It was another thirteen years before that great work would be published in Moscow; three years later, in 1968, it was published in English.

In the 1950s and 1960s, Bakhtin's work began entering into intellectual circulation. Victor Shklovsky and particularly Roman Jakobson drew increasing attention to Bakhtin's contributions. But it was the young literary scholars in the Soviet Union, particularly Vadim Kozhinov, who revived interest in Bakhtin and saw to it that the Dostoevsky book was republished. Bakhtin began to receive recognition among western intellectuals in the late 1960s, particularly as a result of the pioneering work of Julia Kristeva and Tzvetan Todorov. Unfortunately, by this point the health of both Bakhtin and his wife was precarious at best and did not allow them to travel or enjoy the pleasures of success. Bakhtin's left leg could no longer bear his weight, and his wife was barely able to walk. Largely through the intercession of the new generation of Soviet intellectuals, Bakhtin and his wife were moved to a hospital and then an apartment in Moscow in 1969. He gave his last public lecture at the age of 75 in 1960, at the old people's home at which he and Elena lived. A year later, in December 1971, his beloved Elena died. For Bakhtin, who was as devoted to her as she to him, it marked the beginning of the end. Although he lived four more years and was increasingly lionized at home and abroad by a wide range of literary theorists, Bakhtin lost much of his zest for life. Although he continued to write brilliantly, his final work is fragmentary. He died early in the morning on March 7. The attending night nurse heard his final words: "I go to thee." To whom the "thee" refers is unclear, but it is not surprising that even in his last words Bakhtin expressed a desire to forge a relationship between self and other.

Toward a Philosophy of Language

In their introduction to *Rethinking Bakhtin*, Gary Morson and Caryl Emerson attempt to make some posthumous sense of Bakhtin's unfolding intellectual history: they see his work "as a complex, and often haphazard, development that may be divided into four periods."[11] These periods are pre-1924, 1924—1930, 1930—early 1950s, and early 1950s—1975. The earliest period "consisted of largely philosophical writing about ethics and aesthetics ... language was *not* a central category of his thought" (RB 5). During 1924—30, Bakhtin formulated his concept of dialogism and the polyphonic nature of language, arguing for his ideas most fully in the Dostoevsky volume. During the 1930s and 1940s, Bakhtin came to see Dostoevsky as part of a long European tradition that he defined as "the novel." He offered an original concept of this genre and developed his ideas, as well, on chronotope, carnival, Rabelais—all of which could be categorized under the heading of "novel." The Bakhtin that we know is largely this Bakhtin, since *Rabelais and His World* and the essays in *The Dialogic Imagination* were composed in those years. During the last period, Bakhtin "returned to the philosophical concerns of the first period, now enriched by his long sojourn through literary history" (RB 5). He revised the Dostoevsky book (available in the excellent Emerson translation), developed ideas on "the nature of the humanities and the kinds of dialogic or creative understanding appropriate to those disciplines" (RB 6) as well as producing fragmentary "essays" that reveal the complexity and richness of his thought. A good bit of this work is available in *The Problem of Speech Genres*.

As even so brief an intellectual history suggests, Bakhtin's concern with language develops from a concern with philosophy, religion, epistemology. Bakhtin wants to know in part who we are, and since his answer is that we can only be known through our language—since we create our language, which, in turn, creates us—Bakhtin necessarily becomes a philosopher of language, a literary critic, a rhetorophilologist in the sophistic tradition. He is, of course, in his thinking a radical revisionist who it might be said devoted himself to a lifelong critique of rationalist approaches to language and text. Our rationalist inheritance from Aristotle through Descartes and beyond leads ineluctably to Saussure who offers a division of language into *langue* (essentialist, formal, abstract analyses of discourse) and *parole* (speech, verbal interplay, the idiomatic and familiar). Subsequent linguists have modified Saussure's insights but not challenged his basic conceptual model of language. According to this kind of linguistic analysis, language must be studied scientifically in an attempt to discover its deep structures, its absolutist principles. Formalist thinking in Russia, as characterized by Eichenbaum, Shlovskii, and others, adopted a similarly scientistic approach in its consideration of aesthetic texts, adhering to a form/content oppositional paradigm, attempting an understanding of a literary work by isolating various elements within it, "subtracting various essential aspects from the word and other elements of the artistic work."[12] The works by Voloshinov, Medvedev, and Bakhtin argued against the essentialist epistemology of Saussure, the Formalists, and others who presumed an underlying homogeneity and stability in the objects/texts they scrutinized. Voloshinov's *Marxism and the Philosophy of Language*, for example, takes Saussure to task explicitly in arguing that language must be analyzed as a fluid medium that is sociologically charged; Voloshinov held that *"what is important for the speaker about a linguistic form is not that it is a stable and always self-equivalent signal, but that it is an always changeable and adaptable sign."*[13] In a similar vein, Medvedev/Bakhtin's *Formal Method in Literary Scholarship* stated that meaning was historically embedded, that Formalist assumptions about literature are reductive because they "reduce both contemplative and creative perception to acts of juxtaposition, comparison, difference, and contrast, i.e., to purely logical acts" (FMLS 170). In "The Problem of Speech Genres," Bakhtin set out to discuss a hitherto ignored aspect of language, "speech genres," which he describes in terms of their "thematic content, style, and compositional structure" (SG 60) but concerning which he wants to claim an essentially social nature: "Utterances and their types, that is, speech genres, are the drive belts from the history of society to the history of language " (SG 65). The Bakhtin school thus presents a sustained, counterpositivist, post-Formalist critique of language and text. Indeed, it might be fairest to place Bakhtin as a post-Formalist, someone who absorbed the teachings of the Formalist school and in response conceived a sociological poetics of language.[14]

Ultimately much of the work of Bakhtin (and Voloshinov and Medvedev) can be said to fall within a discipline that has come to be called "translinguistics" or "metalinguistics." As a translinguist, Bakhtin argues for a view of language in which grammar, lexicon, syntax, morphology, and phonetics, are all "dynamic elements in constant dialogue with *other* features that come into play only in particular acts of communication."[15] In discussing Bakhtin's revisionist theory of language, it is I think most useful to start with Voloshinov's "Discourse in Life and Discourse in Art," which offers many fundamental translinguistic principles in an abbreviated fashion. Those principles are more fully articulated in Voloshinov's brilliant polemic, *Marxism and the Philosophy of Language*, and then applied as a psychoanalytic critique in *Freudianism: A Critical Sketch*. Finally, Bakhtin's "The Problem of Speech Genres" renews the assault on conventional linguistic theory, and, like *Marxism and the Philosophy of Language*, offers important insights and arguments on the nature of language in society.

Although language is for Bakhtin the sine qua non of humanity, it poses nearly insurmountable problems in terms of analysis because of its embeddedness in human culture. In "Discourse in Life and Discourse in Art," Voloshinov contrasts the study of language to the study of scientific subjects by drawing an important distinction between scientific and sociological methodologies. His purpose here ultimately is to argue that no appropriate sociological approach to poetics has yet been offered. As Voloshinov states:

> Physical and chemical bodies or substances exist outside human society as well as within it, but all products of ideological creativity arise in and for human society. Social definitions are not applicable from outside, as is the case with bodies and substances in nature — *ideological formations are intrinsically, immanently sociological.* ... The most subtle formal nuances of a law or of a political system are all equally amenable to the sociological method and only to it. But exactly the same thing is true for other ideological forms. They are all *sociological through and through*, even though their structure, mutable and complex as it is, lends itself to exact analysis only with enormous difficulty.
>
> Art, too, is just as immanently social; the extraartistic social milieu, affecting art from outside, finds direct, intrinsic response within it. This is not a case of one foreign element affecting another, but of one social formation affecting another social formation. The *aesthetic*, just as the juridical or the cognitive, is *only a variety of the social*. Theory of art, consequently, can only be a sociology of art. No "immanent" tasks are left in its province.[16]

Bakhtin here is not arguing for a psychoanalytic approach to literature; on the contrary he is opposed to such a position just as he is opposed to the "fetishization" of the artistic work ("Discourse" 96–97), that is, to a New Critical methodology. In its place, Bakhtin wants to contextualize art within social, dialogic, interactive frameworks "which take us beyond the border of the verbal altogether" ("Discourse" 107). The claim being made here is an important one that will hold great significance for Bakhtin's work; as Todorov explains it:

> Linguistic matter constitutes only a part of the utterance; there exists another part that is nonverbal, which corresponds to the context of the enunciation. The existence of such a context has not been unknown before Bakhtin, but it had always been looked upon as external to the utterance, whereas Bakhtin asserts that it is an integral part of it. (MBDP 41)

For Bakhtin, social elements — the setting, the identities of the speakers, their relation, their gestures, the ideological content and value of the hero, tone, movements — all enter into the semantic content: *"the situation enters into the utterance as an essential constitutive part of the structure of its import"* ("Discourse" 100). Poetic utterance differs in degree, not in kind, for it too must be understood as *"a powerful condenser of unarticulated social evaluations* — each word is saturated with them. *It is these social evaluations that organize form as their direct expression"* ("Discourse" 107). Thus does Voloshinov return us once again to the essential role of the social in all utterance.

Voloshinov's example of a simple speech act illustrates many of these principles. He posits two people sitting in a room. One of them says, "Well." The other remains silent. In terms of conventional linguistic analysis, this utterance possesses no semantic content because traditional linguistics fails to take into account the "extraverbal context" ("Discourse" 99): a day in May, snow falling, the two speakers looking out the window, a shared weariness of the Russian winter. Suddenly, the "well" possesses meaning; the word takes on semantic value because of the extraverbal context, indeed the word is empty except for the context which fills it with meaning. The importance of context is so significant that, in Bakhtinian terms, the word — any word — is nonrepeatable; each time a word is uttered its meaning changes because the context in which that word is uttered or written changes. Its quicksilver nature makes the word impossible to study in any formalized way; it can only be glimpsed, seen out of the side of the eye, induced. Yet for all its elusiveness, indeed because of it, the word holds the key to understanding consciousness and sociological reality. What makes the word even harder to analyze (at least the printed word) is that much of its meaning and value depends on intonation as well as gesture and an implicit, shared understanding. These factors make it impossible to study the word, as it were, within the objectified environs of a dictionary or on the structuralist dissecting table of a traditional philologist.

Voloshinov then asks an important question: to whom is the "well" directed? Certainly not toward the other speaker, who need not interact in any way whatsoever. Rather, the "well" is directed toward a third participant whom Voloshinov calls "the hero":

> Who is this third participant? Who is the recipient of the reproach? The snow? Nature? Fate, perhaps?
>
> Of course in our simplified example of a behavioral utterance the third participant — the "hero" of this verbal production — has not yet assumed full and definitive shape; the intonation has demarcated a definite place for the hero but his semantic equivalent has not been supplied and he remains nameless. ("Discourse" 103)

If we grant Voloshinov his position, we must agree with his inevitable conclusion, a conclusion that is one of the bedrock principles of Bakhtinian theory:

> *any locution actually said aloud or written down for intelligible communication* (i.e., anything but words merely reposing in a dictionary) *is the expression and product of the social interaction of three participants*: the speaker (author), *the listener* (reader) and *the topic* (the who or what) *of speech* (the hero). ("Discourse" 105)

Voloshinov's formulation grants equivalent (although not inevitably equivalent) status to speaker, listener, and hero; each is conceived as a kind of speaking subject, not as a passive object or mere recipient. Heroes enter into discourse, into utterances and texts and novels and

essays, just as do listeners and speakers. All verbal discourse, whether
in life or in art (for the difference is one of degree not of kind), is a
"*'scenario' of an event*" ("Discourse" 107); it is engaged with speakers,
heroes, and listeners and participates within a living context in which
meaning is a function of relation. "Verbal discourse is the skeleton that
takes on living flesh only in the process of creative perception —
consequently, only in the process of living social communication"
("Discourse" 107).

In *Marxism and the Philosophy of Language*, Voloshinov infuses
semiotic analysis with a social-historical consciousness. Through a fairly
linear argument, he makes a number of important claims beginning
with the basic statement that "Everything ideological possesses
meaning ... In other words, it is a *sign*" (MPL 9). Furthermore,
every sign possesses a kind of double consciousness since it both is
"part of a reality" and "reflects and refracts another reality" (MPL 10).
Consciousness itself is constituted by these signs, a process that is
essentially, inevitably social in nature. Because signs "can arise only on
interindividual territory" (12), they are inherently social; thus "*The
individual consciousness is a social-ideological fact*" (MPL 12). As is
clear, the word and the self are inextricably bound into one another, a
claim that leads Voloshinov ultimately to author *Freudianism: A Critical
Sketch* (about which more later) and, in *Marxism*, to claim that "it is
not experience that organizes expression, but the other way around —
expression organizes experience. Expression is what first gives experience
its form and specificity of direction" (MPL 85). For Bakhtin, this is a
totemic statement; it represents the fundamental importance of language
to humanity — and also justifies the recursive self-reflexivity that is
necessary to study a phenomenon that privileges consciousness itself.

Throughout *Marxism and the Philosophy of Language*, Bakhtin
(Voloshinov) develops this sociological theory of the word. He argues
that the "*word is a two-sided act* ... As word, it is precisely *the
product of the reciprocal relationship between speaker and listener,
addresser and addressee*" (MPL 86). Speakers and listeners anticipate
meanings and responses, create contexts, forge a kind of semantically
intuitive bond. Thus,

> *Any true understanding is dialogic in nature.* Understanding is to
> utterance as one line of a dialogue is to the next. ... Therefore, there
> is no reason for saying that meaning belongs to a word as such. In
> essence, meaning belongs to a word in its position between speakers;
> that is, meaning is realized only in the process of active, responsive
> understanding. (MPL 102)

Because the word is social, it possesses both meaning and value. After
all, "Every utterance is above all an *evaluative orientation*" (MPL 105),

and part of the responsibility all of us have as speakers and listeners is
to develop an acuity to read value in language. In part what we must
"listen" for is social value converted into morphological text, that is,
the kinds of gesturing, intonation, and contextualizations that are
forged within the word when it is placed onto the page. Such thinking
leads Voloshinov to offer a catalog of different speech types in the
third part of *Marxism and the Philosophy of Language*, which he
entitles "Toward a History of Forms of Utterance in Language Constructions" (MPL 107–59). He is particularly interested in the relations
among speaker, listener, and subject (or in Bakhtinian terms "hero")
as they get played out in various kinds of direct and indirect forms of
speech. After all, I can speak (write) directly about my brother, I can
create a narrative structure within which my brother can be given
dialogue (quoted speech), I can indirectly quote my brother's speech
(indirect discourse) — or, in the most dialogized form, my speech and
my brother's can merge and fuse. In this latter instance, which Bakhtin
labels "quasi-direct speech" but which is known more commonly as
"free indirect discourse," "authorial intonations freely stream into the
reported speech" (MPL 146). The hero speaks, in a sense, with two
mouths — his own and the author's, somewhat the way that Bakhtin
himself is "speaking" in this essay outside the quotations marks, his
voice refracted through my editorial reconceptualizations.[17] By the end
of his analysis, Voloshinov essentially claims that virtually all language
study must center on quasi-direct speech:

> The categorical word, the word "from one's own mouth," the *declara-
> tory* word remains alive only in scientific writings. In all other fields of
> verbal-ideological creativity, what predominates is not the "outright"
> but the "contrived" word. All verbal activity in these cases amounts
> to piecing together "other persons' words" and "words seemingly
> from other persons." (MPL 159)

Indeed, the Bakhtinian view is that all language exists on the border
between self and other, that I receive language from others and must
find a way to invest these words with my own meanings, values,
accents. The world is filled with a multiplicity of languages, dialects,
intonations; we live in an environment charged with semantic alterity.
R. B. Kershner puts it this way:

> For Bakhtin, both written and spoken language and inner monologue
> are made up of a great variety of conflicting variants — "languages" of
> officialdom, vernaculars, occupational jargons, technical, literary, and
> subliterary languages, all polyphonically resounding. Language variants
> often are undetectable simply through diction and semantics, but rely
> upon *intonation* and upon context; thus Bakhtin in his attack on
> formalism stresses the need for a "translinguistics" to represent the

reality of communication through utterance. The condition of our existence is thus heteroglossia, a conflicting multiplicity of languages; dialogism is the necessary mode of knowledge in such a world, a form of relationship between or among different languages that, like dialectics, defines a sort of logic. Because for Bakhtin consciousness is always language, and thus unavoidably ideological, the linked processes of perception and interaction with the human world are always dialogical.[18]

This drama of multiple speakers, multiple meanings and languages, plays itself out continuously as long as the world is voiced.

In *Freudianism*, Voloshinov develops a sociological, Marxist critique of Freudianism based on his theories of language. Freud's conceptions of self and psyche were grounded in two biological constants: sex and age. Voloshinov contrastingly advocates a Marxist psychology that argues "first, that a Marxist psychology must deal with the cultural and historical specificity of human consciousness; and, second, that a Marxist psychology must be grounded in objective methods."[19] Since Voloshinov holds that there is no self without language, it follows necessarily that consciousness rests upon a semiotic foundation. Indeed, the subconcious does not differ from the conscious in kind but in degree: "Freud's unconscious can be called the 'unofficial conscious' in distinction from the ordinary 'official conscious'" (FR 85), a formulation that may say as much about repression of speech in Soviet Russia as it does about psychoanalytic theory.

As in *Marxism*, Voloshinov here is articulating a social theory of personality. After all, the methodology that Freud employs in psychoanalysis is the interview, the dialogue, the dream narration, the confession — linguistic forms all. Words, social experience, class awareness are the essential constituents of consciousness and the subconscious. As Caryl Emerson states in her excellent comparison of Bakhtin and Vygotsky:

> The assumption that the psyche is, at its base, a "social entity," a space to be filled with ideological signs, sets the Bakhtinian concept of consciousness at odds with much of Western thinking since Freud on the subject. In his remarkable descriptions of the transitions from "social intercourse" to "outer speech," and from "outer speech" to "inner speech" and to consciousness, Bakhtin fundamentally rethinks both the relation of consciousness to the world around it and the relation of the self to others.[20]

Although no explicit mention is made of Vygotsky's work by Bakhtin (or vice versa), it is clear that both were thinking along similar lines. Vygotsky argues for a view of language development from a socioideological perspective; Voloshinov's *Freudianism* rests on a translinguistic foundation in order to critique a Freudian theory of mind that denied the self a social reality grounded in the word.

In "The Problem of Speech Genres," Bakhtin further articulates his theory of translinguistics by developing a theory of utterance that emphasizes the speaker/listener dimension of language. He distinguishes an utterance from a sentence, a word spoken in the world from a word printed in a dictionary. In each of the latter instances, language is defined only in terms of its formal properties. A sentence, for example, "is grammatical in nature. It has grammatical boundaries and grammatical completedness and unity" (SG 74), qualities it possesses by virtue of its static nature. An utterance, contrastingly, is defined in terms of communication: its boundaries "are determined by a *change of speaking subjects*, that is, a change of speakers" (SG 71). Through this definition, Bakhtin grounds language in a humanly populated world. In part, he offers an abstract description of the various kinds of utterances that are developed within typical situations, producing a somewhat unsatisfactory typological analysis. What is much more fruitful are the insights he offers about language as utterance, particularly his analyses of the speaker/listener dimension of utterance. He is keenly interested in the ways that various utterances are created in a world shot through with the speech of others. Since all of us live in a world of prior, current, and anticipated speech, our own utterances are created in relation to our understandings of the speech of others: "The expression of an utterance always *responds* to a greater or lesser degree, that is, it expresses the speaker's attitude toward others' utterances and not just his attitude toward the object of his utterance" (SG 92). After all,

> any speaker is himself a respondent to a greater or lesser degree. He is not, after all, the first speaker, the one who disturbs the eternal silence of the universe. And he presupposes not only the existence of the language system he is using, but also the existence of preceding utterances—his own and others'—with which his given utterance enters into one kind of relation or another (builds on them, polemicizes with them, or simply presumes that they are already known to the listener). Any utterance is a link in a very complexly organized chain of other utterances. (SG 69)

Utterance can never exist in a social vacuum: "addressivity, the quality of turning to someone, is a constitutive feature of the utterance; without it the utterance does not and cannot exist" (SG 99). For Bakhtin, this concept of responsiveness is an essential one; it grounds utterance in the social. As Bakhtin argues:

> The fact is that when the listener perceives and understands the meaning (the language meaning) of speech, he simultaneously takes an active, responsive attitude toward it. He either agrees or disagrees

with it (completely or partially), augments it, applies it, prepares for
its execution, and so on. . . . Any understanding of live speech, a live
utterance, is inherently responsive, although the degree of this activity
varies extremely. Any understanding is imbued with response and
necessarily elicits it in one form or another: the listener becomes the
speaker. (SG 68)

Bakhtin is arguing here for a kind of speaker/listener identification;
indeed, speakers (writers) and listeners (readers) must forge such a
sympathetic identity in order to create utterance. And the utterance
itself embodies this relation — that is the speaker/listener relation is
constitutive of the utterance itself. Seen in this way, the word is always
invested with other voices; it inevitably takes into account what has
been, is, and will (possibly) be said. Because it is produced by a
speaker in a world filled with other subjects and listeners, because it
anticipates a listener who is also another speaker, because it is formed
within a genre (or speech plan) that frames it constitutively, utterance
is a dialogized category of language that cannot be understood in
traditional linguistic terms. As Holquist states:

> Bakhtin is remarkable for the comprehensiveness of his vision of
> dialogue and the central role he assigns utterance in shaping the
> world. His insistence on authorship as the distinctive feature of con-
> sciousness is a particularly powerful way of giving meaning to the
> definition of man that says he is a sign.[21]

Given its atemporal, transpersonal nature, utterance thus becomes a
synecdochic aspect of humanity's transcendent nature.

Dialogism and Novel

Another way of coming to terms with Bakhtin's theories is to approach
them through his lifelong concern with self/other relations. In their
critical biography, Clark and Holquist offer a theory of Bakhtin's
intellectual development that explains his work as an attempt to "write
the same book, to which Bakhtin never assigned a title but which is
here called *The Architectonics of Answerability*" (MB 63). Although
this theory has been variously received by other Bakhtinians, it offers a
useful focus for Bakhtin's thinking about the relationship between self
and other, self and world.[22] Clark and Holquist argue:

> *The Architectonics* looms large in Bakhtin's later work because of its
> emphasis on action, movement, energy, and *performance*. Life as
> event presumes selves that are performers. To be successful, the relation
> between me and the other must be shaped into a coherent performance,
> and thus the architectonic activity of authorship, which is the building
> of a text, parallels the activity of human existence, which is the
> building of a self. (MB 64)

The self is "never whole, since it can exist only dialogically. It is not a substance or essence in its own right but exists only in a tensile relationship with all that is other and, most important, with other selves" (MB 65). Far from constituting a threat, this philosophy of alterity celebrates otherness, for the more there is of the other, the more there is of the self:

> Dialogism ... is a merry science, a *froliche Wissenschaft* of the other. As the world needs my alterity to give it meaning, I need the authority of others to define, or author, my self. The other is in the deepest sense my friend, because it is only from the other that I can get my self. (MB 65)

According to Clark and Holquist, Bakhtin sketches out a fairly elaborate theory of the architectonics of answerability, focusing in part on the deed, that is, on the necessity of the self authoring an action, an event, in order to create a relationship between itself and the other. He attempts to mediate between the Kantian categories of mind and world (MB 77), in part by revising the conventional understanding of time/ space dimensions. Bakhtin speculates "that self and other are characterized by a different space and a different time" (MB 79), that the self is always in flux while the other (at least from the perspective of the self) is always fixed and completed; eventually, Bakhtin's ideas on the temporal/spatial dimensions of literature lead to his essay on the chronotope in *The Dialogic Imagination*. At this early stage of his thinking, however, Bakhtin attempts less to articulate a critical understanding of language than to sketch out a self/other theory of the world that can be seen as essentially philosophic and religious—a kind of theoretical moral theology.

For Bakhtin, authorship becomes a model of human action. Just as we author words and essays, so do we author ourselves—and simultaneously are authored by others—within the social world of family, school, nation, and world—and are authored by the forms of discourse themselves. A text is therefore a kind of "self" created through an orchestration of reciprocal relations among various voices. Just as an utterance can be characterized in terms of its responsiveness and addressivity, its anticipation of prior and subsequent responses, so can the word, the novel, the essay be similarly characterized. For Bakhtin, this is ultimately not so much an anthropologic, paleontologic, or narrowly historic truth as it is a religious conviction, an essential value of what it means to be human within a culture, within a social context. According to Michael Holquist, Bakhtin participates in the "kenotic" tradition, a form of Russian Orthodoxy whose basic thesis was

> that men define their unique place in existence through the responsibility they enact, the care they exhibit in their deeds for others and the world. Deed is understood as meaning *word* as well as physical

act: the deed is how meaning comes into the world, how brute
facticity is given significance and form, how the Word becomes flesh.[23]

However much Bakhtin immersed himself in mystical Christianity, his
theories of language are suffused with notions of immanence and
secular sacredness: he argues for a kind of semantic radiance which
suffuses the word.

This concept allows Bakhtin to think of texts as alive in some
sense, as participating in a continuous dialogue with writer and world,
as possessing a speaker-hero-listener dimension that is as complex
and vital as in any rhetorical situation involving human speakers.
Novels, stories, the word itself become anthropomorphized, and this
view of the word as "alive" in a variety of senses is formative to the
very notion of the dialogic, that embracive principle that occupied so
much of Bakhtin's thinking. By dialogism, Bakhtin intends two somewhat distinguishable qualities that characterize language.[24] In a general
sense, all language is dialogic because it is born of an interaction
between speaker and listener, each of whom creates words from necessarily different ideological positions:

> The dialogic orientation of discourse is a phenomenon that is, of
> course, property of *any* discourse. It is the natural orientation of any
> living discourse. On all its various routes toward the object, in all its
> directions, the word encounters an alien word and cannot help en-
> countering it in a living, tension-filled interaction.[25]

For Bakhtin, all discourse is characterized by an unceasing struggle to
achieve meaning with words themselves being both agent and agency.
This struggle is a kind of "war" with neither violence nor victory, only
endless attempts to share and merge boundaries without giving up
one's own small bit of property. Words, after all, come to us from
outside — from parents, siblings, books, media, culture. Words come to
us filled with the meanings, intentions, accents and values of other
people, other contexts, other historical eras: "The word is born in a
dialogue as a living rejoinder within it" (DI 279). We absorb this
language and introject it with our own intentions, although the words
can never be fully ours. Indeed, were they to become altogether ours,
they would cease to have any living meaning. Part of the paradoxical
beauty of Bakhtin's theory of the dialogic is that the more there is of
the other, the more there is of the self. Self in language can only be
realized in this dialogic exchange between itself and the other. Thus
that which is foreign, alien, different, is never threatening and must be
neither suppressed nor oppressed: in its very oppositeness, it forms a
dialogic relation which brings to life both self and other. According to
Bakhtin, dialogism "penetrates from within the very way in which the
word conceives its object and its means for expressing itself, refor-

mulating the semantics and syntactical structure of discourse" (DI 284):

> There are no "neutral" words and forms—words and forms that can belong to "no one"; language has been completely taken over, shot through with intentions and accents. For any individual consciousness living in it, language is not an abstract system of normative forms but rather a concrete heteroglot conception of the world. ... [language] lies on the borderline between oneself and the other. The word in language is half someone else's. It becomes "one's own" only when the speaker populates it with his own intention, his own accent, when he appropriates the word, adapting it to his own semantic and expressive intention. (DI 293)

The dialogized word is always aware of the word of the other. It lives on the border between various speakers, various communities of language.

Bakhtin's second sense of the dialogic is a more particularized version of this first one. For Bakhtin, some spoken and written utterances exploit the dialogic potential more fully. When Bakhtin states that "*the polyphonic novel is dialogic through and through*" (PDP 40), he means it in this second sense, that is, that the language of the polyphonic novel derives from a position of unfinalizability, of openness and interaction. Bakhtin most fully develops this second sense of the dialogic in his literary analyses. In *Problems of Dostoevsky's Poetics*, for example, Bakhtin articulates (in a pseudo-Aristotelian manner) categories of dialogized, metalinguistic usages, including various forms of parody, irony, and double-voiced discourse. He uses descriptions such as "internally polemical discourse—the word with a sideward glance at someone else's hostile word" (PDP 196) and "hidden dialogicality" (PDP 197), a discourse by one speaker who incorporates within his or her own text the influences and accents of the interlocutor. Dialogized speech in its very formation conceives of the hero and the listener as speaking subjects, as interactive interlocutors. This formulation allows Bakhtin to claim that in Dostoevsky:

> Dialogue ... is not the threshold to action, it is the action itself. ... in dialogue a person not only shows himself outwardly, but he becomes for the first time that which he is—and, we repeat, not only for others but for himself as well. To be means to communicate dialogically. When dialogue ends, everything ends. (PDP 252)

Such a statement might well be taken as a credo for Bakhtin's entire body of work.

The engagement of a reader with a text, the engagement of a speaker with a hero and a listener, the engagement of a teacher with a student, an essay with the essayistic tradition, a novel with a novel, an

author with a multitude of speaking subjects, an utterance with the
diachronic and synchronic world of utterance — these are necessarily
dialogic activities. The word "engagement" is an apt one for this
relationship is one of betrothal, of negotiated terms, of uneasiness.
When the engagement ends, either in the likely totalizing condition of
marriage or the equally totalizing condition of solitariness, we may say
that the relationship is now best characterized as monologic. Thus it is
not the fact of having a dual or multiple relationship that characterizes
the dialogic; it is the nature of that relationship:

> The idea *lives* not in one person's *isolated* individual consciousness —
> if it remains there only, it degenerates and dies. The idea begins to
> live, that is, to take shape, to develop, to find and renew its verbal
> expression, to give birth to new ideas, only when it enters into
> genuine dialogic relationships with other ideas, with the ideas of
> *others*. Human thought becomes genuine thought, that is, an idea,
> only under conditions of living contact with another and alien thought, a
> thought embodied in someone else's voice, that is, in someone else's
> consciousness expressed in discourse. At that point of contact between
> voice-consciousnesses the idea is born and lives. (PDP 88)

What makes this relation difficult is that it is an immanent one: quali-
tative, invisible, felt. Dialogism is the means by which culture lives and
renews itself through language.

The dialogical as a concept is perhaps most fully addressed in two
books, *The Dialogic Imagination* and *Problems of Dostoevsky's Poetics*,
though the books are complementary rather than repetitive. *The
Dialogic Imagination* opens with two shorter essays, "Epic and Novel"
and "From the Prehistory of Novelistic Discourse," which describe two
polar tendencies that conform to his understanding of monologic and
dialogic. His terms for these oppositional genres are epic and novel.
Epic, Bakhtin believes, possesses a tendency toward monologizing
language. That is, according to Bakhtin, central to the notion of epic
form is a unitary understanding of the word. Epic forms (drama,
poetry, essay, etc.) evolve out of "absolute" understandings of meaning,
intention, national history. Epic is a genre that celebrates the past, the
completely finished. Epic discourse posits formalized relations between
and among characters, author, reader. It is centripetal, hierarchical: it
assumes a certain order of meaning, reifies "truth," dissolves mutually
conflictual and contrastive voices and points of view. Although Bakhtin
clearly prefers the dialogic, there are forms of speech and writing
which brilliantly realize the monologic potential in language.

Novel, on the other hand, is the most dialogized of genres. It is
less a form than a dialogic quality that inheres in texts as varied as a
Menippean satire, a Socratic dialogue, or *Crime and Punishment*.

Novel destabilizes author/character relations, celebrates multiple ideologies, lives on the borders of various languages. It is reflective of the
centrifugal forces in the language, the forces that stand for "decentral-
ization and disunification" (DI 272). Novel is not categorizable; one of
its essential features is its unfinalizability, the ways in which open,
free-ranging dialogue penetrates its very words and structures. Bakhtin
informs us that "the novel is not merely one genre among other
genres. Among genres long since completed and in part already dead,
the novel is the only developing genre. ... Compared with them, the
novel appears to be a creature from an alien species. It gets on poorly
with other genres. It fights for its own hegemony in literature; wherever it
triumphs, the other older genres go into decline" (DI 4). The novel
displaces other genres: it incorporates them parodically. It refuses to
acknowledge its own borders, thus spilling over into alien territories
and claiming those inhabitants as its own. The novel denies itself,
disclaims its own constitutive status as novel. The novel is carnivalistic
(a not-unacknowledged close-cognate of cannibalistic); it defies the
conventional, violates the seemly traditions of community while simultaneously celebrating communal rites of identification.

In "Forms of Time and Chronotope in the Novel," the third essay
in the volume, Bakhtin attempts a post-Kantian collapse of time and
space into a concept he calls "the chronotope." Bakhtin's interest here
is in depicting narrative time, in distinguishing the different kinds of
time/space categories present in novelistic texts. He reveals his substantial understanding of folkloric literature as well as classical and
medieval texts. Much of his analysis focuses on Rabelais in whose
work one finds a culmination of certain tendencies: "a transformation
of the rogue, the clown or the fool" (DI 165), "extraordinary *spatial
and temporal expanses*" (DI 167), an immersion in the grotesque and
carnivalesque. Bakhtin will further develop his celebration of Rabelais
in *Rabelais and his World*; in "Forms of Time," his agenda is a
different one, namely to provide a metaphysical rationale for a category
of narrative that is itself generative:

> They [chronotopes] are the organizing centers for the fundamental
> narrative events of the novel. The chronotope is the place where the
> knots of narrative are tied and untied. It can be said without qualifi-
> cations that to them belongs the meaning that shapes narrative. (DI
> 250)

It is precisely this metalinguistic quality that makes the chronotope so
opaque a subject, even to Bakhtin.

"Discourse in the Novel" is probably best paired with *Problems of
Dostoevsky's Poetics*, since both texts argue for a reconceptualization
of our understanding of novelistic texts. In "Discourse in the Novel,"

Bakhtin formulates his understanding of the dialogic and argues for an understanding of style and poetic language (indeed, virtually all language) as "stratified and heteroglot in its aspect as an expressive system" (DI 288). Although Bakhtin primarily concentrates his analysis on what we would call "fictions," his definition of "novel" is open and allusive: "The novel can be defined as a diversity of social speech types (sometimes even diversity of language) and a diversity of individual voices, artistically organized" (DI 262). The novel, therefore, embraces texts as diverse as plays, poems, essays — as long as they possess an artistic aspect that develops meaning dialogically. "Novelistic" in this usage becomes a descriptive term denoting texts saturated with ideological content, filled with voices, engaged with other speakers, heroes, and listeners as speaking subjects. Novelistic texts are double-voiced; every idea, every word in a novelistic text is contested and shares boundaries with other words, other genres, other ideologies. Part of the difficulty of coming to terms with Bakhtin's thinking here, as usual, is his refusal to think in accepted categories; he signals this originality from the opening paragraph of "Discourse in the Novel" when he announces that "form and content in discourse are one, once we understand that verbal discourse is a social phenomenon" (DI 259).[26] Bakhtin resists cutting off one aspect of a text from the other; texts can only be seen when viewed holistically, as utterances in which all linguistic aspects come into play at once. "Discourse in the Novel" is one of Bakhtin's most difficult essays, in part because it covers so much ground (the novel, epic, dialogism, style, historical development of the genre, forms of the dialogic in speech), and in part because it reads more like "inner speech" than "finished essay."

For Bakhtin, novel is the dialogic made textual; nowhere is this more true than in the works of Dostoevsky. Bakhtin's revised and enlarged *Problems of Dostoevsky's Poetics* celebrates the polyphonic (a near-synonym of "dialogic) qualities of Dostoevsky. Moreover, by anchoring his observations within a consideration of Dostoevsky's novelistic genius, many of Bakhtin's arguments become clearer. Bakhtin sees Dostoevsky as the quintessential contemporary exemplar of the novelist, someone who was able "to visualize and portray personality as another, as someone else's personality, without making it lyrical or merging it with his own voice" (PDP 13). Dostoevsky's characters, ideas, language — the very ideological fabric of his novels — remain open and unfinalized: the "essence of polyphony lies precisely in the fact that the voices remain independent and, as such, are combined in a unity of a higher order than in homophony" (PDP 21). Each thought of a Dostoevsky hero "lives a tense life on the borders of someone else's thought, someone else's consciousness" (PDP 32). Dostoevsky's novels are less conventional plots than dramas of voice and idea, explorations of consciousness seen from multiple perspectives.

Problems of Dostoevsky's Poetics considers many major Bakhtinian subjects: evolution of dialogic forms, carnival, Menippean satire, Socratic dialogue, stylistics. Perhaps more than any other single work by Bakhtin, it offers both specificity and broad, speculative sweep in its analysis of the word as dialogic. Part of Bakhtin's genius in this volume is to describe aspects of Dostoevsky's dialogism that transcend language. Two examples should suffice. First, Bakhtin explores the recursivity of Dostoevsky's worldview, the ways in which words double back on themselves in the novels. Bakhtin's term for this is "the loophole," which is "the retention for oneself of the possibility for altering the ultimate, final meaning of one's own words" (PDP 233). The loophole is not a word but a position of open-endedness, a banishment of monologized thinking from one's own discourse: "The loophole makes the hero ambiguous and elusive even for himself" (PDP 234). One can see in this device of the loophole a strategy near and dear to Bakhtin himself. Second, Bakhtin offers a characteristic feature of Dostoevsky's novelistic vision: "Dostoevsky always represents a person *on the threshold* of a final decision, at a moment of *crisis*, at an unfinalizable — and *unpredetermined* — turning point for his soul" (PDP 61). There are many literal and symbolic threshold situations in Bakhtin: heroes webbed within conflicting ideologies, heroes literally standing within doorways or between rooms or on various borders. For Bakhtin, these thresholds situate the Dostoevsky world in that shifting world between self and other. The concepts of the loophole and the threshold represent only a small and barely representative fraction of the insights Bakhtin offers in his study of Dostoevsky.

This discussion of the threshold does introduce one other central concept that Bakhtin identifies within the novelistic tradition: carnival. In Rabelais, Bakhtin finds perhaps the greatest modernistic expression of the carnivalesque, though one can see it as well in Dickens, Dostoevsky, Faulkner, and Conrad. In the history of folk culture which culminates in Rabelais, Bakhtin discovers a wealth of structures and activities that vitalize literature and society: carnival celebrations, the feast, the spectacle, the grotesque, parodistic forms of laughter and language, oaths, insults and abusive usages that overturn traditional forms of speaking and yet depend upon them. Carnival taps into a powerful force in human life. Bakhtin names this the world's "gay matter" and it "is born, dies and gives birth, is devoured and devours; this is the world which continually grows and multiples, becomes ever greater and better, ever more abundant. Gay matter is ambivalent, it is the grave and the generating womb, the receding past and the advancing

future, the becoming."[27] Carnival as a public form is being smothered
by the conventional constraints of an increasingly middle-class and
technological society, but it is still observable in various underclass
customs (i.e., "the dozens"), mardi gras, folk tradition, and novel.

Bakhtin's celebration of carnival issues from his interest in folk
culture and in history of laughter, both of which undermine and dises-
tablish hegemonic forces. In a sense, carnival can be read as the voice
of the other in culture:

> The opposing voice — really a sort of super-voice, in that it is linked
> with folk-consciousness and is capable of overturning any other
> language — is carnival. As a "theater without footlights" in which all
> are participants, the carnival festival undermines the concept of
> authoritative utterance, and through its characteristic rituals of mock-
> ery, crowning and decrowning of fools, billingsgate, nonsense, and
> the degrading of everything held noble or holy, carnival presents a
> "contradictory and double-faced fullness of life.[28]

The Rabelaisian worldview inverts the world; it denies the vertical
ascent of humanity and instead celebrates the horizontal, the corporeal,
the digestive, the excretory. It is distortive of life and of language, it
laughs at all seriousness, if offers the grotesque as the normative. The
language and worldview of Rabelais is situated on the threshold — that
borderline between classical and vernacular Latin, official and folk
culture. Ultimately Bakhtin's argument serves as a corrective to the
increasing sterility and homogeneity of contemporary culture. Rabelais
is difficult for us to appreciate because we have strayed so far from our
folk roots and abandoned that world of laughter and the grotesque in
our desire to inhabit the bureaucratized neighborhoods and cities
sanctioned by the official.

In many ways, it is fitting to end on this theme. Bakhtin grants that
Rabelais is a difficult author for contemporary readers, that he is "the
least popular, the least understood and appreciated" (RHW 1). For
much of his life, so was this state of affairs also true for Bakhtin.
Living in almost complete obscurity, his work all but forgotten, his
words uttered in a terrible kind of isolation, Bakhtin must have imagined
himself to be a kind of Rabelais gone wrong, a dialogist trapped in a
monologic world. It is heartening to remember that he was, at the very
end, lionized at home and abroad; more importantly, it is increasingly
rewarding to "live into" his ideas and insights and find in them a
continuing source of speculative insight. What Bakhtin says about
Dostoevsky's novels might just as well be applied to his own works of
theory and criticism: *"Nothing conclusive has yet taken place in the
world, the ultimate word of the world and about the world has not yet
been spoken, the world is open and free, everything is still in the future
and will always be in the future"* (PDP 166; italics in original).

Bibliographical Note

In spite of disputes over authorship I still recommend that new readers to Bakhtin begin with "Discourse in Life and Discourse in Art" (available in *Freudianism: A Critical Sketch*) and *Marxism and the Philosophy of Language* by V. N. Voloshinov. "Discourse" maps out some of the essential features of dialogism, and *Marxism* analyzes current linguistic thinking and finds it wanting, proposing in its stead a more Bakhtinian view of language that emphasizes multivoiced discourse and genuinely dialogical qualities that inhere within linguistic structures. In essence, Voloshinov argues for a reconception of the rhetorical paradigm and a revisionary science of linguistics that would embrace aesthetics and speech-act theory. Although much more Marxist in its thinking than work explicitly authored by Bakhtin, Voloshinov's conceptions of language are, I believe, more readily understandable, in part because they come close to existing within a systematic framework. With the now added caution that both texts must be considered "Bakhtin Circle" productions rather than by Bakhtin himself, I still recommend them as a useful departure point for the inevitable long journey through dialogism.

For those wishing to move directly into Bakhtin, *Problems of Dostoevsky's Poetics* is perhaps the most central and approachable work. In part this is the result of its publishing history, for the book stands with one foot in the 1920s and the other in the 1960s. Bakhtin's original (1929) text was *Problemy tvorcestva Dostoevskogo* (in English, *Problems of Dostoevsky's Creative Work*). It has not been translated into English. At the request of Kozhinov and others, Bakhtin revised and expanded this study, publishing it in 1963 under the title *Problemy poetiki Dostoevskogo* (*Problems of Dostoevsky's Poetics*), which was first translated into English in 1973 by R. W. Rotsel (Ann Arbor: Ardis, 1973) and now is available in a magnificent translation by Caryl Emerson. Emerson's Editor's Preface (xxix–xliii) offers a sensitive, cogent appreciation of Bakhtin's thinking and composing process. Indeed, Emerson is one of the finest and most articulate Bakhtinian critics now writing. *Problems of Dostoevsky's Poetics* is extremely useful as a starting point because it functions as a double-sided mirror, reflecting Bakhtin's thinking from both his second and fourth phases; major new material that Bakhtin added in the later edition includes "the history of menippean satire, its relation to other forms of literature, and its connection with such extraliterary phenomena as carnival and other discrowning rituals" (MB 240). A similar perspective is offered by *Speech Genres and Other Late Essays*; this volume contains essays spanning almost forty years that were first put together in a Russian volume entitled *Estetika slovesnogo tvorchestva* (*Aesthetics of Verbal*

Creativity) published in Moscow in 1979, edited by Sergey Averintsev and Sergey Bocharov. It includes a fragment from the now-lost *The Novel of Education and Its Significance in the History of Realism* on the bildungsroman, the important essay on "The Problem of Speech Genres," and two of his latest and most fragmentary manuscripts: "From Notes Made in 1970—71" and "Toward a Methodology for the Human Sciences." The latter two are all the richer for being so elliptical.

Rabelais and His World represents Bakhtin's fullest exploration of carnival and folk culture from the Greeks and Romans through the twentieth century. It includes chapters on the history of laughter, the language of the marketplace (oaths, blazons, insults, etc.), feasts and festival images, and grotesque images of the body. Finally, there is *The Dialogic Imagination*, the most theoretically complex volume of Bakhtin's work in English. This primarily includes essays on the novel written and published by Bakhtin during the 1930s and early 1940s and includes "Discourse and the Novel" as well as "Forms of Time and Chronotope in the Novel." Bakhtin's theories of dialogism and heteroglossia are most fully developed in these essays.

A number of texts published under the names of V. N. Voloshinov and P. N. Medvedev are also worth reading because they develop various aspects of Bakhtin's theories. Of particular interest are Voloshinov's *Freudianism: A Marxist Critique*, appended to which is the important essay "Discourse in Life and Discourse in Art" as well as two other essays: Voloshinov's "A Critique of Marxist Apologias of Freudianism" and Neal Bruss's "V. N. Voloshinov and the Basic Assumptions of Freudianism and Structuralism." Another version of "Discourse in Life" (translated by John Richmond under the title "Discourse in Life and Discourse in Poetry: Questions of Sociological Poetics") can be found in Ann Shukman's edition of *Bakhtin School Papers*. Included in this small volume are additional essays by Voloshinov and Medvedev. Also worth reading is P. N. Medvedev and M. M. Bakhtin, *The Formal Method in Literary Scholarship*. This book was published in 1928, with a subsequent revised edition (entitled *Formalism and the Formalists*) appearing in 1934. *The Formal Method* develops a critique of formalism and maps out the limitations a formalist methodology imposes on critics: though it is unclear how much Bakhtin contributed to the book, it does offer an account of genre (Chapter 7, "The Elements of the Artistic Construction") that parallels his account in *Speech Genres*. For a fuller analysis of the debate concerning the Voloshinov-Medvedev-Bakhtin disputed texts, see Chapter 6 in *Mikhail Bakhtin* by Katerina Clark and Michael Holquist, and Gary Morson and Caryl Emerson's Part Two of the Introduction to *Rethinking Bakhtin*. I. R. Titunik's essay in the "Forum" (cited below) is also essential.

One of the most useful secondary works is Clark and Holquist's biography, *Mikhail Bakhtin*. The book alternates chapters on Bakhtin's life with chapters exploring his theoretical positions. It also contains an excellent bibliography of primary texts. Holquist's entry on Bakhtin in the *Handbook of Russian Literature* (New Haven: Yale Univ., 1985) is short but informative. Gary Saul Morson edited *Bakhtin: Essays and Dialogues on His Works*: it includes a number of important essays that engage in an invigorating Bakhtinian polemic, including Wayne Booth's praise for Bakhtin's liberatory criticism. Perhaps a more rigorous debate can be found in a "Forum" that appeared in *Slavic and East European Journal*, 30 (Spring 1986); contributors particularly debated the "disputed texts" of Medvedev and Voloshinov. My own essay "Mikhail Bakhtin as Rhetorical Theorist" (*College English*, 47 [October 1985], 594–607) may provide some initial help, particularly for those interested in Bakhtin's implications for composition specialists. The Morson-Emerson introduction to *Rethinking Bakhtin* is splendid, especially in summarizing Bakhtin's fragmentary early essay "Toward a Philosophy of the Act" and exploring certain other essential concepts such as "live entering." The essays in *Rethinking Bakhtin* are exclusively literary in focus; contributors include among others Morson, Emerson, Shukman, and De Man.

Tzvetan Todorov's *Mikhail Bakhtin: The Dialogical Principle* works hard to make sense of Bakhtin. The book is extremely useful and offers a fine bibliography of primary works by the Bakhtin school, but I think Todorov's structuralist approach deadens the dialogic. I respond similarly to Wayne Booth's affirmations of Bakhtin, even though I appreciate his feminist critique of Bakhtin's Rabelais book in "Freedom of Interpretation" (see Morson, *Bakhtin* 145–76). Much better is Julia Kristeva's "Word, Dialogue and Novel," which was first published in 1969 (though written in 1966); it is an excellent reading of the concepts of dialogism and carnival from someone moving to poststructuralist thinking. A provocative postmodernist perspective of Bakhtin can be found in Brian McHale's *Postmodernist Fiction* (London: Methuen, 1987), 162–75. Don Bialostosky is a thorough and provocative reader of Bakhtin; see in particular "Dialogics as an Art of Discourse in Literary Criticism," PMLA 101 (1986), 788–79. My own debt to Don Bialostosky in first introducing me to the work of Bakhtin and Voloshinov is one I must acknowledge.

The PMLA bibliography lists over three hundred essays and books that analyze or apply Bakhtinian principles. Scholars interested in engaging dialogically with Bakhtin would be best advised, I believe, to read Bakhtin's work firsthand with occasional sideward glances at the bibliographical items I have listed and to which I have made reference in this essay. Although not available yet, Saul Morson and Caryl

Emerson have coauthored two books that should also prove worthy of attention: *Mikhail Bakhtin: Creation of a Prosaics* and *Heteroglossary: Terms and Concepts of the Bakhtin Group*, both forthcoming from Stanford University Press.

In Conclusion?

There is neither a first nor a last word and there are no limits to the dialogic context (it extends into the boundless past and the boundless future). Even *past* meanings, that is, those born in the dialogue of past centuries, can never be stable (finalized, ended once and for all) — they will always change (be renewed) in the process of subsequent, future development of the dialogue. At any moment in the development of the dialogue there are immense, boundless masses of forgotten contextual meanings, but at certain moments of the dialogue's subsequent development along the way they are recalled and invigorated in renewed form (in a new context). Nothing is absolutely dead: every meaning will have its homecoming festival. The problem of *great time*. (SG 170)

The last word can never be Bakhtin's, nor can it be the last word.[29]

Notes

1. Mikhail Bakhtin, *Speech Genres and Other Late Essays*, trans. Vern W. McGee, ed. Caryl Emerson and Michael Holquist (Austin: Univ. of Texas, 1986), p. 111. Hereafter SG.

2. Ken Hirschkop, "A Response to the Forum on Mikhail," *Bakhtin: Essays and Dialogues on his Work*, ed. Gary Saul Morson (Chicago: Univ. of Chicago, 1988), p. 74.

3. Clive Thomson, "Bakhtin's 'Theory' of Genre," *Studies in Twentieth Century Literature*, 9 (1984), p. 32.

4. Katerina Clark and Michael Holquist, *Mikhail Bakhtin* (Cambridge: Belknap Press of Harvard Univ., 1984), p. 152. Hereafter MB.

5. Mikhail Bakhtin, *Problems of Dostoevsky's Poetics*, ed. and trans. Caryl Emerson (Minneapolis: Univ. of Minnesota, 1984), p. 293. Hereafter PDP.

6. Tzvetan Todorov, *Mikhail Bakhtin: The Dialogical Principle*, trans. Wlad Godzich (Minneapolis: Univ. of Minnesota, 1984), p. 11.

7. Albert J. Wehrle, Introduction to *The Formal Method in Literary Scholarship* (Baltimore: Johns Hopkins Univ., 1978), p. xiv.

8. Ann Shukman, Introduction to *Bakhtin School Papers*, ed. Ann Shukman (Old School House, Somerton, Oxford: RPT Publications, 1983), p. 1.

9. Michael Holquist and Caryl Emerson, Introduction to *The Dialogic Imagination*, trans. Caryl Emerson and Michael Holquist, ed. Michael Holquist (Austin: Univ. of Texas, 1981), p. xxv.

10. Julia Kristeva, "Word, Dialogue and Novel," *Desire in Language*, trans. Thomas Gora, Alice Jardine, and Leon S. Roudiez, ed. Leon S. Roudiez (New York: Columbia Univ., 1980), pp. 88–89.

11. Gary Saul Morson and Caryl Emerson, Introduction to *Rethinking Bakhtin: Extensions and Challenges*, ed. Gary Saul Morson and Caryl Emerson (Evanston: Northwestern Univ., 1989), p. 5. Hereafter RB. See also Clark and Holquist's alternative interpretation of Bakhtin's career (MB 3).

12. P. N. Medvedev/M. M. Bakhtin, *The Formal Method in Literary Scholarship: A Critical Introduction to Sociological Poetics*, trans. Albert J. Wehrle (Baltimore: Johns Hopkins Univ., 1978), p. 61 Hereafter FMLS.

13. V. N. Voloshinov, *Marxism and the Philosophy of Language*, trans. Ladislav Matejka and I. R. Titunik (Cambridge: Harvard Univ., 1973, 1986), p. 68. Italics Voloshinov's. Hereafter MPL.

14. See Todorov, who states that Bakhtin is postformalist in that "he exceeds Formalism, but only after having absorbed its teachings," p. 40.

15. Michael Holquist, "Answering as Authoring: Mikhail Bakhtin's Trans-Linguistics," in *Bakhtin: Essays and Dialogues on his Work*, p. 63.

16. V. N. Voloshinov, "Discourse in Life and Discourse in Art," Appendix I, *Freudianism: A Critical Sketch*, by V. N. Voloshinov, trans. I. R. Titunik, ed. in collaboration with Neal Bruss (Bloomington: Indiana Univ., 1976, 1987), pp. 95–96. Hereafter "Discourse." All italics in my quotations from this source are Voloshinov's.

17. For a fuller analysis, see my essay "Mikhail Bakhtin as Rhetorical Theorist," *College English*, 47 (1985), pp. 594–607.

18. R. B. Kershner, *Joyce, Bakhtin, and Popular Literature; Chronicles of Disorder* (Chapel Hill: Univ. of North Carolina, 1989), pp. 15–16.

19. V. N. Voloshinov, *Freudianism: A Critical Sketch*, trans. I. R. Titunik, ed. in collaboration with Neal Bruss (Bloomington: Indiana Univ., 1976, 1987), p. viii. Hereafter FR.

20. Caryl Emerson. "The Outer Word and Inner Speech: Bakhtin, Vygotsky, and the Internalization of Language," in *Bakhtin: Essays and Dialogues on his Work*, p. 25.

21. Holquist, "Answering," p. 70.

22. For example, see *Rethinking Bakhtin*, pp. 42–44.

23. Michael Holquist, "The Politics of Representation," in *Allegory and Representation: Selected Papers from the English Institute, 1979–80*, ed. Stephen J. Greenblatt (Baltimore: Johns Hopkins Univ., 1981), p. 176.

24. Gary Saul Morson is the only critic I have seen who explicitly characterizes Bakhtin's ambivalent usage of the term "dialogic." See his essay "Dialogue, Monologue, and the Social," in *Bakhtin: Essays and Dialogues on his Work*, pp. 83–84.

25. Mikhail Bakhtin, *The Dialogue Imagination*, trans. Caryl Emerson and Michael Holquist, ed. Michael Holquist (Austin: Univ. of Texas, 1981), p. 279. Hereafter DI.

26. Todorov devotes considerable discussion to this topic, noting that "when Bakhtin adopts a critical stance in this matter, it is not against form or against content (as he was 'against' the individual), but against those who isolate the study of one or the other: the pure ideologists and the pure formalists." *Mikhail Bakhtin*, p. 35.

27. Mikhail Bakhtin, *Rabelais and His World*, trans. Helene Iswolsky (Cambridge: MIT, 1968), p. 195. Hereafter RHW.

28. Kershner, p. 16.

29. This essay was written in 1989–90. In the past year or so, additional scholarship—both primary and secondary—has appeared that further illuminates Bakhtin as a philosopher of language. Unfortunately, it was not possible to incorporate that work within this essay. I wish to state my gratitude to Caryl Emerson (Princeton University), whose careful reading of the typescript has prevented me from making any number of foolish statements in print. I also wish to thank Dana Beckelman (University of Wisconsin—Milwaukee) for her extensive research on my behalf; her efforts allowed me to produce this essay in a timely fashion.

The Revival of Rhetoric

Introduction

George H. Jensen

Hans-Georg Gadamer recently wrote: "It seems, some of my colleagues have been trying to 'save my soul' from such dishonest things as rhetoric! They think that hermeneutics is no noble pursuit and that we must be suspicious of rhetoric."[1] As we are now in the midst of a momentous revival of rhetoric, we find it surprising that Gadamer's colleagues are trying to save his soul. Indeed, in most intellectual circles, it is now difficult to function without either bandying about the term "rhetoric" or seeing everything from the visual arts to sexual intercourse as part of the greater scheme of rhetoric. So how is it that rhetoric could ever be so neglected that it would need reviving and how is it that, even today, people in some circles still disdain rhetoric? To understand these questions, they must be placed in a broader historical perspective: the revival in which we currently participate is but one of many revivals, and the status of rhetoric has always been rather tenuous.

Even though the teaching and practice of rhetoric was pervasive in ancient Greece, rhetoricians were constantly attacked. Plato's *Gorgias*, one of the earliest diatribes against rhetoric, is by no means unique.[2] Such critiques must evolve, in part, from a fear of the power of rhetoric that seems as natural to humans as the use of language. Indeed, Jung would argue that this primordial fear can be illustrated by our reactions to the trickster archetype.[3] But the belief that rhetoric is somehow dishonest involves more than the stories we encounter in myth and religion. When invention was historically viewed as an integral part of rhetoric, when rhetoric was considered to be more than mere persuasion, it was less the tool of the trickster than the companion of the philosopher. During such periods, rhetoric was less likely to be viewed as the purveyor of opinion (*doxa*) than the creator of truth (*episteme*). The hostility toward rhetoric also surfaced during eras of cultural adaptation. When rhetoric was introduced into Roman culture or later when the Roman Empire began its conversion to Christianity and adopted the Christian ethic, critiques of rhetoric flourished.[4]

That rhetoric has experienced some difficulty adapting to new contexts is in part related to the character of its original formulation. Rhetoric was first conceptualized in ancient Greece as a primarily oral art in the service of a unique culture. During historical periods and in cultural contexts that encouraged oral deliberation, the importance of rhetoric was quickly recognized. In autocratic or totalitarian contexts, its importance waned.[5] During the Middle Ages, rhetoric was seldom taught because there was little opportunity to practice it, but rhetoric experienced a revival during the fourteenth, fifteenth, and sixteenth centuries in Italy, largely due to the country's active civic life.[6]

With the numerous rocky transitions of rhetoric from one context to another, important classical texts were temporarily or permanently lost. Thus, during some historical periods, rhetoric was taught by scholars who had access only to watered-down commentaries. When classical texts were periodically rediscovered, allowing for a fuller reconceptualization of rhetoric, revivals typically followed. For example, when the texts of Cicero and Quintilian became available in America during the early eighteenth century, largely a result of the Scottish revival spearheaded by George Campbell, rhetoric soon formed the core of most college curricula.[7]

Of course, the availability of texts could not effect a revival without an intellectually powerful advocate. When thinkers comprehensively adapted Greek rhetoric to a new age and a new context, the importance of rhetoric was more widely recognized. For example, Cicero was instrumental in adapting Greek rhetoric to Roman culture, and Campbell was instrumental in synthesizing classical rhetoric and the work of British Empiricists.[8] When more limited thinkers such as Peter Ramus reduced the scope of rhetoric, it became more vulnerable to attack. It was easier to dismiss rhetoric as style that creates only opinion.

Ramus was one of the key figures in the reduction of the scope of rhetoric to style, or the deemphasis of invention, a trend that George Kennedy calls the *letteraturizzazione* of rhetoric.[9] When rhetoric was viewed as being merely a catalog of figures and tropes, a collection of textual ornaments, it could be more easily dismissed by the Enlightenment. The proponents of an emerging scientific method sought a transparent discourse that would not distort their objective data; they had no use for textual ornaments. The Romantics treated rhetoric no kindlier. They were not opposed to style as such, but their emphasis on natural genius and inspiration — rather than rhetorical invention — was also incompatible with a technical approach to creating style.

Given the double blow by the Enlightenment and Romanticism against an eviscerated rhetoric, it is not surprising that it entered a period of general decline. Given the current intellectual climate, it is also not surprising that rhetoric is experiencing a vibrant revival. Classical texts are now widely available, and a number of original thinkers — Kenneth Burke, Chaim Perelman,[10] Stephen Toulmin,[11] I. A. Richards,[12], James L. Kinneavy,[13] and others — have worked to update and extend them. Research on orality and literacy by figures like Eric A. Havelock,[14] Walter Ong, Jack Goody,[15] and others has added to the vitality of current discussions of rhetoric. And the assault on foundationalism among contemporary philosophers has fostered the view that rhetoric is epistemic; communication, in other words, is inseparable from the creation of knowledge.[16] This view has opened a number of new areas of rhetorical research, including studies of the rhetoric of science, a topic that would have been inconceivable even thirty years ago.[17] What has emerged in the twentieth century, it could be argued, is the transformation from rhetoric's being primarily viewed as oral persuasion to its being viewed as communication in the broadest sense: oral and written, persuasive and scientific, verbal and visual, conscious and unconscious, logical and mythic, dialectical and paralogical. A sampling of this broad view of rhetoric will be presented in the following chapters on Burke, Ong, and White.

Notes

1. Hans-Georg Gadamer, "The Hermeneutics of Suspicion," in *Hermeneutics: Questions and Prospects*, eds. Gary Shapiro and Alan Sica (Amherst: Univ. of Mass, 1984), p. 35.

2. Even Plato is not consistent in his attitudes toward rhetoric. Even though he criticizes rhetoric in *Gorgias*, he acknowledges the value of rhetoric in *Phaedrus*, a later dialogue.

3. C. G. Jung, *Four Archetypes* (Princeton: Princeton Univ., 1959, 1969), pp. 135–152.

4. For a discussion of the tension between philosophy and rhetoric, see Samuel Ijsseling's *Rhetoric and Philosophy in Conflict: An Historical Survey*, trans. Paul Dunphy (The Hague: M. Nijhoff, 1976), passim.

5. Tzvetan Todorov writes: "The flowering of eloquence was linked to a certain form of government, democracy; with the disappearance of democracy, eloquence can only decline." *Theories of the Symbol*, trans. Catherine Porter (Ithaca: Cornell Univ., 1977, 1982), p. 64.

6. George A. Kennedy, *Classical Rhetoric and Its Christian and Secular Tradition from Ancient to Modern Times* (Chapel Hill: Univ. of North Carolina, 1980), pp. 189, 195.

7. Robert J. Connors, Lisa S. Ede, and Andrea A. Lunsford, "The Revival of Rhetoric in America," in *Essays on Classical Rhetoric and Modern Discourse*, eds. Robert J. Connors, Lisa S. Ede and Andrea A. Lunsford (Carbonale: Southern Illinois Univ., 1984), pp. 1–2.

8. Kennedy, pp. 91, 232.

9. Ibid., pp. 110–11, 210–12.

10. Chaim Perelman and L. Olbrechts-Tyteca, *The New Rhetoric: A Treatise on Argumentation*, trans. John Wilkinson and Purcell Weaver (Notre Dame: Univ. of Notre Dame, 1958, 1969), and Perelman, *The Realm of Rhetoric*, trans. William Kluback (Notre Dame: Univ. of Notre Dame, 1982).

11. Stephen Toulmin, *The Uses of Argument* (Cambridge: Cambridge Univ., 1958).

12. I. A. Richards, *The Philosophy of Rhetoric* (New York: Oxford Univ., 1936).

13. James L. Kinneavy, *A Theory of Discourse* (New York: W. W. Norton, 1980).

14. Eric A. Havelock, *Preface to Plato* (Cambridge: Belknap, 1963), *Origins of Western Literacy* (Toronto: Ontario Institute for Studies in Education, 1976), and *The Literate Revolution in Greece and Its Cultural Consequences* (Princeton: Princeton Univ., 1982).

15. Jack Goody, *The Domestication of the Savage Mind* (Cambridge: Cambridge Univ., 1977) and *The Logic of Writing and the Organization of Society* (Cambridge: Cambridge Univ., 1986).

16. Much of the current theory of epistemic rhetoric began as a reaction to Robert L. Scott, "On Viewing Rhetoric as Epistemic," *Central States Speech Journal*, 18 (1967), pp. 9–17. Also see his "On Viewing Rhetoric as Epistemic: Ten Years Later," *Central States Speech Journal*, 27 (1976), pp. 258–66.

17. For an introduction to the growing line of research into the rhetoric of specific disciplines, see John S. Nelson and Allan Megill, "Rhetoric of Inquiry: Projects and Prospects," *Quarterly Journal of Speech*, 72 (1986), pp. 20–37. See also *The Rhetoric of the Human Sciences: Language and Argument in Scholarship and Public Affairs*, eds. John S. Nelson, Allan Megill, and Donald N. McCloskey (Madison: Univ. of Wisconsin, 1987), passim.

7

Dramatism and Dialectic
Kenneth Burke's Philosophy of Discourse

Joseph J. Comprone

Kenneth Burke left Peabody High School in Pittsburgh at the age of seventeen with doubts about college. Already he and his later equally illustrious classmate, Malcolm Cowley, had set themselves apart, reading European and American literature and philosophy, developing interests in music, art, and culture. By the time he left high school in 1917, Burke had become somewhat of a youthfully jaded intellectual, already suspect of formal learning. His friend Cowley went off to Harvard, from which he graduated several years later, after an extended stay in Europe. Burke tried Ohio State for a semester, then Columbia for another, but he gave up formal education for good in 1918, to become — he asserted, half seriously, half tongue-in-cheek — a "Flaubert" in New York City.[1]

Burke never really left behind this romantic yearning for new intellectual territory. His career is itself a drama of exploration and discovery, with intellectual systems and perspectives replacing the exotic lands of more conventional romantic journeys. Unlike his lifelong friend Cowley, Burke did not go overseas until 1969, and then only to Italy and France (Jay 360). But far more than Cowley, who was later to make his intellectual home in American literary history, Burke remained a rambler among both strange and known intellectual movements. He was, as he said to Cowley in a letter, always interested in explaining and interpreting the process of interpretation itself (Jay 206).

A Sketch of Burke's Career

It is perhaps most useful to see Burke's career as moving through five progressive stages. In each stage in this developmental process Burke moves from a prescribed circle of interest into an area of larger connection and intellectual circumference, until in the 1940s, 1950s, and 1960s he progressed to the point where, retrospectively considered, he seemed to be headed from the beginning — with language and dialectical action as the stage on which human beings, the symbol-using animals, play out their intellectual dramas. The remaining parts of this first section sketch out in general form Burke's career from both professional and personal perspectives. This background clarifies general themes and concepts that are elaborated on in later sections.

Burke as Would-Be Artist: Stage 1, 1917–1926

Burke left college to return to New York and its environs (actually he commuted from Andover, New Jersey, to New York City), dedicated to writing fiction. But the twenties were financially difficult for Burke; actually he wrote as much criticism (his essays made him more money) and did as much editing (he prepared Eliot's *The Waste Land* for publication in *The Dial* magazine) as he wrote fiction in the twenties. He published his collection of short stories, *The White Oxen*,[2] in 1924, to mixed reviews, and his novel (or collection of related epistles, as it is more aptly described), after much struggle and domestic strife (his first marriage to Lily Batterham ended in 1930), was published in 1932. It was both a critical and financial failure. Burke was never again to give sustained attention to writing imaginative material.

Still, it is not accurate to see Burke's critical career as completely the result of his failed literary efforts. Even while writing *The White Oxen* stories, he tells us that he discovered more about form in literature than he did about writing fiction. Always to a large degree a critic and theorist, Burke's work in this early stage (1917–1926) was marked by its total immersion in the intellectual milieu of the modernist period, especially as that milieu was influenced by European artistic movements such as Dadaism or Art for Art's Sake. He grounded himself in literary and artistic theory even while producing fiction himself; later, he was to use this grounding in fiction writing as a source of representative or explanatory anecdotes in his own theory building (Jay 385).

Critic Versus Artist: Stage 2, 1926–1932

Toward the end of the twenties and into the thirties Burke continued to develop his theories as he struggled to finish his novel. He seemed at many points to ground his critical thinking in his experiences with writing, as in this passage from a letter he wrote to Malcolm Cowley, where he asserts that "all the resources of prose thought [criticism, in this comparison] must be developed in order that the poetic can be given its only genuine safeguards. That is: only a thorough body of secular criticism, secular thought 'carried all the way round the circle' can properly equip a society against the misuse of its most *desirable* aspects, the *poetic* or *religious* aspects" (Jay 205). This tendency to elevate critical over artistic production was simply brought to a climax by the negative critical and commercial responses to his novel. The publication of *Counter-Statement*[3] in 1931 brought Burke far more positive response than had either his story collection or novel; this, coupled with his enormous intellectual curiosity, led him to put criticism above imaginative writing for the rest of his career. But he always remained convinced that his having experienced imaginative writing from the inside had given him the advantage of a double perspective compared with critics who had always written only as critics.

The Social Awareness Period: Stage 3, 1932–1941

Social and political circumstances also contributed to Burke's turn toward theory. The economic tragedy of the early thirties, and the rise of totalitarian governments in Europe and Russia in the 1930s, influenced Burke's critical theories, moving them decidedly to the Left, resulting in a search for an overarching framework that would enable him to bring together the aesthetic and social dimensions of language. Burke had become in the twenties increasingly dissatisfied with narrow aesthetic formalism. Indeed, *Counter-Statement*, in its search for an organic theory of form rooted in a combination of depth and Freudian psychology, had in the twenties foreshadowed this need in the thirties to integrate social and aesthetic theory.

Burke's struggles with Marxist theory in the thirties functioned as a way for him to distance himself from the more aesthetic and elitist perspectives on culture he had consistently maintained as a "Young Flaubert," as a contributor to modernist, antibourgeois sensibility. Along with many other late-modernist intellectuals, his friend Cowley included, Burke was intensely influenced by the economic hardship and rising totalitarianism of the thirties, but his social leanings never really, as did Cowley's, become social*ist*. Rather he took on Marxist thought as another in a series of "perspectives by incongruity," using it as a counterstatement to his modernist formalism, but always in a way that combined the social with the aesthetic, one commenting upon and clarifying the other.

It was during the thirties that Burke shaped the foundation for his entire philosophy of discourse. He wrote and published two books, *Permanence and Change* (1935)[4] and *Attitudes Toward History* (1937),[5] that were to function as chronicles of his interest in the interdependency of social and aesthetic cultural processes—he had left imaginative writing and purely literary criticism behind with the publishing of *Counter-Statement* and *Towards a Better Life*[6] in 1931 and 1932—and as groundwork for the dramatistic theory of culture that he was to produce in the 1940s and 1950s. Burke, in the thirties, moved away from provincialisms of all kinds—in his case, the literary and imaginative provincialism of modernism—and toward an intellectual eclecticism that was to become rare in the highly specialized academic world of the second half of the twentieth century.

The Rhetorician Develops: Stage 4, 1941–1950

Having created the philosophical and historical background for his dramatistic theory in the thirties, Burke used the forties to construct his massive epistemological and rhetorical theory of the drama of human history. He began the decade by assembling several previous essays on aesthetics and politics into what he felt, when edited and published together in 1941 as *The Philosophy of Literary Form*,[7] was a definitive statement on how organic theories of form, developed through time and social contest, came to *inform* the texts that we read and produce. Even in this primarily literary effort one finds numerous examples of Burke's application of aesthetic theory to political and social events of a nonliterary kind.[8] Burke's drive toward rhetorical analysis of all texts is prevalent in *The Philosophy* well before he had established the tenets of rhetorical dramatism later in the forties, and with the publication of *A Grammar of Motives*[9] in 1945 Burke established the basic principles of his entire dramatistic system. All human texts, he argued, evolved out of a basic structural system composed of the interactions or *ratios* among five essential elements in an ongoing, progressive, and recursive drama: *act* (or the particular verbal gesture that a text performed within the ongoing drama of human expression), *agency* (or the means through or by which a text reaches its audience), *agent* (the individual, group, or institution that motivates a text, understood either indirectly or directly), *scene* (the background, considered philosophically and historically, against which a text is developed and expressed), and *purpose* (a text's reason for being, considered in broad ontological as well as more specific historical terms). This structural system he labeled the pentad (see the opening section of *A Grammar* for a brief account). Throughout *A Grammar* Burke devoted most space to the relationships existing between scene and act, explaining how the broad contextual backgrounds and schools of thought he had outlined in *Attitudes Toward History* actually function as scenes encompassing particular texts, and how these texts and scenes, and the agencies and agents producing them, function within a progressively unfolding intellectual-verbal drama. The scene against which a text was written became a perspective by incongruity superimposed on the perspective that an individual writer put into the text itself. Out of this integration of perspectives developed original philosophies.

By 1950, with the publication of *A Rhetoric of Motives*,[10] Burke had moved from an exposition of the symbolic structures behind his system to an application of that system to representative traditional and contemporary texts. In the process of producing *A Rhetoric*, Burke also redefined the Aristotelian notion of analyzing textual effects to include both larger and more organic senses of audience and purpose. It was in *A Rhetoric of Motives* that Burke expanded Aristotle's notion of persuasion to include every kind of text, and it was also in this book that he developed his concept of identification, where readers are both *part of* and *different from* the texts they read. The pentad and Burke's expanded notion of persuasion became a means of expanding traditional notions of textuality. The concept of text itself became a lens (a "perspective by incongruity") through which larger and more dynamic social and intellectual forces came to influence human action. Motivation and rhetorical action were combined in one dramatic process, and all forms of discourse commented on one another.

From Rhetoric to Language Theory: Stage 5, 1950–Present

Burke has devoted most of his efforts during this later stage of his career to refining his philosophy of language. Two books written in this stage best represent this broadening out into language theory. *The Rhetoric of Religion: Studies in Logology*,[11] published in 1961 but written during the late fifties and early sixties — and partially supported by a fellowship from the Center for Advanced Study in the Behavioral Sciences — defines a dialectical perspective on language in which "we can finally develop a considerable body of conceptual instruments for shifting back and forth between 'philosophic' and 'narrative' terminologies of motives, between temporal and logical kinds of sequence"(RR 33).[12] This process of terminological shifting became Burke's focus in these later years as he attempted to show how the original struggle between nature and human agency, at first mediated by language, came, as cultures progressed, to be constructed by language. The collection of essays entitled *Language as Symbolic Action*,[13] published in 1966 but written throughout the fifties and early sixties, carried this study of general dialectical origins in *The Rhetoric of Religion* into specific textual applications. What Burke had treated as an ontological historical drama in the thirties and forties became a study of language and epistemology in the fifties and sixties.

Burke's Personal and Professional Situation

Burke's definitive biography is still to be written.[14] But for our purposes, several patterns in his personal and professional life are relevant.

Burke was always a professional outsider. His early career was characterized by work on modernist journals such as *Broom*, *Secession*, and *The Dial* that were consistently inveighing against conventional bourgeois culture and academic formalism. His imaginative writing was often considered too intellectual by admirers of concrete poets and fictional realists, and his critical work was often considered too theoretical by new critics and aesthetic formalists.[15] This intellectual marginalism was compounded by the fact that he never completed college or took a permanent academic position. His letters to Malcolm Cowley, in fact, mention over and again the difficulties he faced while teaching full time on part-time salary (Jay 337–38, 339). Added to this professional life on the fringe was his ongoing love for country places relatively near the city. His home in Andover, New Jersey, kept him both away from but near New York City.

This intellectual and professional in-between life had its good and bad effects. Intellectually, his keeping to the fringes kept Burke in close touch with cutting-edge work in many disciplines — philosophy, the social sciences, depth and Freudian psychology and psychoanalysis, economic theory, and, of course, literary criticism and rhetoric. It supported the incredible range of his work, and its applications to texts as varied as Hitler's *Mein Kampf* and St. Augustine's *Confessions*. And it most importantly encouraged his willful, often obstinate, tendency to believe that he was in touch with sources of information and ideas that his more specialized colleagues ignored.

But, of course, Burke's life situation also resulted in texts that made for very difficult reading for those highly specialized academic readers who were members of very closely knit discourse communities. Burke was, and is, more at home with the Cowleys, Edmund Wilsons, Irving Howes, Alfred Kazins, and Norman Podhoretzs of the intellectual world than he ever was or could be with those who see themselves as card-carrying members of defined academic disciplines. He is, as Richard Ohmann points out in a recent *College English* essay (vol. 52 [March 1990], pp. 247–57), the kind of intellectual who was put out of a job by the rising professionalism and specialization of twentieth-century academic life. His books do not have the kinds of integrated cross references to current scholarship that characterize today's academic texts; they range too far and too wide in their citations, and they often seem to ignore the near-at-hand. But more significantly, Burke's texts do not define problems in the way that current scholarship does; he is constantly deconstructing issues back into broader and more complex issues of linguistic epistemology. His texts, in other words, do not address members of defined discourse communities, but instead speak to readers who are interested in broader redefinition of disciplinary issues. And there are simply fewer of such readers than there used to be. Burke's work, then, is difficult to integrate into most of today's academic communities, even in the humanities, where the scientific paradigm of a specialized scholar working along with other members of his or her discourse community on a defined issue or "problem" remains dominant.

But, taken as a whole, Burke's work is dialectic-in-process; it does not simply extol dialectical literacy, it is a living example of it. For dialectical method was his way of composing himself, not merely a surface metaphor for superficially resolving essential differences in thought and action.

"The Body That Learns Language"

An introduction to work as copious and eclectic as Burke's must be selective. Basically, I intend to examine three larger elements of his philosophy — his essential belief in mind-body relationships of an organic kind, his creation of a dramatistic system for explaining how that relationship influences human history and social relations, and his consistent advocacy of a particular kind of dialectical intertextuality. Developing these three central motifs, in the end, can help us define the spirit behind all Burke's thought as effectively as any more complete adumbration of his concepts.

Capturing that spirit and using it to inform our own ways of understanding discourse requires seeing all Burke's particular concepts (the pentad, perspectives by incongruity, terminological screens, identification) as parts of a greater whole. That whole is perhaps best described in the brief title to this section: "the body that learns language."[16] In interpreting and applying Burke, it is important to recall the social-intellectual context in which he did his foundational work — that of the 1930s and 1940s. Consider these lines from the Prologue to *Permanence and Change*:

> This book, *Permanence and Change*, was written in the early days of the Great Depression, at a time when there was a general feeling our traditional ways were headed for a tremendous change, maybe even a permanent collapse. It is such a book as authors in those days sometimes put together, to keep themselves from falling apart. (PC xlvii)

This search for stability amidst instability helps explain the central features of Burke's logology. Burke was not to define *logology* fully until 1961 when he published *The Rhetoric of Religion* (see its Foreword and Preface). But he laid the foundation for his logological system in both *Permanence and Change* and *Attitudes Toward History*, written in the thirties. Simply put, logology is the study of "words about words" (RRI). But implied in logological study is the sense that languages contain within themselves the bases of all human hierarchies and systems of knowledge. In turn, every system of knowledge is structured around some kind of central metaphorical transformation. For Augustine in *The Confessions* it was the transformation of spirit into physical or bodily terms (RR 37), where Burke finds a hierarchical dialectic of physical and supernatural terms that is controlled by Augustine's pervasive sense of *charitas* (the love of the physical world because one knows through faith that it is a manifestation of God's will and spirit). For Burke in the thirties, and those, like Burke, who found the process of metaphorical transformation itself the primary object of study, the central metaphorical transformation was situated in the verbal dialectic between positivistic epistemology and its conviction that truth could be found by removing objects of study from their *locus* in language. A logologer, as Burke might have called himself, is interested first in how human systems of knowledge are constructed out of and by words. Burke's motives are always directed toward finding a balance that will explain how the languages of different fields evolve out of the interests and perspectives of practitioners, and how those languages include within themselves the seeds of resistance and change.

In *Permanence and Change* and *Attitudes Toward History* Burke builds a dialectical system in which language places human beings between the extremes of material and intellectual realities. It is a system composed of body *and* mind, individual *and* social-cultural restraints. Individuals are preeminently language users (his essential pragmatism, with its roots in William James and Charles Peirce, is made clear in *Attitudes Toward History*, 3—14); they strive to create systems and realities out of their collectively developed terminologies. Those systems are themselves derived from terms that have roots in human biology, in collective thought, and in individual initiative. In responding to bodily needs, human beings appropriate collective languages to their own particular uses. Burke's logology, his system of words about words, is a way of seeing verbal dialectics as influenced by biology (the individual and his physical needs), and philosophy (used in its broadest sense, to describe the individual's intellectual needs). The meanings human beings make with words are always the result of a dialectic among these forces. Certainly, in retrospect, we can understand how this Depression-driven context moved Burke toward a system that recognized physical constraints at the same time as it sought, through language, to free individuals from those constraints. Words, developed partially out of bodily needs, can paradoxically free human beings from those needs.

How does Burke's sense of social structure and history function in *Permanence and Change* and *Attitudes Toward History*? And, perhaps a more important question, how can the theory of language posited in these books serve as an overall frame for the kind of dramatistic perspective on rhetoric that Burke puts forth in his more interpretive works?

For Burke, it is important that we establish the interdependency of biological and conceptual dimensions of discourse. Working in the Hegelian dialectical tradition, Burke rejects both Kantian idealism and the extreme positivism of much of modern science.[17] This interdependency, what Burke and Heidegger would call the "paradox of being," acts through and in every human utterance, no matter how objective or subjective the discourse may be trying to be.[18] This aspect of Burke's language theory is perhaps most explicitly apparent in his theory of the negative. Only affirmative statements can be referred back to the physical world; only affirmative statements can exist in the world. Negative statements, characterized by the Christian decalogue, can exist only in and through language. Only human beings, capable of symbolic action, can say no to what is true in nature. Killing, for example, happens. But only language can bring the concept of "not-killing" into being. Nowhere in nature can we find a physical expression of "not-killing," unless we find it in a *symbolic* act of kindness that is essentially a negative assertion against a positive evil.[19]

This ability to say no, this negative capability, becomes the base on which Burke constructs his entire symbolic drama. It is also from this base in the negative that Burke's logology evolves. At this point, one must reconsider Burke's use of the term *logology* — a combination of Greek *logos*, embodied in the deeper rationalism of the essential word-thing relationship, and the *−ology* of biology, the study of living organisms. Burke's logology is built on a mind-body relationship that is extrinsically and intrinsically symbolic, with the intertwinings of nervous and endocrinal systems and their counterparts in the symbolic systems of language. For Burke, people are essentially "bodies that learn language"; our language activities can never be effectively dissociated from bodily functions, nor can those bodily functions ever be dissociated from language.[20] The two acting together, the body and its language, make for the symbolic action, the drama, that is for Burke composing.

Burke most pointedly brings together logology (language + body) and the negative capability in a representative anecdote that appears on pages 371 and 372 of *Attitudes Toward History*.[21] Imagine, he says, a person who has just had a good meal and is digesting it while sitting dreamily by a pond on a balmy day. He has recently been "sexually appeased and [has] received word of a legacy." The result is an almost somnambulant state in which all the man's systems are operating in balance. Such rudimentary pleasure, Burke suggests, can never result in the kind of higher consciousness we associate with language.

Linguistic, or logological pleasure or fulfillment would demand that this ideal pastoral scene be interrupted by some kind of internal or external stimuli. At such an interruptive point, "awareness" would develop out of the interaction of internal (in this case, pleasurable) and external forces, with words acting as symbolic intermediaries. We become aware or "conscious" when we are awakened from a rhythmic and lulling physical state by external processes that are then mediated by symbolic action. States of pure physical, or mystical, or intellectual functioning are impossible. We by nature live in a mediated, or symbolically organized world.

It is significant that Burke coined his phrase "the body that learns language" within a "retrospective prospect" written some thirty years after the original publication of *Permanence and Change*.[22] In that informal Afterword to the new University of California edition of *Permanence and Change*, Burke named the informing theory behind his entire, dramatistic system. But, to understand the full significance of "the body that learns language" one needs to review Burke's perspectives on history and social processes. The best method of doing that is to turn to Burke's terminology itself, particularly to his concepts of *frame*, *scene*, *attitude*, *perspective by incongruity*, and the *comic*. These terms shape Burke's entire historical and social perspective.

Key Burkean Terms: Integrating Social, Biological, and Historical Perspectives

We can best define *frame* by referring to Burke's conception of history as it is put forth on pages 111–75 of *Attitudes Toward History*. In representing what he calls the "curve" of history, Burke posits five frames on recent Western "historic drama" (ATH 159): Hellenism on the decline–Christian Evangelism emerging; feudal-medieval synthesis; the Renaissance; the Reformation; naive capitalism; and emergent collectivism. Obviously, this is not the place to explain this system in detail. To understand the term *frame* all we need to do is emphasize the role language has in mediating the elements on this historical curve. In every succeeding period, frames of reference are created out of terms that are at least partially derived from the previous period. Metaphorical clusters of terms are appropriated by a later frame of reference and used to represent and create a different reality than was imagined in the former period. Evangelical Christianity lent its terminological screens to later medieval Christian philosophy, but in the medieval frame these earlier evangelical terms were translated into a new kind of dramatic action. What happens, in other words, as individuals mediate between internal and external environments through language is replicated as language functions to create cyclic systems of thought on an historical level.

We can expand on this Burkean perspective on evolving verbal frameworks by analyzing his discussion of Periclean Athens and its concept of individualism:

> If a philosopher of Periclean Athens ... speaks of a man as the measure of all things, and means thereby the *individual* man, you must discover how many *collective* ingredients, how much deference to custom, was *assumed* in his statement before you know whether his words are representative or compensatory. That is, one may call individual man the measure of all things precisely because he *isn't*, precisely because one may be using a collective grammar that *permits* this luxury. (PC 113; all italics are Burke's)

Here Burke sets out the essential paradox behind contemporary perspectives on the individual in society. As Althusser and Gramsci and other revisionary Marxist theorists have argued,[23] our concepts of the individual must themselves be revised to include the social construction of self.[24] For Burke, it is the terministic screens through which we remake our selves that come to mediate our actions as selves in a larger social world. The individual Athenian, then, was partially constructed by the social milieu within which he or she lived, and more specifically by the way in which his or her language represented Athenian cultural perspectives. Reading another culture, whether Athenian or modern, always involves this overlapping and contrasting of verbal systems, where the reader's terms are mixed with, yet separate from, the "other" culture's.[25]

It is within this theater of competing and merging terminologies and frames of reference that we can best understand Burke's overall dramatistic perspective on rhetoric. Of the five terms of the pentad, *scene* is perhaps his most pervasive because it ties in so neatly with Burke's linguistic orientation. Every discourser composed within a particular scenic background. This scene is constructed out of the languages of all those terminological frames that have influenced the writer, but the writer also is capable of bringing frames and terms together in new combinations and forms. In *A Grammar of Motives*, pages 3–20, Burke explains how scene operates on individual writers, both constraining and freeing symbolic action. Writers must to some degree be captives of the linguistic frames within which they have evolved. But writers, at least the more serious, adventurous, and imaginative ones, are never totally dominated by the words they have appropriated from others. For a short while they may be stilled by the complex verbal influences residing in their own texts, but in the end they become rhetoricians rather than linguistic technicians. At this point of transition, a text maker uses tropes — themselves often defined by the group within which a writer writes, but nonetheless capable of individualizing an evolving text — to translate inherited frames of reference into new dramatic scenes. All the old linguistic components remain, but they are rearranged into an original social and terminological perspective.

To use a negative example, we might refer to Burke's analysis of Hitler's rhetoric in *Philosophy of Literary Form*,[26] pages 191–220. Here Burke sets the context for his discussion of *Mein Kampf*, gives it what he would call "sub-stance" (a base on which one can imagine the text being constructed), by describing the prewar Vienna and postwar Munich that served respectively as background and foreground for Hitler's coming to power. Vienna, Burke tells us, provided the base for Hitler's antiparliamentary hatred of contending ideas, which he felt weakened the will of German patriots. Hitler's jousts with communists in Vienna at first confused, then enraged him (PLF 197). Later, after Hitler's humiliation at Germany's defeat in World War I, and his revulsion for what he felt was the disorderly and weak Weimar Republic, Hitler turned to Munich as foreground for the Third Reich; Munich, with its "folkish architecture" representing pan-German nationalism, became Hitler's symbol of a reborn Aryan superiority (PLF 215). These cities, taken together, formed the physical scene from which Hitler built his demagoguery in *Mein Kampf*. They were, Burke suggests, consistently present in Hitler's mind, directing his choices as he composed *Mein Kampf*. These material situations formed the *motives* behind his writing. These scenic backgrounds became the physical base for *Mein Kampf*. But Burke suggests spiritual sources for *Mein Kampf* as well:

> The church ... had proclaimed an integral relationship between Divine Law and Natural Law. Natural Law was the expression of the Will of God ... it was a result of natural law, working through tradition, that some people were serfs and others nobles. And every good member of the Church was 'obedient' to this law ... the serf resigned himself to his poverty, and the noble resigned himself to his riches ... the pattern was made symmetrical by the consideration that each traditional 'right' had its corresponding 'obligations'. (PLF 208)

This reliance on spiritual obeisance in Christianity became the basis for Hitler's appeal to his highly secularized but still for the most part Christian, German, middle-class audience. Postwar Germans, Hitler demanded, must be prepared to fight, to sacrifice themselves to an evolving and larger social order, just as medieval Christians had accepted their roles in a higher order. This appeal to order, to goals, to regimentation, would offset the frustration Hitler had felt amidst Vienna's swirling political and intellectual controversy. Physical and spiritual aspects of the *scene* from which *Mein Kampf* is created thus become Hitler's means of appeal to his audience, as he remakes that audience with images and tropes growing out of his own frustration and anger.

Frames, composed of terms, are the channels we follow as we become part of history's ongoing conversation; *scenes* are the particular influences, the intellectual "situations" surrounding our constructions of text. How, then, does *attitude* fit in? Burke consistently saw texts as inextricably related to the scenes in which they were created and read. Frames on experience developed into systems of thought, ways of seeing and knowing the world. Particular scenes, representative situations, were, in turn, the structural components upon which writers based their specific textual strategies. These textual strategies Burke called "attitudes."

In the opening pages of *Philosophy of Literary Form*, Burke argues that poetry should be understood as a writer's attempt to develop "strategies for the encompassing of situations." Burke goes on to say that "strategies size up the situations, name their structure and outstanding ingredients, and name them in a way that contains an attitude towards them" (PLF 1). Attitudes are writer's ways of ordering the frames and scenes with which they are working. Hitler brings *Mein Kampf* together around the polemics that evolve from the language frames and scenes, spiritual and material, within which his text was written (and here we should expand the act of writing to include influences reaching far beyond the actual putting of words on paper). Every significant text has been "written" out of the verbal life of its author. It is the result of an ongoing conversation or dialectic process, not of a single act of authorship. Attitudes are built into writers by the logologies, the frames and scenes, within which they exist as users of language. Attitudes also come to *inform* the texts their users produce. They become the "perspectives by incongruity" through which a particular text is made.

A Marxist, angered by the hypocrisies of capitalism, constructs an "angry" text, one calling on the frames and scenes of earlier anticapitalist polemics. But always there is the possibility that anger will join with other attitudes, perhaps one more sympathetic to some forms of capitalist exchange, and the result will be a text that transcends its originating attitude and develops a form that represents a more complex attitude — perhaps anger mixed with ironic affection for ownership of material goods. This type of hybrid text, informed by conflicting or paradoxical attitudes, would develop appeals to an audience of an equally complex kind, with elements of both Marxism and capitalism in dialectical interplay.

Human history and social process, to Burke, is one large and dynamic verbal drama, and those who study and teach discourse must view the writer as an agent, a temporary protagonist, within that dialectical drama. Human action is influenced through and through by past and present uses of language. Only when those who work with language realize that every new text is made out of verbal systems created in the past will they fully comprehend the need to connect text and context. Every text-making agent in this dialectical drama is motivated by attitudes endemic to the scene in which they were developed. Attitudes, what Burke in another context calls "incipient actions" (PC 253, referring to I. A. Richards's *Principles of Literary Criticism*), evolve out of verbal frames and scenes, but as these frames/scenes are brought into interaction with one another by a writer confronting a problematic issue, new attitudes and actions become possible. Here Burke's notion of *recalcitrance* can help resolve the tension between convention (restrictions imposed by preexisting verbal *frames* and current dramatic *scenes*) and intention. A teacher or researcher of writing might call this merging of attitude and situation *revision*, as Burke himself suggests in *Permanence and Change*: "A statement [text] is *an attitude rephrased in accordance with the strategy of revision* made necessary by the recalcitrance of the materials employed for embodying this attitude" (PC 255; italics are Burke's).

Here Burke moves from considerations of historical-social perspective to a focus on the individual composer. A writer's attitudes, once he begins to make a text, run up against the "recalcitrance," or the built-in resistance of the materials used to construct the text. This recalcitrance—cognitive psychologists might call it "dissonance"—works against a writer's attitudes to create a language that is hybrid, composed of both the frame embodied in the writer's attitude and the frame implied in the materials (ideas, evidence, assertions, whatever the writer actually puts into words) themselves. The result is a kind of plural textuality, a textual dialectic, a "scene" that the writer must strive to "encompass" by whatever formal inventions that are available. Serious text is always the product of such verbal dialectic.

Perhaps a final, more practical example is necessary before going on to define the final two remaining concepts, perspectives by incongruity and comic transcendence. Let us imagine a student engaged in writing a text on abortion. She comes to the situation equipped with attitudes that are the result of long-standing verbal frames on the issue. She also comes into this writing situation with particular scenic elements in place. Perhaps another student has just presented his position on the issue. Or more likely, the class of which the student is a part has read several different texts on the issue, each developing a different attitude. This combination of inherited frames and scenic elements work directly on our student as she begins to construct her text. As she writes, her own words may argue with her, seeming at times to represent ideas counter to her original intention, causing her to lose her verbal equilibrium. This "recalcitrance" causes her to revise, in the process working different language seams together into a textual fabric that, as Burke would put it, gradually comes to "encompass the situation" in which she finds herself engaged. The result is a text, if successful, that is decidedly *her* text, although it has been created out of a larger social context that has had its influence on her. The text represents the dialectical balance that created it, and the writer in the process has been recomposed as well.[27]

What, then, happens when a writer truly masters a textual situation? The answer lies in Burke's concepts of perspectives by incongruity and comic transcendence. In fact, the perspectives-by-incongruity concept also provides Burke's most convincing explanation of how social context and individual action combine during the composing process. Drawing from Nietzsche's reactions against Hegelian dialectical idealism, Burke situates the individual writer within a world of swirling, interactive languages (PC 1v, and ATH 410). The job of the writer is to take action within the swirl, employing these different languages as tools in creating new perspectives and eventually new scenes for subsequent symbolic action. In *Permanence and Change*, pages 125−63, Burke illustrates this process by showing how different models of psycho-analysis rooted in the study of affective sources for human behavior, were themselves influenced by scientistic perspectives on behavior that ignored the affective domain. In the process of developing these "new" clinical, psychoanalytical methods, theorists such as Adler, Rivers, Freud, and MacDougall appropriated the language of the "older" perspectives — objective scientism and religion — and combined it with a "new" language to create yet another scenic perspective on human behavior.

Individual writers, working among these often conflicting perspec-tival scenes, must strive to embody their perspectives in attitudes (strategies of incipient action) which, in turn, become the informing principles behind their work. In essence, then, writers must be both immersed in and "above" the scenes that surround them. They work to fashion symbolic actions that work within, against, and for the perspec-tival scenes that provide the backdrop for their own texts. Writers cannot separate themselves from the social-cultural contexts within which they work, but, at the same time, they must "transcend" the scenes within which they work, taking action against the language posed by existing perspectives to create texts of their own (ATH 338; also see PC 230−55, where Burke provides an extended discussion of the balancing acts required of individual composers writing in the midst of competing scenes).

Burke, in fact, carries this analogy between individual composers as actors within cultural scenes even further when he argues in *Attitudes Toward History* for "the comic frame." Writers can keep from losing themselves in this terministic welter only by distancing themselves from the scenes within which they operate:

> A comic frame of motives avoids these difficulties [of extreme negative and extreme positive response], showing us how an act can "dialecti- cally" contain both transcendental and material ingredients, both imagination and bureaucratic embodiment . . . The comic frame should enable people *to be observers of themselves, while acting.* Its ultimate would not be passiveness, but maximum consciousness. (ATH 166– 67, 171)

Comic distance enables a writer to transfer a term from one scene into the context of another. In so doing, the term in its new context carries with it the connotations of both old and new scene. Effective composers are active "fusers of languages," individuals who take verbal actions from one scene and use them to name and frame the actions of other scenes. They master perspectives by incongruity by merging them metaphorically into one dialectical text.[28]

Burke's comic perspective "transcends" through the writer's use of tropes (GM 503–17), for through metaphor, synecdoche, metonymy, and irony, a writer is able to transform one frame into another, to, in essence, combine dramatic contexts and terminological systems. Literary scholars do this when they use scientific perspectives and terms within fictional or poetic contexts; natural or social scientists do it when they use narrative or metaphorical techniques in describing deductive science. "Serious" writers, straightforwardly developing an argument, do this when they create ironic twists by playing with the words of the opposition.

We need to close our discussion of Burke's philosophy of language with some general remarks on how texts are produced out of often competing word systems, and how social contexts are both represented and mastered by the dialectical interaction of languages within texts. Burke's is essentially a dialectic sense of history, its cycles defined by terms that grow out of the physical and social conditions of different periods. That sense of history provides the frame within which his dramatistic system operates. *Permanence and Change* best summarizes the cumulative and sequential nature of this historical/social process. Social thought moves through stages of orientation, disorientation, and reorientation (PC 308). This rhythmic, social interaction is both bio- logical and verbal. The physical destitution caused by the Depression exerts its pressure on the free-enterprise system dominant in America at the time. This biological pressure (people feel the effects of economic depression in their bodies, which in turn causes the "body" to respond negatively to free enterprise throughout the social system), felt across an entire society, begins to develop a "collective" language of its own, which is itself premeated by terms appropriated from socialist and communist movements in Europe. This collectivist language, with its own positive, dialectical, and ultimate terms, begins to merge with its capitalist counterpart, creating a hybrid logology (a mixture of socialist and capitalist terms) characteristic of the 1930s in America (PC 295–336). Burke's dialectical mergers of terms and frames are ways of tracking the dynamics of social "thought," from its beginnings in the orientation of system-building action, through its clash with other systems (disorientation) and the resulting conflicts in terms, to its merger with competing systems through metaphor, synecdoche, metonymy, and irony (reorientation).

Individual writers who are aware of this overall process become more sensitive to the epistemological and cultural implications of language. They are prepared for recalcitrance and opposition, even expect and exploit it. They see themselves as operating within a scene, while they attempt to transcend particular scenes by partaking of even larger frames of reference. And they realize that even these larger frames are themselves biologically and verbally motivated.

The Burkean Perspective on Text

Against this sweeping historical and cultural backdrop, individual text makers confront the problem of working within shifting logological frames. It is at this point of considering individual composers that Burke's pentad becomes most useful. An individual composer uses the master tropes as tools to fashion dynamic relationships among act, scene, agency, agent, and purpose. Nathaniel West, in *Miss Lonely-hearts* (1933), uses synecdoche to bring together the individual suffering and isolation and the social context brought about by the Depression. His characters, caught in the economic and psychological webs of a shattered social and material dream, speak to readers as human objects acted upon by forces beyond their individual understanding or control. They stand as parts representing a whole society in West's vision of Depression-era suffering.

The ironic trope works in West's fictional world not in the novel's internal structure but through his narrator's relationship with implied readers, or through what Burke might call West's and his readers' "comic transcendence" of the world that is represented in the novel itself. The main characters, identified with as suffering and forlorn individuals within the novel, become to some degree sentimentalized comic figures as readers look at them from their positions outside the novel. The interdependence of both tropic positions — synecdochic and intimate from within, ironic and distant from without — creates in

Burkean terminology a complex, dramatic relation between scene and agency in *Miss Lonelyhearts*, accomplished through West's use of the synecdochic and ironic master tropes.

This brings us to a consideration of Burke's concept of "terministic screens," which is central to understanding his overall sense of how language works to construct human reality (LSA 44–62). Here is Burke's description of his screens metaphor:

> When I speak of 'terministic screens,' I have … in mind some photographs I once saw. They were *different* photographs of the *same* objects, the difference being that they were made with different color filters. Here something so 'factual' as a photograph revealed notable distinctions in texture, and even in form, depending upon which color filter was used for the documentary description of the event being recorded. (LSA 45)

Language, or our particular logologies, are our verbal ways of "coloring" the objects and ideas we see and then express. The infusions of the language of one intellectual, cultural, or social scene into another is our way of using language to avoid what Burke calls "reduction" (GM 507). We "reduce" when we use language in a one-dimensional way. We might, for example, carry the denotative and technical language of science to its extreme in describing the natural world *as if* it were actually completely knowable through the quantifications and statistics of technical science. Such an extreme referential perspective on nature "reduces" nature to things existing completely separate from human cognition. The world becomes a taxonomer's dream. Such one-dimensional verbal perspectives need to be mixed, Burke argues, with dramatistic perspectives on language that include the idea that human language at least partially creates the world that it describes. Physical objects themselves exert their pressures on words (Burke's ongoing sense of the biological motives inherent in language). The result is a need to see language whole, to have one perspective overlayed on another, to use terministic screens to mix our languages, and to mix our perspectives on the world. Readers, then, when processing plural texts, have their attention directed first one way — perhaps toward a technical description of natural phenomenon — and then another — perhaps back toward a narrative perspective or story.[29]

The Appropriation of Burke's Thought by Different Academic Fields

Literary critics and rhetoricians have consistently focused primarily on Burke's more literary and philosophical works: *Philosophy of Literary Form*, *Counter-Statement*, *Language as Symbolic Action* (a collection

of language-oriented essays), and the more rhetorical works—
Grammar of Motives and *Rhetoric of Motives*. The result of this somewhat restricted appropriation of Burke is an overemphasis on his
reactions to new critical formalism and its approaches to text. Wayne
Booth, in his incorporation of Burke into his own pluralistic critical
theory, compares Burke's broadly based rhetorical formalism, informed
by rhetoric, psychology, and language theory, to what Booth believes
are the equally pluralistic perspectives of R. S. Crane and Meyer
Abrams. All three, Booth makes clear, go beyond textual formalism
without ever threatening the central place of text in developing critical
perspective.[30] These critics, Booth says, "overstand" the texts they
criticize, using them as a base on which to construct interpretations
that bring together diverse perspectives on culture, history, and
language. What Booth deals with in only peripheral ways, however, is
Burke's whole theory of language, particularly as it serves as a basis
for his dramatistic approach to text. Booth seems to ignore the fact
that the pentadic ratios themselves develop out of Burke's logology.

Frank Lentricchia, in his poststructural analysis of Burke's dramatism, uses Burke to broaden the critical perspective of poststructuralism.
Burke, Lentricchia suggests, can help us avoid the intricate but in the
end debilitating focus on "traces" and subtle *difference* in the decon-
structionists, who, to Lentricchia, lack political-cultural perspective.
And Burke can also provide the radical neo-Hegelian Marxists and
cultural critics with a more balanced sense of dialectics and plan of
verbal action than they have to this point been able to achieve. In
essence, Lentricchia correctly sees Burke as a social reconstructionist,
rather than as a deconstructionist. But, by giving much less attention
to Burke's social theory books (*Permanence and Change* and *Attitudes
Toward History*) than he has to his literary studies, Lentricchia fails to
exploit Burke's dynamic sense of logology in its full sociocultural
meaning.[31] Lentricchia, in other words, uses Burke's pentad with its
emphasis on human discoursers as influenced both by internal and
external forces to inject a sense of being, reality, or experience back
into literary theory. But he supplies his own cultural reading of Burke,
rather than doing a close analysis of *Attitudes Toward History* and
Permanence and Change, those books where Burke's logology and his
sense of social history are linked.

Meanwhile, rhetoricians using Burke have committed a different
kind of oversimplification. They often find in Burke's more psychological
perspective on organic forms created by internal rather than external
conditions the ground for a flexible sense of how form works both to
constrain and elaborate discourse. Frank D'Angelo uses Burke's theory
of form as the fulfilling of "created expectations" (see "Lexicon Rhetoricae," in CS 123–83) in *A Conceptual Theory of Rhetoric*, where

he argues for a "paradigmatic" perspective on form as a means of explaining how conceptual-formal paradigms are used by composers as they move from text to text.[32] Richard Coe, in an advanced rhetoric text entitled *Form and Substance*, has used Burke's concept of "progressive form" to explain the rhetorical modes of narration, process-analysis and causation. As does D'Angelo, Coe finds an overarching theory in Burke that helps him explain how general forms come to "in-form" individual texts.[33] But both D'Angelo and Coe fail to acknowledge that Burke's theory of form is part of a larger social project, which again is best explained in *Attitudes Toward History* and *Permanence and Change*.[34]

In Conclusion

Understanding Kenneth Burke, and using his work to interpret and explain the many kinds of pluralistic texts we find around us every day, demands an interdisciplinary perspective on language and knowledge itself. Burke's work is not very useful if we think of using it to close off texts into strictly defined generic categories. But it is rich in its potential to open up textual criticism to a search for new connections, for tracking elusive but important intellectual influences from one generic field to another. His work could provide us with useful strategies for understanding where and how the specialist knowledge constructed by different fields can be combined into a larger, more complex and dynamic understanding of how the texts we make shape us as well as our knowledge of the world.

To return to the reference to metainterpretation that opens this essay, we can conclude by asserting the value that Burke's kind of critical theory has for practitioners in any field. Burke does not give us much help when it comes to stabilizing the meanings of given texts. But he is a close and useful friend when it comes to understanding the dynamically interacting substances out of which our interpretations evolve. And in that collective enterprise we need all the help we can get.

Notes

1. Paul Jay, ed., *The Selected Correspondence of Kenneth Burke and Malcolm Cowley* (Berkeley, CA: Univ. of California, 1990), p. vi. Hereafter cited parenthetically as Jay. The biographical information for this first section is drawn from two primary sources: the various prefaces and introductions Burke wrote for different editions of his major works, and the introductions and letters in *The Selected Correspondence*.

2. *The Complete White Oxen: Collected Short Fiction of Kenneth Burke*, 2d augmented ed. (Berkeley, CA: Univ. of California, 1968). First published 1924.

3. *Counter-Statement* (Berkeley, CA: Univ. of California, 1931). Rev. ed. published 1953, 1968. Hereafter CS.

4. *Permanence and Change: An Anatomy of Purpose*, 3d ed. with new Afterword (Berkeley, CA: Univ. of California, 1984). First ed., 1935; rev. 2d ed., 1954. Hereafter PC.

5. *Attitudes Toward History*, 3d ed. with New Afterword (Berkeley, CA: Univ. of California, 1984). First ed., Editorial Publications, 1937; rev. 2d ed., Hermes Publications, 1959. Hereafter ATH.

6. *Towards a Better Life, A Series of Epistles, or Declamations*, rev. ed. (Berkeley, CA: Univ. of California, 1968). First ed. 1932.

7. *The Philosophy of Literary Form*, rev. ed. (Berkeley, CA: Univ. of California, 1967). First ed. 1941. Hereafter PLF.

8. Burke's analysis of Hitler's *Mein Kampf*, which appears in PLF and is discussed later in this essay, is a good example of his application of literary theory to political texts.

9. *A Grammar of Motives*, rev. ed. (Berkeley, CA: Univ. of California, 1969). First ed. 1945. Hereafter GM.

10. *A Rhetoric of Motives* (New York: Prentice-Hall, 1950). Second ed. with Introduction added, Georges Brazilier, 1955. Paperback ed., Univ. of California, 1969. Hereafter RM.

11. *The Rhetoric of Religion: Studies in Logology* (Boston: Beacon, 1961). Paperback ed., Univ. of California, 1970. Hereafter RR.

12. Burke put this idea even more succinctly in a letter to Malcolm Cowley: "Experimentally, I often turn the usual perspective around, and think not of us as using language but of language as using us to get itself said ..." (Jay 332).

13. *Language as Symbolic Action* (Berkeley, CA: Univ. of California, 1966). Hereafter LSA.

14. Burke has remained professionally active into his nineties. For example, he addressed the Conference on College Composition and Communication in Seattle, Washington, in 1989 at the age of ninety-one.

15. Burke described some of his differences with concrete poet and imagist William Carlos Williams in a letter to Malcolm Cowley, written in 1921: "I see now why I am interested in Williams; because he has frequently done to perfection just the sort of thing I do not want to do" (Jay 109).

16. See "In Retrospective Prospect," (PC (295–336), where Burke uses this maxim to explain his entire theory of language and its social function.

17. Samuel B. Southwell, *Kenneth Burke and Martin Heidegger* (Gainesville, FL: Univ. of Florida, 1987), pp. 62, 66.

18. Ibid., pp. 38, 40. Southwell also makes a distinction between Burke and Heidegger. Whereas Heidegger posits an uncloseable gap between "life-world" and metaphysics, between being "in" the world of experience and talking and thinking about that world, Burke sees the two realms as inextricably related, with body *informing* mind and mind, in turn, *reinforming* body. ATH includes a succinct summary of Burke's body-mind dialectic (370–75). Burke closes this summary with a list of moral prerogatives for secular education. Heidegger's existential leanings ask us to consider the need to immerse ourselves in Being; Burke's dramatism is a recipe for rhetorical action that picks up where Heidegger leaves off.

19. LSA (419–79) provides Burke's most self-contained and complete account of his linguistic theory of the negative. Burke, however, refers continuously to language's capability of engendering this sense of nonaction whenever he refers to symbolic action in general (see also GM, where Burke applies this negative capability to ladders of abstraction in human thought).

20. Current debates among composition theorists might be edified by a close look at Burke's dialectical perspective on the physical and intellectual rhythms of composing processes. See Stephen P. Witte, "Pre-text and Composing," *College Composition and Communication*, 38 (1987), pp. 397–425.

21. Burke describes the concept of "representative anecdote" in GM (323–25): "A writer's selection of a case with which to illustrate a more general theory comes to serve as the base or substance upon which that theory is erected. The 'scope' of the theory itself is in turn defined by the substantive anecdote used to represent it. In other words, once a writer translates a general theory into particular anecdotal terms, she or he has already begun the process of arranging the terminological screen through which all further discourse about the theory will be filtered."

22. PC was originally published in 1935; it was written during the Great Depression. Burke revised it and added a Prologue and Afterword, explaining the context of its earlier writing, in the second edition of 1954 (written in 1953). A third edition, with an introduction by social scientist Hugh Dalziel Duncan, was published in 1965 (Bobbs Merrill). The definitive University of California edition used here appeared in 1984 with Burke's Afterword ("In Retrospective Prospect") added to all earlier afterwords and prefaces.

23. Louis Althusser, *Lenin and Philosophy*, trans. Ben Brewster (London: New Left Books, 1971); Antonio Gramsci, *Selections from the Prison Notebooks*, ed. and trans. Quintin Horare and Geoffrey Smith (New York: International, 1971).

24. Althusser problematizes the concept of *ideology*; he, in fact, uses the term to explain how the cultures from which individuals evolve cause them to perceive and organize reality according to tacit political frameworks (or by what Burke might call "terminological screens"). Gramsci problematizes the term *hegemony*, using it to explain how particular ideologies come to dominate over others within the larger social framework that provides contexts for individual writers.

25. Burke's discussion of *ultimate*, *dialectical*, and *positive* terms in RM (183−88) enriches the preceding discussion of the term *individualism*. *Positive* terms are those that members of a discourse community use to refer to physical aspects of their perceived environments; *dialectical* terms are those that members use to refer to arguable abstractions within these environments; and *ultimate* terms are those that members use to refer to abstractions that represent higher-order principles the community uses to control its perspective on reality. Ultimate terms, such as *profit* or *money* in capitalistic systems or *labor* in socialistic ones, often are reified and remain unexamined by those within the communities that are governed by them. A term such as *individualism*, then, might function as an ultimate in one system and as a dialectic in another; Burke's approach would suggest that such terms require dialectical analysis before any sense of comprehensive meaning could for them be established.

26. A more positive example of the same textual phenomenon can be found in Burke's interpretation of Keats's "Ode on a Grecian Urn" in "Symbolic Action in a Poem by Keats," an Appendix to GM (447−63). In this Appendix, Burke explains how Keats turns the terms of aesthetic "spirit" into body and back again into spirit, primarily through his uses of the tropes of metonymy and synecdoche.

27. This notion of *balance* is treated by Burke in ways similar to Jean Piaget's use of the concept. Piaget's concept of "equilibration," in which an organism attempts to find a stable blend of *assimilation* (the adaptation of external stimuli to the organism's internal structure) and *accommodation* (the organism's adaptation of external stimuli to its internal structure) is similar in the biological realm to Burke's use of *balance* in the verbal realm.

28. Recent discussions of Mikhail Bakhtin's notions of heteroglossic texts are yet another gloss on this dialectical social-individual interaction in textual analysis and interpretation. The overlaps between Burke's "perspectives by incongruity" and Bakhtin's "heteroglossia" are provocative and potentially useful. Whereas Burke, in PC, argues that the author's comic perspective ultimately transcends all other textual voices because it asserts the author's control (through the master tropes) over the voices he or she projects into any individual text, Bakhtin argues in *The Dialogic Imagination* (Austin: Univ. of Texas, 1981) that textual voices, both authorial and narratorial, exist in an equal but contending dialectical interaction, with no one voice ever dominating all others — at least not for the open and discerning reader (361). Gary Saul Morson's *Bakhtin* (Chicago: Univ. of Chicago, 1986) serves as a useful critical introduction to the ongoing dialogue concerning Bakhtinian textual dialectics.

29. Much of the writing of essayists such as Stephen Jay Gould, Oliver Sacks, and Lewis Thomas, as well as the best of the current science journals, mix technical and narrative forms of knowing in a way that is similar to what Burke says of Saint Augustine's mixture of theological and narrative epistemologies and forms in *The Confessions*.

30. Wayne Booth, *Critical Understanding* (Chicago: Univ. of Chicago, 1979).

31. Frank Lentricchia, *Criticism and Social Change* (Chicago: Univ. of Chicago, 1979), p. 19.

32. Frank D'Angelo, *A Conceptual Theory of Rhetoric* (Cambridge, Mass.: Winthrop, 1975).

33. Richard Coe, *Form and Substance* (Glenview, Il.: Scott Foresman, 1981), pp. 278–320.

34. Burke's three most succinct discussions of form are found in the "Lexicon Rhetoricae" section of CS (123–83), where he discusses form psychologically, in RM (65–78), where he discusses form rhetorically and stylistically, and in the Appendix of GM (447–63), where he discusses "master tropes."

8

Ong's Theory of Orality and Literacy
A Perspective from Which to Re-View Theories of Discourse

Michael Kleine

In his 1975 award-winning article, "The Writer's Audience Is Always a Fiction," Walter Ong gestures at a "growing literature on the differences between oral and written verbalization," but complains that "many aspects of the differences have not been looked into at all, and many others, although well known, have not been examined in their full implications."[1] The overlooked difference that concerns Ong most in his 1975 article involves the concept of audience. Whereas speakers interact with an audience that is both present and responsive, writers must construct — or "fictionalize" — an audience. As Ong writes, "The writer must construct in his imagination, clearly or vaguely, an audience cast in some sort of role." Moreover, the audience "must correspondingly fictionalize itself."[2] Ong implies that a writer's ability to fictionalize an audience, and a reader's ability to assume the role of a fictionalized audience, is an intertextual process that has led to increasingly complicated audience fictions, and increasingly sophisticated writers and readers. When script was first developed, writers and readers were so close to the oral tradition that "written narrative was merely a transcription of oral narrative" and "the fictionalizing of readers was relatively simple."[3] But as written texts began to interact with each other over time, they became increasingly distanced from the original oral audience:

> If the writer succeeds in writing, it is generally because he can fiction-
> alize in his imagination an audience he has learned to know not from
> daily life but from earlier writers who were fictionalizing in their
> imagination audiences they had learned to know in still earlier writers.[4]

The thesis regarding orality and literacy that Walter Ong develops and
advances in a later book-length study, *Orality and Literacy*, is strongly
implied in "The Writer's Audience Is Always a Fiction": writing is
an invention, a technology, that forever changed — and continues to
change — the nature of human discourse and consciousness. Like all
technologies, writing is evolutionary, changing not only itself, but also
those who use it. Like most technologies, writing engenders among its
users a kind of ambivalence. In Ong's case, writing is "more interesting,
although perhaps less noble than speech."[5] It is, then, both a thesis
and an ambivalence concerning writing as a technology that unifies the
corpus of Ong's work, and that enables the reader of Ong's work to
gain from it a powerful perspective from which to examine, to "review," contemporary discourse theory. Seen through the lens that Ong
provides, discourse is not only a communicative interaction between
human beings over time and across space, but also an interaction that
bears the imprint of a chirographic and typographic technology.

In the pages that follow, I draw mainly from *Orality and Literacy*[6]
in an effort to summarize and explicate the orality/literacy perspective
that Ong's work offers to the discourse theorist. Although other book-
length works by Ong, *The Presence of the Word*[7] and *Rhetoric, Romance,
and Technology*,[8] offer similar versions of Ong's orality/literacy perspective, no other work so completely and clearly reviews the historical
and anthropological work that influenced Ong. I then explain how an
orality/literacy perspective enables Ong to construct a powerful critique
of New Critical and poststructural theories of discourse and literature.
Finally, I assume the orality/literacy perspective in an effort to construct
my own critique of contemporary writing theory, especially the developmental theory of James Britton. I hope to demonstrate not only that
Ong's work is interesting and comprehensive, but also that it provides
an invaluable perspective for re-viewing various contemporary theories
of discourse, and for understanding our own discourse.

Ong's Orality/Literacy Perspective

In the corpus of his work, and particularly in *Orality and Literacy: The
Technologizing of the Word*, Walter Ong argues that the advent of
literacy has influenced ineluctably the nature of human discourse,
consciousness, knowledge, and personality. Ong's own perspective
grows from his extensive reading of the written scholarship of historians
of the ancient Greek shift from orality to literacy,[9] cultural anthropol-

ogists,[10] sociolinguists,[11] cognitive psychologists,[12] and media theorists.[13] By maintaining both a historical and a cultural view of the difference between orality and literacy, Ong is able to argue that the advent of literacy both significantly changes the discourse and consciousness of a particular culture *and* forever differentiates that culture from other cultures that remain oral.

Ong's central thesis is both simple and powerful: literacy is a technology that bears the linguistic traces of an oral past, but at the same time radically alters the way a culture discourses (both orally and in print), perceives reality, interacts with the world, and thinks. So significant is the advent of literacy in a culture that it continues to exercise its influence even when the culture reverts to a mode of discourse that seems primarily oral. Thus, Ong differentiates between "primary orality" (a condition of pure orality that is nearly impossible for us "literates" to imagine) and "secondary orality" (the kind of orality that seems to replace literacy when new electronic technologies, like broadcasting, supplant the old alphabetic print technology). Secondary orality, however regressive it may seem, still bears the traces of a prior literacy in much the same way that literacy itself bears the traces of a prior primary orality. Echoing McLuhan, Ong asserts that a particular technology, like television, is its own message, but Ong is more concerned with an evolutionary and ecological view of the succession and interdependence of technologies. Thus, Ong notes that the secondary orality of television has been both influenced and structured by the preceding and concurrent existence of writing. As Ong points out, secondary orality is both planned and scripted, and removed from the immediate lifeworld of the culture.

By placing literacy into opposition with primary orality, especially, Ong is able to bring to consciousness what we literates so often take for granted: literacy has slowly and inexorably changed human discourse and thinking. In *Orality and Literacy* Ong writes: "abstractly sequential, classificatory, explanatory examination of phenomena or of stated truths is impossible without writing and reading" (OL 8–9). He argues that even our ability to bring literacy to consciousness and consider its difference from primary orality is itself a result of literacy. Before considering the impact of literacy, then, let us first understand the nature of the primary orality that Ong reconstructs with the help of scholarship in history and anthropology.

Ong considers both the epistemological and the pragmatic concerns of primary orality. Fundamentally, primary orality is concerned with the preservation ("conservation" is Ong's biological metaphor) of prior discourse and knowledge. Influenced by Parry's and Havelock's writing about the advent of literacy in ancient Greece, and especially their focus on the Homeric epic tradition, Ong argues that the function underlying and motivating primary orality is the retrieval and display of knowledge that has already been constructed rather than the construction of new knowledge. The epic poet, for example, does not create a literary work that is "novel" and that is advanced through linear plotting; instead, he starts "in the middle of things," in the middle of the discourse and immediate concerns of the culture, and attempts to remember the epithets, the stock characters, and the "stories" of the past. Thus, the epic poet enters into a collaborative relationship with other epic poets and storytellers, but it is a collaboration that looks back on past linguistic formulations of knowledge instead of pushing ahead with new formulations of knowledge.

Because primary orality is backward-looking and conservative, and because its function is to retrieve linguistic formulations of knowledge from cultural memory (and thus maintain them), the speaker uses mnemonic and formulary devices instead of the heuristic systems that enable invention in writing. In the Homeric tradition, for example, the hexameter line and the frequent use of epithets ("wily Odysseus," the "wine-dark sea," etc.) helped the poet maintain prior linguistic formulations. Moreover, by using a structure that was essentially episodic, the poet was able to remember the past in chunks that could be presented in the order they were remembered. Arrangement, then, was never sequential and hierarchical; it was, instead, the fortuitous result of randomly remembering the past in chunks, in stories.

If it is the function of retrieving and preserving prior knowledge that motivates the production of primary oral discourse, then it is the immediacy of the rhetorical situation that controls its content and nature. In Ong's terms, primary oral discourse involves the immediate presence of one or more "interlocuters," and thus its effort to retrieve the past is inextricably bound to a "human lifeworld" that is present and active. Because the immediate needs of the interlocuter are often voiced and heard by the speaker, or at least understood and felt, the discourse tends to be "empathetic" and "situational" instead of "distant," "abstract," and "analytical." In other words, memory serves the immediate needs of the audience. Furthermore, because the values and attitudes of the interlocuter may clash with the values and attitudes of the speaker, the discourse can become confrontational and "agonistic." When this happens, the memory of the speaker is used to retrieve and select past knowledge (stories, proverbs, adages, etc.) that discredits or undermines the past knowledge evoked by the interlocuter. Thus, primary oral dialogue, like epic formulation, depends on memory of the past instead of on complex analysis and logical argumentation.

In a chapter of *Orality and Literacy* entitled "Some Psychodynamics of Orality" Ong constructs a list of the salient characteristics of primary orality (OL 37–57). It is helpful to consider the list in its entirety since it provides a contrastive basis for understanding the radical difference that literacy, in Ong's view, imposes on human discourse and thought. As opposed to literate discourse, oral discourse is:

1. "Additive rather than subordinative." At both macro and micro levels, oral discourse is structured by addition (coordination) rather than hierarchical subordination and embedding. Thus, oral discourse is paratactic, not hypotactic.

2. "Aggregative rather than analytic." Oral discourse develops as one remembered formulation is added to another. Because of its temporal, nonspatial nature, oral discourse does not tend to "partition" and "categorize" (both space-related operations that are enabled by the visual display of text).

3. "Redundant or 'copious.'" Since oral discourse depends on memory of prior linguistic formulation, it requires the kind of repetition that enhances the conservation of form and meaning in long-term memory.

4. "Conservative or traditionalist." Oral discourse intends to preserve and retrieve prior knowledge. Thus, it relies on rigid lexical and syntactic conventions.

5. "Close to the human lifeworld." Because oral discourse is situated among participating human beings, it tends to privilege active human agency and concrete reference to human experience instead of passive and nominalized sentences, and abstract reference.

6. "Agonistically toned." Oral discourse evinces the struggle among discourse participants. The "knower" and the "known" are inseparable as the speaker utters his knowledge during moments of immediate conflict and in a context that is both present and visible.

7. "Empathetic and participatory rather than objectively distanced." A speaker experiences empathy as he interacts directly with his interlocuters. In the immediacy of oral discourse, it becomes impossible to distance the self from meaning and knowledge, and to regard knowledge as an object that can be considered and analyzed by itself.

8. "Homeostatic." As Ong writes, "Oral societies live very much in a present which keeps itself in equilibrium or homeostasis by sloughing off memories which no longer have present relevance" (OL 46).

9. "Situational rather than abstract." In oral cultures, conceptual understanding, and definition, is operational rather than categorical. Thus, a "bear" might be understood as an "animal that once raided our village and killed a child" instead of as a "fur-bearing mammal that hibernates during the winter."

Ong's list prepares us to understand how the technology of writing changed the nature of human discourse and thought. Against each of the characteristics of primary orality we can infer and oppose a characteristic of literacy:

1. Hypotactic and hierarchical. Chirographic and typographic texts, because they are expandable spatial entities, are capable of displaying old knowledge in the form of subordinated propositions and textual components while allowing space for the addition of new knowledge.

2. Planned and analytic. By conserving knowledge textually, literate discourse frees writers from the burden of remembering and enables them to concentrate on textual planning and on high-level cognitive operations.

3. Streamlined and efficient. Literacy, because it is a technology that spatially conserves knowledge, eliminates much of the redundancy required by primary orality.

4. Creative and sometimes unconventional. Discourse that is conservative and culturally circumscribed tends to be conventional. Because literate discourse is more decontextualized than oral discourse, and frequently detached from its cultural field, it is somewhat liberated from cultural convention and constraint.

5. Distant from an immediate human lifeworld. Because a written text can be separated from an immediate human context by both time and space, "the writer's audience is always a fiction."

6. Nonagonistic (separates "knower" from "known"). When human beings engage in active oral dialogue, knower and known are one. Literacy, however, separates textually constructed knowledge from the producer of the text.

7. Detached from immediate rhetorical context. In its detachment from immediate rhetorical context, writing loses the empathy required by speaking.

8. Nonhomeostatic. Literacy enables the preservation of all written knowledge, not just selective knowledge that is situationally relevant.

9. Abstract. Literacy enables intertextuality and abstraction. Over time, literate discourse gestures more and more at language, and less and less at an immediate lifeworld.

What is it, though, about alphabetic literacy, and about writing, that so radically changes human discourse and consciousness? Ong suggests that the answer to this question has something to do with the relationship between textual presence and space, and long-term memory. As a technology, as a tool, writing diminishes the necessity of preserving knowledge through memory. Because writing makes knowledge textually and visually available, writers no longer need to focus on maintaining old knowledge. Instead, they can count on textual space to hold what they have already constructed (and "know") and push ahead with the construction of new knowledge. Their liberation from long-term memory enables them both to invent and plan. Memory, then, can be used to store not only old knowledge, but also the goals and plans that will guide construction of new knowledge. Though Ong does not develop the relationship between short-term memory and writing, it seems safe to assume that they are related in much the same way that long-term memory and writing are related, but at the micro rather than the macro level of composing.

Furthermore, writing has led to the ascendancy of the "grapholect," a normative written dialect that subsumes and standardizes countless oral dialects and discourses. By subsuming the linguistic resources of different oral dialects and by abstracting underlying formal patterns and potentials, the grapholect is a technological refinement that enables writers to transcend their particular lifeworlds and memories, and enter remote cultures and discourses with their own writing. Thus, the grapholect enables both abstraction and distance from immediate situation and reference, and exploration of what is not already known and remembered.

Ong argues that the technology of literacy begets new technologies. The alphabet is succeeded by writing, and writing is succeeded by printing. With the printing press, a new kind and sense of discourse space is born. Typographic, justified, and evenly spaced, print literacy imposes its own order and enables a new kind of discourse. The kind of typographic space created by printing is conducive to lists, hierarchical organization and headings, and paragraphs. Moreover, when printed texts are widely read and written, they become embedded in each other and responsible for each other. Human discourse becomes "intertextual," and its ability to preserve and construct knowledge is increased, its scope expanded both temporally and spatially. With print literacy, then, human consciousness, at least in part, is removed from a world of memory and immediate context and relocated in a vast temporal and spatial world of hierarchically organized texts and complicated intertextual relationships. The writer, then, is distanced from both discourse and knowledge, but as a result can advance the construction of knowledge with objective analysis and linguistic precision.

Extending the biological metaphor that underlies his work, Ong contends that the phylogenetic manifestations of the shift from orality to literacy are recapitulated ontogenetically:

> The interaction between the orality that all human beings are born
> into and the technology of writing, which no one is born into, touches
> the depths of the psyche. Ontogenetically and phylogenetically, it is
> the oral word that first illuminates consciousness with articulate
> language, that first divides subject and predicate and then relates
> them to one another, and that ties human beings to one another in
> society. Writing introduces division and alienation, but a higher unity
> as well. It intensifies the sense of self and fosters more conscious
> interaction between persons. Writing is consciousness-raising.
> (OL 178–79)

Just as literacy slowly promotes the sort of detachment that enables a
culture as a whole to examine and understand itself, it promotes the
rapid recapitulation of that growth in the individual. Ong contends that
concurrent with the rise of romanticism, literate individuals began to
examine and analyze themselves, to gain distance from themselves and
differentiate themselves from their discourse with others. In terms of
personality, then, literate individuals are more "interior," more self-
conscious. As far as Ong is concerned, diaries, journals, and autobiographies are not genres that accommodate a kind of prior interiority;
they are, instead, forms of literacy that enable and promote cultural
and personal interiority.

Finally, Ong's orality/literacy perspective includes the kind of
"secondary orality" that seems to be succeeding literacy as a technology
in our own electronic culture. Although secondary orality seems to be
a regressive return to primary orality, Ong argues that it is, instead, an
orality that is profoundly affected by the literacy that preceded it and
exists alongside it:

> At the same time, with telephone, radio, television and various kinds
> of sound tape, electronic technology has brought us into the age of
> "secondary orality." This new orality has striking resemblances to the
> old in its participatory mystique, ... but it is essentially a more
> deliberate and self-conscious orality, based permanently on the use
> of writing and print, which are essential for the manufacture and
> operation of the equipment and for its use as well. (OL 136)

Thus, literacy and secondary orality exist interdependently in an ecology
of discourse and consciousness.

In a chapter in *Rhetoric, Romance, and Technology* entitled "The
Literate Orality of Popular Culture Today," Ong discusses at length
the phenomenon of a dynamic social orality that is interdependent
with, and transformed by, literacy. Noting the apparent similarity
between primary orality and secondary orality, Ong writes, "Sound
always tends to socialize. The drive toward group sense and toward
participatory activities, toward 'happenings,' which mysteriously

emerges out of modern electronic technological cultures is strikingly similar to certain drives in preliterate cultures" (RRT 284). However, he goes on to argue that secondary orality, unlike primary orality, is both scripted and highly visual, and that resultantly it evinces the same kind of spatial orientation, compartmental organization, distance, and abstraction that is characteristic of literacy. Moreover, though secondary orality is laden with clichés that seem to work in a formulary way, secondary oral discourse uses the clichés pragmatically rather than mnemonically, and is both self-conscious and ironic about its own use of them. The advertising proposition "It's the real thing," as spoken on television, does not aim to help a culture remember that *Coca Cola is a real thing*. Instead, it aims to persuade a culture to buy a product. Once voiced in secondary oral discourse, the proposition can be detached from original context and used ironically: "I hope the newly elected President will be 'the real thing.'"

Ong's diachronic and synchronic opposition of orality and literacy offers a unique perspective from which to view discourse. If literacy is indeed a technology that has transformed the nature of human discourse and knowledge, then its powerful and pervasive impact must be considered as we attempt to construct theories of discourse and theories of how theory itself is constructed. Indeed, the orality/literacy perspective helps us understand that the construction of theories of discourse is enabled by literacy, that without writing as a means of inquiry, we could not understand writing as an object of inquiry.

The Orality/Literacy Perspective and Literary Theory

In *Interfaces of the Word*, a collection of essays that focus on problems of textuality and literary discourse, Ong examines the evolution of contemporary literary theory.[14] In an essay entitled "The Poem as a Closed Field," he opposes the New Criticism to the "old rhetoric" (the rhetoric of Aristotle), and in so doing is able to demonstrate that the New Criticism is one of the fruits of the growth of literacy. Whereas the "old rhetoric," as an abstract study of discourse, was first made possible by the advent of literacy (*The Rhetoric* is a written study), it originally focussed on oral discourse and was, itself, close to the oral tradition that was its own subject:

> When writing first appeared, it did not immediately wipe out or supplant oral-aural modes of thought and verbalization. Rather, it accentuated and codified them. Writing made scientific analytic thought possible. Directed to the consideration of communication such analytic thought produced "rhetoric" as a formal, reflective *techne* or art. (IW 214–15)

It was an oral tradition, then, that led Aristotle to locate the subject of his study (human communication) in an open contextual field that included not only the spoken words, but also the participation of speaker and hearer. The New Criticism of the 1930s and 1940s, however, evolved a theoretical discourse that intended to make sense out of texts, out of written artifacts. Because of the dislocation of literary texts from ostensible context, the New Criticism treated writing as what it appeared to be: text without rhetorical context, a closed rather than an open field.

Throughout *Interfaces of the Word*, Ong argues that literary theory has increasingly separated text from rhetorical context—not only because the literary text in fact seems to be a lifeless artifact that is removed from its own human lifeworld, and that takes on its own independent life, but also because literary theory is itself a kind of writing. In Ong's view, writing dissociates the knower from the known; as a result, literary theorists who write literary theory risk becoming alienated from the texts they attempt to know. It was inevitable, then, that new critics, themselves alienated from the literary discourse about which they were writing, began to assert that the poem was a kind of "closed field," a monument to discourse rather than itself a discourse. In Ong's view, then, The New Criticism evolved not only because it focussed on written rather than on spoken discourse, but also because it was itself advanced in writing, and thus was removed from the kind of primary orality that was still nearly a memory when Aristotle began to develop the "old rhetoric."

In another essay, "Voice and the Opening of Closed Systems," Ong argues that closed-system approach of the New Critics and early structuralists is now beginning to give way to open-system approaches, such as poststructuralism. Ong explains:

> Whatever the role of structuralism in advertising current openness-closure crises, consciousness has evidently shifted in recent times to favor open-system paradigms in many areas of verbalization, at least in the West. (IW 310)

In Ong's view, an open-system mentality is one that locates language—be it oral or scripted—in living human contexts. Thus, poststructuralism, in its effort to locate the text in a number of contexts and discourses, is the result of open-system thinking.

In general, Ong believes that literacy as a technology has tended to promote closed-system thinking (he points especially to Kant's belief in a closed-system, decontextualized logic), but he believes that poststructural literary theory, though it is advanced in writing, is a noteworthy exception. Indeed, throughout *Interfaces of the Word*, Ong associates poststructural discourse—especially Derrida's *De la grammatologie*—with the regeneration of open-system thinking. Though he never overtly commends Derrida's work, it is clear that Ong is sympathetic to the kind of open-system deconstruction of Western dualism and logocentrism that Derrida's work advances.

However, Ong's orality/literacy perspective, while helping him to appreciate the contextual awareness and openness of poststructuralism, leads him to a critique of Derrida's effort to privilege writing and separate it from orality. Derrida's assertion of the difference between speaking and writing is, of course, a strategic move that enables him to demonstrate the indeterminacy of language, critique logocentrism, and deconstruct the binary oppositions that thrive in Western discourse. But whereas Derrida tries to cleanly escape from orality, and the illusions of logocentrism and direct referentiality, Ong's perspective maintains a connection between orality and literacy, and even celebrates orality as a force of openness. It is writing itself, Ong argues, that promotes the closure of a discourse.

Ong believes that Derrida's assertion of difference between speaking and writing is problematical for several reasons:

1. It denies the evolutionary relationship between orality and literacy. Ong believes that though literacy as a technology radically changed human discourse and consciousness, literate discourse still bears traces of primary orality.

2. It denies the ecological interdependence of orality and literacy. Ong believes that literate discourse coexists with secondary orality; thus, literate discourse is continuously reinvested with direct referentiality, and it can never be completely dissociated from speaking and from a present lifeworld.

In *Orality and Literacy*, Ong complains:

> Jacques Derrida has made the point that "there is no linguistic sign before writing." But neither is there a linguistic "sign" after writing if the oral reference of the written text is adverted to. Though it releases unheard-of potentials of the word, a textual, visual representation of a word is not a real word, but a "secondary modeling system." Thought is nested in speech, not in texts, all of which have their meanings through reference of the visible symbol to the world of sound. (OL 75).

In Ong's view, then, not even open-system philosophies like poststructuralism have treated adequately the relationship between orality and literacy. Derrida's movement toward open-system deconstruction of writing denies the primacy — and resonance — of the spoken word.

An orality/literacy perspective, then, leads Ong to value both spoken and written discourse, and to be skeptical about literary theories that attempt to dissociate writing from speaking. Contemporary human discourse enjoys a dynamic of opening and closing, of gesturing at the world and gesturing at language about the world. It enjoys such a dynamic precisely because literacy is *not* a technology that has supplanted orality and left it behind, but because it is a technology that has contributed to the dynamic evolution of human discourse and consciousness.

The Orality/Literacy Perspective and Writing Theory

Contemporary writing theorists are by now well aware of the important relationship that holds between speech and writing. By maintaining a developmental view of the anteriority of speech, they are able to better explain both the production of written discourse and the nature of written texts. The work of Piaget, Vygotsky, and Perry has been so completely incorporated into writing theory that phrases like "cognitive decentering" (Piaget),[15] "inner-speech" (Vygotsky),[16] and "moral development" (Perry)[17] have become commonplace. The development of writing ability is now strongly associated with the cognitive, social, and moral growth of the individual writer.

Perhaps no work with the development of writing competence has been more influential among writing theorists and teachers than James Britton's study of school writing in England — *The Development of Writing Abilities* (11–18).[18] Although Britton's research is not longitudinal and includes only written scripts, his report begins by advancing a developmental theory that purports to consider and to explain an individual writer's movement from speech to writing, and the subsequent development of writing competence over time. Although Britton's research does not provide a solid basis for inducing the theoretical model with which he and his colleagues begin their book, it is the model itself that most writing theorists remember and that still influences contemporary writing theory and pedagogy.

In brief, Britton proposes that speech provides the "expressive" basis for the development of writing competency. Writing, then, always maintains this expressive basis, but also moves away from it in two opposite and continuous directions: toward either a "poetic" or "transactional" pole. As Britton explains, poetic discourse results when writers assume a "spectator role" in relationship to the world they are writing about, attempting to observe it and frame it rather than interact with it and change it. Transactional discourse, on the other hand, results when writers assume a "participant role" and attempt to interpret and change the world as they interact with readers who cohabit the world with them. As writers develop, they gain distance from the speech-based "expression" that drives all discourse; thus, while maintaining to some degree a competence and energy that derives from self-expression, they are able to move toward transactional writing that is more "analogic" and "tautologic" (analytical and theoretical), and poetic writing that is more depersonalized and self-reflexive.

Britton models his developmental theory of writing in the following way:

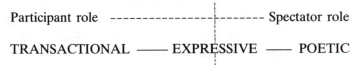

Participant role ----------------|-------- Spectator role

TRANSACTIONAL —— EXPRESSIVE —— POETIC

As Britton acknowledges, the model, with its expressive core, derives from Sapir's work in linguistics. Britton writes:

> We drew on Sapir's theory of the essentially expressive nature of all speech and the way in which it moves to a greater explicitness at the expense of its expressive features when the need to communicate increases. Expressive language signals the self, reflects not only the ebb and flow of a speaker's thought and feeling, but also his assumptions of shared contexts of meaning, and of a relationship of trust with his listener. (DWA 10)

For Sapir and Britton both, the expressive function is close to the self and "signals the self" with the "I" pronoun, a feature of self-reference. Moreover, Britton's model credits the expressive function with learning, suggesting that it is a "means of exploration and discovery" (DWA 82). Britton implies, then, that speech-based expression is in large part responsible for the construction of new knowledge.

Clearly, Ong's orality/literacy perspective challenges Britton's privileging of the expressive function and complicates his developmental theory of writing. Although an orality/literacy perspective supports Britton's view that writing ("literacy") develops into analogic and tautologic modes of discourse and thought, it argues against his view that expression is anterior to, and responsible for, the ability to write and the nature of writing. Furthermore, the orality/literacy perspective argues that it is literacy, not "expression," that enables exploration and the construction of new knowledge; and it argues that it is literacy, not "expression," that enables consideration of the self and interiority. Finally, the orality/literacy perspective challenges the assignment of the "poetic" function to writing and to spectatorship.

In *Orality and Literacy*, Ong differentiates not between personal expression and public writing, but between orality and literacy. In so doing, he draws his line of historical and personal development within a context of technological impact, cultural difference, and social change. In Ong's view, orality is anterior to literacy both in the discourse of the world and the discourse of the literate individual. Literacy does not succeed orality on an unbroken continuum. Instead, literacy represents a radical break in the developmental line and a moment in historical, cultural, and personal time when primary oral development splits into two lines of development (secondary orality and literacy) that remain separated, but intertwined. Unlike Britton, Ong abandons Sapir's theory of language, specifically complaining that Sapir, among other structural linguists, "resisted the idea of the distinctiveness of spoken and written languages" (OL 17). Thus, Ong's orality/literacy distinction offers a perspective for constructing a developmental theory of discourse that is based more on the opposition of communicative modalities than it is on the continuation and transformation of communicative competence.

In the following space, I will attempt to re-model the work of Britton by assuming the perspective offered by Ong:

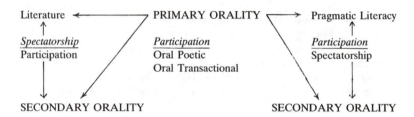

In this revised model, primary orality replaces expression as the term that is anterior to writing. In this privileged anterior position, primary orality, unlike expression, is seen as being both participatory and transactional. As Ong argues, primary orality is highly participatory: close to the immediate lifeworld, speakers attempt to retrieve old knowledge as they actively participate in agonistic discourse—or else they epically re-present old knowledge in light of present activity in order to maintain it homeostatically. Moreover, primary oral poetry (i.e., the epic) is classified as participatory: the spectatorship of epic poets was far less important than their participation in the immediate lifeworld of the culture. Literacy is seen not so much as a developmental continuation of primary orality, but as a new technological order that breaks the developmental line and brings about both the divergence and interdependence of literate and secondary oral discourse.

If literate discourse moves toward spectatorship, it then becomes "literature," and subsumes not only written poetry (epitomized by the lyric, not the epic), but also the personal essay, the drama, and es-pecially the novel. As Ong suggests, it is literacy itself that makes spectatorship possible. Distanced from both the world, themselves, and their own texts, literary writers are able to attend to form, script dramatic conversation and action, and establish point of view. As spectators, they can even observe themselves and write personal essays, autobiographies, journals, and diaries—"literary nonfiction" such writing might be called. Indeed, the orality/literacy perspective suggests that Britton's "expressive writing" needs to be reclassified as literature that observes the self of the writer. Highly personal and exploratory, such writing leads to the kind of interiority that Ong associates with romanticism and the triumph of literacy.

If, on the other hand, literate discourse retains the participation characteristic of primary oral discourse, it becomes what I have called "pragmatic literacy," subsuming "expository" and "persuasive" writing that intends to interpret and change the world. Most obviously, professional and academic writing reflect the onset and evolution of pragmatic literacy; both kinds of writing are responsive to social demands for the maintenance of old knowledge and the active construction of new knowledge.

Finally, even secondary orality is seen as a break from primary orality, influenced as it is by the effects of literacy on human consciousness and discourse. Secondary orality in the spectator mode (the songs we listen to on the radio, the movies we watch) can only move toward spectatorship because literacy has created a space for such movement. In the same way, secondary orality in the participant mode (the news broadcasts that inform us and the television commercials that influence us to buy new products) reflects the influence of pragmatic literacy in both its compartmental organization of time and its effort to construct the new rather than conserve the past.

Conclusion

In the *Domestication of the Savage Mind*, Jack Goody, an anthropologist who is in many ways a proponent of an orality/literacy perspective, warns of the danger of claiming too strongly that literacy has transformed the nature of human consciousness. Goody is concerned that some versions of the orality/literacy perspective may in fact promote the ethnocentric view that literate cultures and individuals are in fact cognitively superior to nonliterate cultures and individuals. In an article entitled "Narrowing the Mind and Page: Remedial Writers and Cognitive Reductionism," Mike Rose, a writing theorist, echoes Goody's concern and further complains that an orality/literacy perspective offers an oversimplified view of discourse. Rose argues that privileging such a bipolar perspective runs the risk of obscuring other important differences — such as "genre, context, register, topic, level of formality, and purpose."[19]

However, the particular version of the orality/literacy perspective that Ong offers in *Orality and Literacy* elegantly responds to such challenges. While it is true that Ong argues that literacy has transformed human consciousness, he never explicitly asserts that literacy has actually changed the nature of human cognition. Because he is careful to specify that literacy is an instrumental technology, a tool, that enables analytical and objective modes of thinking, he is able to avoid the dangerous claim that the possession of literacy brings about a cognitive change that makes analytical and objective thinking possible. Literate people, then, are not people who are cognitively superior to oral people; instead, they are people who possess a tool that helps them think in unique ways, a tool that is external to the brain, but one that enables it to do special work.

Moreover, Ong is careful not to privilege literacy. Orality, as he argues in *Interfaces of the Word*, is itself capable of enabling unique modes of discourse and thinking—open-system and contextualized modes that unify the knower and the known.

Finally, Ong's orality/literacy perspective prevents a bipolar and discontinuous view of discourse by situating orality and literacy not only in an evolutionary relationship, but also in an ecological relationship. Throughout his work, Ong suggests that literacy and secondary orality have become so interdepedent in the modern world that they cannot be understood in isolation. Literacy is embedded in secondary orality; secondary orality is embedded in literacy. Thus, Ong's perspective avoids explaining differences between contemporary discourses solely on the basis of an orality/literacy opposition, but at the same time it recognizes the reality of an orality/literacy interrelationship.

Notes

1. "The Writer's Audience Is Always a Fiction," *Publications of the Modern Language Association*, 90 (1975), p. 9.

2. Ibid., p. 12.

3. Ibid.

4. Ibid., p. 11.

5. Ibid., p. 20.

6. *Orality and Literacy: The Technologizing of the Word* (London: Methuen, 1982). Hereafter OL.

7. *The Presence of the Word* (Minneapolis: Univ. of Minnesota, 1981).

8. *Rhetoric, Romance and Technology: Studies in the Interaction of Expression and Culture* (Ithaca: Cornell Univ., 1971). Hereafter RRT.

9. See Eric A. Havelock, *Preface to Plato* (Cambridge: Belknap, 1963), and Milman Parry, *The Making of Homeric Verse*, ed. Adam Parry (Oxford: Clarendon, 1971).

10. See Aleksandr Luria, *Cognitive Development: Its Cultural and Social Foundations*, trans. Martin Lopez-Morillas and Lynn Solotaroff, ed. Michael Cole (Cambridge: Harvard, 1976), and Bronislaw Malinowski, "The Problem of Meaning in Primitive Languages," in *The Meaning of Meaning: A Study of*

the Influence of Language upon Thought and of the Science of Symbolism, eds. C. K. Ogden and I. A. Richards (New York: Harcourt, Brace, 1923).

11. See Jack Goody, "Introduction," in *Literacy in Traditional Societies*, ed. Jack Goody (Cambridge: Cambridge Univ., 1968); Goody, *The Domestication of the Savage Mind* (Cambridge: Cambridge Univ., 1977); Wallace Chafe, "Integration and Involvement," in *Speaking, Writing, and Oral Literacy*, ed. Deborah Tannen (Norwood, N.J.: Ablex, 1982); and Deborah Tannen, "A Comparative Analysis of Oral Narrative Strategies: Athenian Greek and American English," in *The Pear Stories: Cultural, Cognitive, and Linguistic Aspects of Narrative Production*, ed. Wallace Chafe (Norwood, N.J.: Ablex, 1980).

12. See L. S. Vygotsky, *Thought and Language* (Cambridge: M.I.T., 1962).

13. See Marshall McLuhan and Quentin Flore, *The Medium Is the Massage* (New York: Bantam, 1967).

14. *Interfaces of the Word* (Ithaca: Cornell Univ., 1968). Hereafter IW.

15. Jean Piaget, *The Language and Thought of the Child* (New York: World, 1955).

16. Vygotsky, passim.

17. W. G. Perry, *Forms of Intellectual and Ethical Development in the College Years* (New York: Holt, Rinehart and Winston, 1970).

18. James Britton, et al., *The Development of Writing Abilities (11–18)* (London: Schools Council Project, 1975). Hereafter DWA.

19. Mike Rose, "Narrowing the Mind and Page: Remedial Writers and Cognitive Reductionism," *College Composition and Communication*, 39 (1988), p. 292.

9

Hayden White and the Kantian Discourse
Tropology, Narrative, and Freedom

Hans Kellner

> I will not apologize for this Kantian element in my thought,
> but I do not think that modern psychology, anthropology, or
> philosophy has improved upon it.
>
> Hayden White[1]

Beginning his career as a historian of the medieval Church, Hayden White (b. 1928) turned to reflection on the cultural significance of historical thought in the 1960s. In "The Burden of History,"[2] White noted that the traditional description of history as *both* an art and a science prevented it from confronting recent developments in either area and justified an antagonism to "theory," which was taken to be the mark of the truly historical mind. White's *Metahistory: The Historical Imagination in Nineteenth-Century Europe* (1973) attempted an ambitious schema of the "Poetics of History," describing four structures of emplotment, four argumentive models, and four ideological strategies. He added to this a fourth category of analysis, also comprising four modes — the theory of tropes. Adapted from Giambattista Vico and Kenneth Burke, the theory of tropes defines the "deep structural forms" of historical thought as the four literary figures of metaphor, metonymy, synecdoche, and irony, each possessing its characteristic means of organizing parts into wholes. White asserts that the vision of a given historian derives not from the evidence, since the vision decides in advance what shall constitute evidence, but rather from conscious and unconscious choices made among possibilities offered by the categories of his historical poetics. Thus, given a basic honesty and competence on the part of the historian studied, White finds no reason to prefer one account over another *on historical grounds alone*. The version of the past we choose depends on *moral and aesthetic* values which ground both the historian and his audience, and are beyond the call of historical evidence.

White has been influenced by existentialism's emphasis on freedom and responsibility in the world; his writings are based on the Kantian notion that the choices among forms of historical representation are in fact choices among possible futures. Structuralism has been a second influence on White's critical method, which typically assumes a mediating stance that strives to get "above" the question at hand in order to discern the system of thought that authorizes the terms of the debate. He sees the tropology described in *Metahistory* and in *Tropics of Discourse: Essays in Cultural Criticism* (1978) as a powerful tool for distinguishing modes of thought because it describes how discursive choices are *pre*figured by one dominant trope. Nevertheless, White does not claim that tropes are laws of discourse; they are instead "conventional" models in Western discourse.

Because the four tropes describe the logically possible part/whole relationships, tropology forms a basic component in the study of narrative, which fashions a unity from the diverse elements of language. In *The Content of the Form: Narrative Discourse and Historical Representation* (1987), White maintains that the decision to narrativize real events as history serves the ideological function of asserting the "beautiful," meaningful nature of the past (and present), and repressing any possible choice of encoding a "sublime," chaotic, terrifying meaninglessness as reality. This "de-sublimation" made possible the professionalization of nineteenth-century history by cutting its traditional ties to rhetoric, which emphasizes choices among possible forms of representation. Thus, history makes the past into an object of desire by giving it the same kind of coherence found in the story. In asking how a nonnarrative history is possible, White does not examine the analytic, socioeconomic history of recent decades (which he considers fundamentally narrative), but rather prenarrative forms—the medieval annals and chronicles. These forms could be replaced by proper historical narrative only when a sense of public order in the modern state prevailed, providing a "subject" for narrative representation. The "content" of the narrative "form" asserts the rationality of any social order dominated by centralized hierarchies and state power; the authority of narrative as a representation of "reality" depends upon its putative "realism" and its condemnation of all utopian choices as politically and artistically *un*realistic.

Although White believes that historical texts are an ideal place to study narrative realism because historians traditionally claim to represent reality itself rather than fictional simulacra, his inquiry into the ideology of narrative forms and his use of tropology extend to all narrative forms. White's work also serves as a warning to any criticism or would-be New Historicism that would ground readings of texts in given historical contexts. History cannot serve as a neutral, factual support for their interpretations, because it has the same hermeneutic foundations as other humanistic studies. Any image of a historical context is itself, taken as a whole, a prior interpretation chosen for a particular purpose and in no way less problematic than the literary text which constitutes its part.

If, as Hayden White often suggests, all of discourse is engaged in a struggle to claim for itself the title of "realistic," then the title of realist must be the one thing worth arguing about and fighting for; virtually all the "−isms" in politics, philosophy, and the arts are in fact nothing more than attempts to establish the reality of a certain vision of things.[3] Even self-professed Utopianism should never be seen as opposed to realism, but only as an alternate view of what may be seen as real. An established, authoritative, realism of almost any stripe is dangerous because of its power in modern culture to repress or marginalize other modes of discourse. To designate a discourse as "utopian" is the prerogative of the authoritarian discourse of realism; as an exercise of authority, it is a political act.[4] In a review of M. M. Bakhtin's *The Dialogic Imagination*, White interprets Bakhtin's work as "nothing less than a phenomenology of the lie on which every claim to authority is based."[5] Yet White is at pains to refute charges that this position is politically irresponsible and could easily engender a voluntaristic rebellion of Right or Left. Indentured to live in a post-industrial world in which power resides in the hands of faceless, decentered networks, we must accept the futility of revolution.[6] "In such a situation, the socially responsible interpreter can do two things: (1) expose the fictitious nature of any political program based upon an appeal to what 'history' supposedly teaches and (2) remain adamantly 'utopian' in the face of any criticism of political 'realism.'"[7]

If Diogenes is thus the implicit type of the "socially responsible interpreter," roaming about with a lantern, looking for an honest discourse, what might count as responsible discourse? Were the quest doomed in advance to eternal failure, White should share with Diogenes the title of Cynic. But this is not the case. Responsible discourse does exist in the form of a self-consciously rhetorical presentation, which assumes an ironic stance toward all forms of authority, including its own. Like Bakhtin and Foucault, White celebrates the responsibility of the "irresponsible" eruptive performance that violates the *doxa* by calling into question the formal grounds on which decisions of "realism" and "responsibility" are made. The carnivalesque or marginalized text reveals the artificiality of every human system of understanding.

White's definition of discourse requires special attention, because it functions in his usage quite differently from the binary Formalist discourse, which contrasts "discourse" with "story," and differently as well from Foucault's epistemic notion of discourse as a mode of power-as-knowledge, embodied in a discourse of madness, a discourse of illness, or a discourse of sex. White views discourse as a dynamic force that mediates between the preliminary and the final stages of linguistic process. Once a field of "data" has been described, the process of discourse engages, acting like a "shuttle" in order to commute between the phenomena and the argument or narrative that the phenomena have been chosen to serve. Thus conceived, discourse is what brings together in textual practice the description of things, and the meaning presented by its encoding in a text. If the descriptive sorting of the "clutter of phenomena" is the province of the classical *mimesis*, and the meaning embodied by the presentation as a whole the province of classical *diegesis*, then discourse occupies a third role, which White calls *diataxis*.[8] The important thing to note about White's "diatactical" definition of discourse is its dynamic function; discourse is always moving back and forth in its shuttle diplomacy.[9] It does not seem unreasonable to think of the ultimate chaos of data as a merely *natural* scatter of things, while the arguments and narrative forms from which one may pick in discourse are *culturally* preexistent molds which enable us both to encode reality as writers and to decode texts as readers. Discourse is the arbiter between the meaning-poor realm of nature and the meaning-saturated realm of culture.

This mediative, shuttle role that White assigns to discourse is remarkably similar to his description of the function of narrative in history. Narrative points in two directions (rather than shuttling): on the one hand toward the events, on the other, toward the chosen story type.[10] Narrative turns a chronicle of events into a proper story by calling the attention of the reader to the plot types supported by the culture. Once this plot type has been recognized, and its congruence with the events presented accepted, the history has been understood. A historical explanation has been produced.[11] If White views discourse as a shuttle diplomat, he is most clear about the protocols by which it effects its negotiations. These are the protocols of tropology, the centerpiece of White's idea of discourse. All "genuine discourse" operates at base like the figurative powers of language, ordering its field of data according to one of the tropic forms of organization, and, what is more, always aware of and making use of the other possibilities. Discourse is more tropical than logical, or rather, the elements of logic are tropological throughout.

In pointing repeatedly to the gap between reality and the discourse of reality on which authority inevitably rests, White returns to Immanuel Kant's distinction between a noumenal world of the "real per se" and the phenomenal world which we can know in our human way. White's analysis of discourse, particularly in its tropological dimension, suggests that this human way of knowing is precisely figurative, tropological. Like Vico, White sees logic and the forms of reason as subsequent to a poetic apprehension of the world, which is primal and probably inexplicable, because it is itself the source of any kind of human explanation.

> How could it be otherwise, when even the model of the syllogism itself displays clear evidence of troping? The move from the major premise (All men are mortal) to the *choice* of the datum to serve as the minor (Socrates is a man) is itself a tropological move, a 'swerve' from the universal to the particular which logic cannot preside over, since it is logic itself that is being served by this move. Every *applied* syllogism contains an enthymemic element, this element consisting of nothing but the *decision* to move from the plane of universal proposi-tions (themselves extended synecdoches) to that of singular existential statements (these being extended metonymies).[12]

As we shall see, it is characteristic of White's strategy that the words "choice" and "decision" are italicized in this passage. They are, quite simply, the key concepts in his entire philosophy of discourse. Linguistic performances of every sort are above all a series of choices regarding what shall count as real and good; any discourse that claims authority to exclude possible choices in these matters, especially on the basis of their formal eccentricity, should be treated as an occasion for laughter and unmasking. Genuine discourse ("as self-critical as it is critical of others") must challenge even its own authority. White's is an ironic formalism, skeptical of the rule-seeking inquiries of narratology, ana-lytical philosophy, and professionally sanctioned academic practice, which hope to define discourse as a "syntactical middle ground" working in a formally constrained way to mediate between a chaos of data and the existing forms of human comprehension. This middle ground, the space of discourse, is precisely the space of human *freedom*, not exactly natural or cultural, but rhetorical. Rhetoric is the realm of choice in language, and it is inextricably tied to the modes of choice, the tropes.

As laid out in *Metahistory*, the "theory of tropes" is but one of four levels of analysis deployed by White in reading the historical texts of the nineteenth century. Ideological and epistemological categories,

drawn from the work of Karl Mannheim and Stephen Pepper, describe
the social and logical dimensions of the texts, their links to political
power and philosophical authority. More literary is White's use of
Northrop Frye's modes of emplotment to map the narrative structures
inherent in any history. Each of these forms of analysis, within its own
province of knowledge, claims the privileged position of *depth*. To the
sociologist of knowledge (or the Marxist), the social (derived from
economic and technological relationships of power) underlies the visible,
ideological appearances of culture. The philosopher, on the other
hand, will look into any argument in order to discover whether the
rational strategies on which it is grounded are valid. To a formalist
critic, all discursive matters are built from an underlying skeleton of
plot options, which themselves embody visions of the world. These
foundational claims, in essence, establish what a sociological, philosophical, or literary approach, might be. To select any one of them as the
bottom line, so to speak, is to identify oneself and one's discourse.
Having described these strategies, enumerated the possible modes of
deployment for each, and suggested how he will use them in his own
reading, White rejects each of them as a foundation. It is tropology
that describes for him the "deep structure" of the historical text. The
base of historical thinking is tropological because tropology is the basis
of all thinking.

   White's contention that the poetic figures of speech or tropes offer
the best model for understanding the organizing powers of thought at
the most fundamental level available to discourse has been much
discussed; tropology in general has generated a vast and growing literature.[13] Metaphor is the model for the primary form of human apprehension, identifying something previously unknown out of the chaos of
phenomena by stating that it is *like* something already known. Metonymy
and synecdoche are both ways of relating parts to the wholes to which
they belong or are contiguous.[14] Following Kenneth Burke's discussion
of the "master tropes," White distinguishes metonymy from synecdoche
by a dynamic or functional definition, just as he defines discourse by a
dynamic definition: metonymy is a citation of the part for the whole
that *reduces* the latter to an aspect of the former, while synecdoche is a
citation of a part for the whole that *represents* the whole, thus characterized and essentialized by the part. Metonymy disperses the field
defined by a previous metaphorical recognition into strictly delineated
categories, and is the enabling procedure of the modern sciences.
Synecdoche unites and integrates into larger fields of comprehension,
particularly those of a symbolic or organic nature. Irony, the last term
in this foursome, is modeled on the logically abusive figures of speech,
catechresis and oxymoron. It reminds us self-consciously of the artificial, created nature of its three companion tropes; it points to "things"

uninterpreted, just as they are, and in so doing unmasks the figures that have represented things as a coherent field offering meaning. Irony always seems to say: "Back to the drawing-board!" And so does White.

The relations among the four master tropes are far from arbitrary. Metaphor and irony both deal with the relations of whole concepts, the former positively, by identifying one with another, the latter negatively, by denying the authority of any such metaphoric identification. Metonymy and synecdoche deal with parts and wholes, metonymy by dividing something into elements that may be manipulated and calculated according to law-governed formulas (as in the sciences), synecdoche by integrating these elements through the discovery of some essential, defining shared characteristic. Thus, metaphor and synecdoche act as integrative discursive protocols, while metonymy and irony disperse their fields. Viewed as a systematic whole, this tropology corresponds in certain ways to Kant's "Principles of Pure Understanding."[15]

In *Metahistory*, White used tropology as a master set of algorithms, an ultimate system of categorization. In discussing Marx, for instance, White presents a remarkable texture of woven categories that outline how Marx's analysis employs different discursive strategies to illuminate the different processes of historical development. In contrast to Kenneth Burke, who had characterized Marx's discourse as *mechanistic*, and hence *metonymic*, given to the deterministic operations of cause and effect, White stresses that Marx grasped and organized all the tropological modes of comprehension, and used them to create a powerful model, adequate to his theoretical goals.

> Burke's analysis is true enough as far as it goes, but it obscures the extent to which, in the *Manifesto* as elsewhere, Marx's thought moved simultaneously on two levels, by appeal to *both* Mechanistic and Organicist conceptions of reality, and utilized two fundamentally different linguistic protocols, Metonymical on the one hand and Synecdochic on the other. So, too, Marx emplotted the historical process in two modes, Tragic and Comic, simultaneously, and in such a way as to make the former emplotment a *phase* within the latter, and so as to permit himself to claim the title of a "realist" while sustaining his dream of a utopian reconciliation of man with man *beyond* the social state.[16]

Thus the world of the bourgeoisie is a tragic tale, governed by strict laws, the cause-and-effect determined by metonymic part/whole relationships; within this historical cosmos develops the proletariat, which will ultimately turn the tragedy of history into a moment in a larger comedy by reconciling the parts of society in a synecdochic classless world by recognizing and realizing the essential humanity within everyone.

Despite its ostensible origin in Giambattista Vico's *The New Science* and numerous features derived from current literary theorists, this system of tropes is White's creation. He may claim that it has been "customary" since the Renaissance and frequently "reinvented" by Western thinkers, but never with the scope he claims for it. Tropology offers White a typology of conceptual strategies so basic as to be a plausible bedrock (or "deep structure") so long sought by modern thinkers in the mold of Marx, Freud, and Lévi-Strauss, and at the same time so protean as to make an unending series of appearances at every level of discourse. It defines the levels of language itself, if we choose to see metaphor as the initial process of naming, metonymy as the process of grammatical distinctions, synecdoche as the form of syntax and its agreements, and irony as the interpretive work of semantics. Moreover, through a remarkable set of correspondences, which White calls "elective affinities," the four tropes reveal the ideological, epistemological, and literary manifestations toward which they "naturally" gravitate, but do not by any means preordain. Indeed, it seems clear that the plot forms (metonymy as tragic, for example) or "world hypotheses" (as in the organicism of synecdoche) reciprocally influenced White's vision of the tropes.[17]

This point is well taken. White tends to describe discourse in which the "affinities" match as "doctrinaire"; for example, a "metonymically" conceived discourse would have a mechanistic and hence tragic vision, suitable to a radical ideology. Marx, however, unlike the doctrinaire Marxist, conceived only the material base as a tragic realm of necessity; history he envisions as a comic, even farcical, play of illusions. His discourse is, consequently, heavily ironic, which is to say, dialectical (*Metahistory* 285–89). The question of the "elective affinities" points to the embarrassing problem that the tropes, however often they are called conventional or customary, look very much like a mental structure, a natural part of human cognition. In more recent work, White, eager to sidestep any taint of presupposing a tropological law of discourse, speaks only of an "interesting quaternary pattern."[18] Yet most explorations of White's tropology have abandoned its ideological, epistemological, and literary counterparts altogether, seeking instead, and finding in abundance, works of history, fiction, philosophy, psychology, etc., that follow the course of the four tropes, one after the other, as a comprehensive model of knowledge.

Another issue arising from White's decision to employ a four-trope model with a strong diachronic pull, as each trope seems to imply the next, is the clear, irreducible conflict with the binary tropology dominant in structuralist circles, and used by such figures as Roman Jakobson and Claude Lévi-Strauss, both of whom have importantly informed White's work. For many structuralists, binarism *is* structuralism, and metaphor/metonymy (or resemblance and contiguity) are the

essence of all formal relationships. White, however, finds this a desic-
cated structuralism, preferring that aspect of the structuralist venture
which seeks to plot out the possible modes of any system. Here, the
four-trope curriculum, which he finds implicitly at work in Foucault,
Lévi-Strauss, and Piaget, comes into play, but always as a mode of
reading (or allegory), rather than as a mode of thought (or structure).

The essays contained in *The Content of the Form* represent an
attempt on White's part to shore up an essential aspect of the view put
forth in *Metahistory* and *Tropics of Discourse* that the nature of things
is chaos and that any dogmatic statement about the world finds no
natural justification in things as they actually are (to use a historical-
sounding phrase). Part of the scandal of White's thought is that he
wants to suggest (but never does) that every statement about the world
of human beings may be "essentially contested," finally resolvable by
no form of discussion, but rather endlessly open to dispute among
rational points of view based upon supportable arguments and ample
evidence.

It is essential to White's view of the ethical thrust of narrative that
it be presented as simply a conventional and not in any way a natural
form of human experience. Thus, he asserts repeatedly that we do not
experience our lives in narrative form because real events do not
present themselves in the form of a story. "No one and nothing *lives* a
story."[19] In other words, the field of occurrences in our lives is fundamentally as formless as the field of historical traces confronted by
the historian. All consciousness of identity, direction, purposefulness,
and meaning in human existence is basically a narrative construction
built with socially available blueprints. To say that "real events" do not
take the form of a story, as White sometimes does,[20] implies that
reality is composed of "events," but White so vehemently denies that
these events have any given meaning until they are defined, bounded
and set in a narrative that they virtually disappear as entities. "Reality,"
he suggests, is a pure, absurd flux; at the very least, one should never
rule out the possibility that this is the case.[21]

White is at pains to demonstrate in *The Content of the Form* that
human history and human consciousness show no continuity with one
another. Within the Western tradition there are epochs without history,
in which "lower," prenarrative forms such as the annals and the
chronicle prevailed, yet these lengthy periods are not taken to be
evidence of a lack of human purpose or intentional activity. Within the
modern era of historical culture, the notion that historical writing is in
any way yoked to historical experience (as a narrative form analogous
to human experience) is everywhere disproved. Histories may mock
the folly of human intentions which bring on the opposite of their
goals, or treat them as pathetic illusions, to be given meaning only by a

comprehension of the intention of the historical process itself, apart from human purpose; in the former case, Tocqueville, in the latter case, Hegel and Marx, come to mind. In both cases, and in many more recent examples such as Fernand Braudel, the historical subject is depicted as living in a world of illusion brought on by the deceptions wrought by cultural patterns of self-understanding. History "itself" has nothing to do with these.

White, however, can point to a certain moment in history when a contemplation of the nonstoried and meaningless essence of things was possible. This was the Western Middle Ages, when the ancient art of historiography virtually died out, to be replaced by other written ways of recording time, ways notable mainly for their nonnarrative form. In a world in which the cyclical pattern of nature and its seasons dominated the lives of men and women in a rural world without a social center, the events were noted by date after the Incarnation but in a form that testified to the sequence of years whose fullness is meaningful only to the divine plan.[22] White's strategy in selecting actual medieval annals and chronicles as his counterparts to the fully narrativized discourse of later times, as opposed to oral tradition studied by anthropologists or the usual elementary and artificial examples beloved of analytic philosophers, enables him to accomplish several things. First, he asserts that even the most random notation of discontinuous and unrelated happenings is not without meaning, but merely without *human* meaning. Second, he maintains that it is the creation of a state as the center of social focus that makes a narrative of events possible by manufacturing a hero, as it were, for such a narrative, and displacing meaningful comprehension from God's plan to human plans. Finally, he suggests that narrative as a form not only follows from but also reinforces the authority embodied by the state, acting as a sort of ideological state apparatus, as Louis Althusser might have put it. It is not that the culture gives us literary forms that we use retrospectively to narrativize our existence, but social existence which demands narrativization once a consciousness of the state as an actor arises. Since the state is an artificial creation, narrative consciousness is hardly a part of our natural being. However, the phenomenologist's notion that any human action requires a sense of the world that is narrative in essence also suggests that this action is precultural, based upon a sense of meaning and intention that are not informed by social or cultural models. Such actions there may be, but it seems wrong to call them specifically human actions.

Having noticed that the question of whether human pragmatic narrativization depends upon the initially variously describable conditions of human reality, we further remark a notable contrast between the goal of a realistic discourse encapsulated in the phrase "as it actually was" by the nineteenth-century German historian Leopold von Ranke, and on the other hand the assertion of the unknowability of the "Things-in-Themselves" of Immanuel Kant. This rather stark opposition is in many respects the same one existing today as modern versus postmodern. The discourse of modernism sees *through* its modes of representation to the phenomena themselves, grasping them more or less absolutely (at least this is the goal) after the manner of the physical sciences, and demoting narrative forms of knowledge as invariably secondary to the realities they represent. The postmodern condition, however, always takes ironic note of the constitutive capacities of its focal aids, the metanarratives of history, society, and culture, with which we are obligated to live in the world.[23]

White's reading of Kant takes as its point of departure the philosopher's late reflections on history, rather than any of the three prior *Critiques*. According to Kant, historical reflection could take one of three forms: the historical process could be seen either as one of continual progress (eudaemonism), continual decline (terrorism), or as neither one, but instead a directionless flux. This last position Kant calls *abderitic*, after the school of Greek philosophers from Abdera. White prefers the term "farcical," calling to mind Marx's famous misquotation of Hegel.[24] For Kant, this last form of thought, the abderitic or farcical, derives from any conception of the past which sees it as an occasion for interest or human persuasion, that is to say, for rhetoric. Such a notion of history, prevalent in the eighteenth century, offended Kant above all on moral grounds, because it entailed a conception of human reality that was essentially chaotic, making either no sense or any number of different senses. Consequently, he concluded, history must be derhetoricized and disciplined, as it would in fact become in the following century. To avoid the moral chaos found in ironic Enlightenment historiography, historical discourse must become *disinterested*. This repressive triumph of intellect over will was, White suggests, the basis of Nietzsche's attacks on Kantian and Schopenhauerian aesthetics and the historical practice of his day.[25]

White, however, turns Nietzsche's view of Kant on its head, using Kant's philosophy of faculties to contradict his horror at rhetoric. White believes that "the aged Kant was right," not in rejecting rhetoric on moral grounds, but in *understanding that the grounds for rejecting rhetoric were moral grounds*.[26]

> Kant's distinctions among the emotions, the will, and the reason are not very popular in this, an age which has lost its belief in the will and represses its sense of the moral implications of the mode of rationality that it favors. But the moral implications of the human sciences will never be perceived until the faculty of the will is reinstated in theory.[27]

Kant's error, apparently, was his failure to recognize that his own position depended upon the freedom of the will that White views as the realm of rhetoric alone. To escape irony, one need only *will* to do so, as Kant, for example, did.[28] However much White may dislike Kant's role in the derhetoricization of history, he must celebrate the voluntarism which enabled Kant's move. What was for Nietzsche a triumph of intellect over will, is for White a triumph of will over intellect, a moral decision, like it or not, brought on for Kant by reflection on the French Revolution and the work of a younger generation represented by Herder.[29]

The apperception of chaos, the fundamentally nonnarrative nature of natural and human reality, was the occasion of the eighteenth century's rediscovery of the sublime, which is thus a historiographic concept as much as an aesthetic one. To elevate the beautiful over the sublime as a model of ethical discourse is to turn away from the chaotic nature of reality in favor of an idea of order. Certainly, the phenomenological championing of a narrative sense of human life, however limited, is an attempt in this direction.[30] Interest in the beautiful, Kant insisted in the third Critique, is the work of a good soul, a characteristic of sociability; and White maintains that the nineteenth-century professionalization of history as a narrative ordering, and hence philosophical beautification, of human events, was aimed at the production of good citizens, willing participants in the social world surrounding them.

> This is not because it may deal with patriotism, nationalism, or explicit moralizing but because in its featuring of narrativity as a favored representational practice, it is especially well suited to the production of notions of continuity, wholeness, closure, and individuality that every "civilized" society wishes to see itself as incarnating, against the chaos of a merely natural way of life.[31]

Awareness of the "chaos of a merely natural way of life," espoused by both Lévi-Strauss and Foucault, is the remythicization of the world, accepting all forms of order as allegorical.[32]

Having been frequently accused himself of radical skepticism, cultural pessimism, nihilism, and the like, White nevertheless comments on the note of sadness in structuralism, which knows too much. Because everything in culture disappoints those who can unfailingly identify the fictional and semiotic essence of it, the game is over in advance, all *"tropiques"* seem *"tristes."*[33] Deconstruction is "absurdist" for this reason. In believing he has transcended the structuralist problematic, Jacques Derrida has simply made it into a fetish. The problem of how to avoid becoming entrapped in the toils of one's system, especially a system as powerful and all-encompassing as tropology, is a difficult one. White's voluntaristic solution is not always convincing, as he seems to know, suggesting that an element of "as if" is to be taken for granted. The relativism implied by any tropological sense of discourse, the vigilant consciousness of alternative points of views and a sensitivity to the fictional nature of one's own discourse, implies on the face of it a paralysis, a loss of nerve of the sort that White found blameworthy in his treatment of Jakob Burckhardt and Friedrich Nietzsche. Burckhardt's irony saw only the fragmented nature of social reality, so his treatment of the past devalued the sense of plot and elevated instead theme. Nothing developed, and Burckhardt was ultimately left with a language about language, a vision of history cleansed of metaphor and based upon simple *being* as expressed in direct declarative sentences. White adds in apparent self-contradiction: "And this anti-Metaphorical attitude is the quintessence of every Ironist's attitude."[34] Nietzsche, unlike his friend and former colleague Burckhardt, rejected all forms of historical consciousness that were *not* fundamentally metaphoric, but this demolition of the fundamental underpinnings of historical semantics in metonymy and synecdoche left him with a past that was "only an occasion for his invention of ingenious 'melodies.'"[35] The effect was to break the bond that holds men together in a common enterprise, just as Burckhardt already both assumed and prophesied the dissolution of cultural bonds.

Such cultural pessimism is not White's. He often denies that the relativism of *his* irony has anything to do with that of the pessimists, or with that of their Enlightenment forebears. Awareness of the figurative, tropological dimensions of all discourse is rather a way out of the dilemmas of historical relativism and the social pessimism engendered by it.

> Because it is a theory of *linguistic* determinism, we can envision a means of translating from one mode of discourse to another, in the same way that we translate from one language to another. This way of conceptualizing this problem of relativism is superior to that which grounds point of view in epoch, place, or ideological allegiance, because we can imagine no way of translating between these, while we can imagine ways of translating between different language codes.[36]

White consistently views linguistic analysis as a higher form of social criticism, always leading to a humanistic tolerance. He sees the Renaissance, for example, as primarily a linguistic purification through analysis of the strangulated world of scholastic discourse. Lorenzo Valla is the model humanist, ushering in a new "culture of criticism." Thus, Vico's philosophy of the rise and fall of cultures, and their close resemblance to the forms of linguistic tropes, is associated with the "higher" Erasmian irony, which views folly, represented here by the figurative understanding, with its poeticization of the world, as dialectically related to reason and responsibility, indeed the base upon which they may be built.[37]

As I have suggested, White has noted a contradiction in Kant's vision of history, and found it a fruitful one. His glance at Kant's late writings on history clarifies the problems brought forth by Frank Lentricchia, who finds that Kant's isolation of the aesthetic idea by an ahistorical subject results in "mere isolation," while artistic practice itself for Kant always deals with a content, "remolding" rather than "molding" the world of phenomena. Thus, Lentricchia maintains, neo-Kantian adherents of "conservative fictionalism" have missed the point, failing to notice that Kant has "trivialized" art by isolating the aesthetic idea. Realism sneaks in the back door, as it were, but it is an impoverished realism.[38] For Lentricchia, the point of this lesson is to view literary discourse in constant engagement with social and political discourses so that the "necessary historicity of literature" is never forgotten.[39] History, however, is not quite a discourse for Lentricchia, not open to meanings in quite the same way that literature is; it is not an aesthetic object. Rather, it assumes precisely the privileged status that White rejects. Remember: for White, all ideological disputes are disputes over Realism, not reality. To invoke history is to invoke the many possibilities of realistic understandings, possibilities which are not fundamentally different from those of literary understanding, and never prior to them. White's Foucault, who systematically displays the tropological possibilities in each of his historical accounts, is not Lentricchia's Foucault, who seems almost a historical determinist of the oldest sort; if White's Kant is similar to Lentricchia's, he has nevertheless chosen to draw quite a different conclusion. The disinterested, derhetoricized idea of history that Kant found morally necessary is equally necessary to Lentricchia's project.[40] Kant, according to White, chose a progressive and rational view of history as a grand illusion to make men struggle and suffer life nobly. Without the hope of such a positive outcome, men would despair and fail to effect the difficult and painful tasks that were necessary to create a human meaning amidst the chaos of things.[41] To suggest that one's vision of history depends on what kind of person you are, as Kant did, cuts two ways. On the one hand, it places the burden of historical discourse on the historian or reader of history; indeed, it almost mandates that positive view of the process that Hegel and Marx would later assume. On the other, it leaves the element of will in plain sight, to be taken up by Schopenhauer and Nietzsche, who found the positive, beautified, vision of nineteenth-century historical thought and the authoritative realism it engendered culturally nauseating.

White insists that the chronicle of historical facts consists of culturally meaningless phenomena (except in the purely formal sense that the chronicle form itself bespeaks a certain type of social consciousness), and that the linguistic protocols of tropology are a set of aesthetic ideas that act upon the phenomena to produce history. To be sure, they are "empty" forms without the chronicled materials to fill them, rather like the empty list of years which the annalist of St. Gall would fill with the most inchoate series of happenings, meaningful, White suggests, only to the Power who has created the fullness of time. Although he will often make reference to conventional historical "causes" like the French Revolution or the influence of Herder, he must always note that an event thus explained—in this example, Kant's late reflection on history—could have been discussed in many different ways. Paradoxically, history cannot explain history, if the former is a series of documented phenomena, and the latter is a discourse of various stories drawn from it.

Most historical and philosophical opposition to White has failed to address this crucial point: *the chronicle as such is not historical.* To state that the fact is meaningless without interpretation is by no means a radical assertion in historical theory; the extreme positivist position by which the facts can speak for themselves has always been more theoretical than actual. It is difficult to point to anyone who effectively holds this position today, or who ever put it into consistent practice. White's intervention here is to define and isolate the role of discourse, as a shuttle, running back and forth between chronicle (already prefigured in its constitution, to be sure, by tropological protocols used in selecting materials to make up the *relevant* chronicle) and history. History proper presents the material under such a form that it can be understood as a culturally recognizable kind of tale; only when this plot form has been tacitly recognized by the reader has a "historical explanation" been achieved. Thus, when White writes: "Our knowledge of the past may increase incrementally, but our understanding of it does not," he is simply distinguishing between the functions of the chronicling of past events and historical discourse proper.[42] Historians turn facts into fictions precisely by being historians, both in the most professional and academic mode supported by any given culture or in an alternate, nonstandard mode that challenges the presuppositions of the trade.

And so, in writing "Our knowledge of the past may increase incrementally, but our understanding of it does not,"[43] White is by no means denying the usefulness of the historical enterprise, but rather stating that "knowledge of the past," characterized by validated facts in the cultural record and embodied in "archival reports," adds nothing to *historical* understanding. The purpose of historical discourse, far from arriving at a single vision of the past, is to generate as many such visions as are possible within the mythic compass of a given culture. "History-writing thrives on the discovery of all the possible plot structures that might be invoked to endow sets of events with different meanings."[44] The progress that might result from this historical invention (in the rhetorical sense of finding all strategies available to a given discourse) is a progress in historical understanding. Thus conceived, the purpose of the writing of history is to sound out the ability of a culture to encode real events with the meanings offered to it by its inherited and developing literary forms. In assuming a historical meaning, reality takes on an imaginary form, the form of an allegory.[45]

> And if the tropes of language are limited, if the types of figuration are finite, then it is possible to imagine how our representations of the historical world aggregate into a comprehensive total vision of that world, and how progress in our understanding of it is possible. Each new representation of the past represents a further testing and refinement of our capacities to figure the world in language, so that each new generation is heir, not only to more information about the past, but also to more adequate knowledge of our capacities to comprehend it.[46]

This echoes White's discovery that Michel Foucault had envisioned his "world without man," not from a reasoned observation of the state of things in his day, but rather through his understanding of the figural possibilities left unfulfilled by his tropological account of the course of Western thought. The comprehensiveness of his vision in *The Order of Things* is an attribute of his cultural inheritance, far more than of his knowledge of the past.[47] Foucault's critics will look in vain for information that will disprove his vision; what they must offer is a vision of their own. Historical discourse and historical understanding are the cultural proving grounds for the mythic power of a culture.

With the question of "more adequate knowledge of our capacities to comprehend," we again confront Kant, this time on the ground of practical reason, with historical thought serving as a moral test of our faculties. And with the question of myth we stand again at the uncertain borderline between the modern and the postmodern.[48] Certainly the project of modernism in all its garbs was to demystify those aspects of the world which claimed some sort of hegemony over human reason; it is hardly surprising that reason and art themselves fell prey to the demystifying discourse of modernism. The structuralist desire of Lévi-Strauss and Foucault is to demystify culture and its authoritarian discourses of power (of which official historical thought has become a major example), in favor of a disordering of the world so that it may reappear as it actually is before representations — "a plenum of *mere* things, no one of which can lay claim to privileged status with respect to any other."[49] In such a world myths again can live and contend, unashamed. At the same time, the mythic form inherent in all narrative, especially through plot, is the basis on which "dominant social groups" build and promote their version of reality.[50] It is only through narrative, that is to say, through *mythos*, that the world can be made to seem livable.

Like White, Jean-Francois Lyotard suggests that the postmodern attitude toward a decentralized world of capital and communications, in which foci of power cannot be located and revolution is neither possible nor desirable as a form of resistance, is another dispute about realism. Yet if ideology, as White presents it, is always a dispute to win the authority to present the Real, then the modern world, instead, asserts what Lyotard calls the unreality of reality.[51] This loss of reality, which was heralded by the decline of academic art and the rise of mass reproduction of images, makes any sense of reality either nostalgic or parodic, hardly a source of reassurance about the world. Although Walter Benjamin, and before him Friedrich Nietzsche, described the consequences of this unreality of reality, it is to Kant again that we must go to find the concept that defines it. In the *sublime* Kant saw a true conflict of the faculties that arises when the imagination cannot present an object that matches what we are capable of conceiving, the unpresentable. Modern art that destroys all faith in realistic representation is incomprehensible without this Kantian idea of the "incommensurability of reality and concept."[52] With a striking similarity to Stendhal's statement that all Classic art was Romantic in its own day, Lyotard suggests that all modern art was first *post*modern, that postmodernism is modernism in its nascent stage.[53] In a phrase reminiscent of the French Romantic debate about Shakespeare's romanticism, Lyotard notes that the postmodern artist is working without rules, is making up the rules, so as to establish "the rules of *what will have been done*."[54] The word itself expresses "the paradox of the future (*post*) anterior (*modo*)." Lyotard concludes:

> Finally, it must be clear that our business is not to supply reality but to invent allusions to the conceivable which cannot be presented. And it is not to be expected that this task will effect the last reconciliation between language games (which, under the name of the faculties, Kant knew to be separated by a chasm), and that only the transcendental illusion (that of Hegel) can hope to totalize them into a real unity. But Kant also knew that the price to pay for such an illusion is terror. The nineteenth and twentieth centuries have given us as much terror as we can take. We have paid a high enough price for the nostalgia of the whole and the one, for the reconciliation of the concept and the sensible, of the transparent and the communicable experience.[55]

For White the essential "unpresentable" is historical reality, that is unpresentable not because of any failure of representation itself, nor even because we humans do not *live* immediately meaningful, storied, lives, but rather because it is possible that the chaos of the historical record is more than a surface phenomenon in need of historical beautification through narrative. To rob history of the possibility of its meaninglessness, as all ideologies do in their arguments over what is Real, is to domesticate mankind and deprive it of a sense of self-responsibility. "In my view, the theorists of the sublime had correctly divined that whatever dignity and freedom human beings could lay claim to could come only by way of what Freud called a 'reaction-formation' to an appreciation of history's meaninglessness."[56]

White always castigates approaches to human understanding that base their authority on a deeper source of knowledge, a scientific discourse of truth. The anthropologies of Lévi-Strauss or Rene Girard, for example, or Fredric Jameson's Marxism, fail in White's view at the moment when they appeal to the authority of their own discourse of the Real. This is not at all to say that White is antistructuralist, or anti-Marxist; it is rather their claims to reality that he distrusts. There may be very good reasons for holding many beliefs, but White will not grant that any but the most trivial can be proven true, for this would require a deeper discourse of authority. Yet because the humanities have fragmented and diverged so widely from an earlier rhetorical center, any research can proceed only on the prior assumption that in at least one area of study, a firm bedrock of undisputed discourse exists.[57] This, however, is not the case.

> If intellectual history, which takes as its special subject matter the ideas, *mentalités*, thought systems, systems of values and ideals of particular societies in the past, simply treats these as data that reflect processes in some way more "basic" (such as economic, social, political, or even psychological processes), then intellectual history is super-erogatory in relation to the historical reconstruction of these other processes, for in that case it can only double accounts given by specialists in these other fields of study, tell the same story, with slightly different material and in a slightly different register, as the story told about these other fields.[58]

Historians, and by implication all discourses of human affairs, reach eternally for a master discourse on which to found the authority of their stories, but they are united in only one thing, the exclusion of the possibility that history's proper place in the human sciences rests upon its status as "the very type of a cognitively responsible art."[59] As an art, historical discourse tests the ability of its culture to create visions of the past, each of which, Kant maintained, was a vision and choice of a possible future.

Kant's late writings on history and politics are little known, even among historians. Their relation to the three Critiques is not always clear, nor is White's professed Kantianism. However, if Claudia Brodsky is correct, Kant is the quintessential philosopher of narrative, establishing in the first Critique the formal presuppositions of narratology; cognitive representation is narrative representation.[60] It is the third Critique that addresses the question of what a nonrepresentational cognition could be like, or how it could be known. In Kant's terms, like those of the structuralists who sought to show the world as mere uninterpreted things, it is a question of understanding only what pertains to a word, divorced from any significance as experience.[61] Here practical reason intervenes:

> Kant's critical theory of cognition, it has been argued, describes cognition in the form of narration. As stipulated in the *Logic*, the single object of real, rather than nominal, narrative knowledge would be the means of narration, words themselves. Finally, our knowledge of reality in coherent, narrative form rests upon the necessity of our knowing the single individual word deduced in the *Second Critique* to mean the absence of all causal and nominal narrative relations: "freedom."[62]

In the twelfth century, students began to clamor to be taught logic at the expense of rhetoric; that same seductive rhetoric that had been denounced for centuries by the Church Fathers had lost its charm and had been replaced as an object of desire by the dry antieroticism of the syllogism. Why? Richard Southern has plausibly suggested that this new curricular turn was an expression of a medieval humanism, a need to focus on an image of order and control in a world arising from chaos.[63] In other words, logic gave the young scholars a renewed sense of freedom, the freedom to grasp the order of things. For Hayden White, the order of things, which everywhere enforces its "realism" and expertise against dreams of a different future and a different past, is too much with us. The authorities hold all the cards. Rhetoric is the battleground of a discourse which is responsive to such a condition, a discourse which has not been co-opted by success and its ability to define what is irresponsible.

Notes

1. *Tropics of Discourse: Essays in Cultural Criticism* (Baltimore: Johns Hopkins Univ., 1978), p. 22.

2. In *History and Theory*, 5 (1966); collected in *Tropics of Discourse*, pp. 27–50.

3. *Metahistory: The Historical Imagination in Nineteenth-Century Europe* (Baltimore & London: Johns Hopkins Univ., 1973), p. 46.

4. *The Content of the Form: Narrative Discourse and Historical Representation* (Baltimore: Johns Hopkins Univ., 1987), pp. 58–82.

5. "The Authoritative Lie," *Partisan Review*, 50 (1983), p. 312.

6. *Tropics of Discourse*, p. 264.

7. *The Content of the Form*, p. 227.

8. *The Content of the Form*, p. 4.

9. The word *diatactic* is no neologism. It traditionally referred to the ecclesiastical power of ordering and arrangement; the diatactical is contrasted with the critical and dogmatical as the three jurisdictions of church assemblies. Cf. "Diatactical," in *The Compact Edition of the Oxford English Dictionary* (Oxford: Oxford Univ., 1971), p. 718.

10. *Tropics of Discourse*, pp. 88, 106.

11. *The Content of the Form*, p. 43.

12. *Tropics of Discourse*, p. 3.

13. Discussions of White's tropology are found in Hans Kellner, *Language and Historical Representation: Getting the Story Crooked* (Madison: Univ. of Wisconsin, 1989), pp. 189–264; in James M. Mellard's *Doing Tropology: Analysis of Narrative Discourse* (Champagne: Univ. of Illinois, 1987). The thrust of both of these works is a discussion of how a four-trope system may function as a cognitive narrative structure, moving discourse forward from initial apprehension and definition to final afterthoughts and denial.

14. White credits the literary theorist Geoffrey Hartman with indicating that these two tropes are the only way of relating parts and wholes in language. *Tropics of Discourse*, p. 94.

15. This correspondence is discussed at greater length in Kellner, *Language and Historical Representation: Getting the Story Crooked*, pp. 242–51.

16. *Metahistory*, p. 310.

17. John S. Nelson has noted the undeveloped nature of the "elective affinities" in *Metahistory*. He writes: "Without a direct treatment of that concept, we seem to be left in a peculiar position where particular works which fit White's patterns do so because of elective affinity, but those which fail to fit do so because of the creative genius of their authors, who incline toward misaffinities for their 'creative tension' among levels of style." See "Tropal History and the Social Sciences," in *Metahistory: Six Critiques, History and Theory, Beiheft*, 19 (1980), p. 94.

18. *Tropics of Discourse*, p. 70.

19. *Tropics of Discourse*, p. 111.

20. *The Content of the Form*, p. 4.

21. *The Content of the Form*, p. 82.

22. *The Content of the Form*, p. 8.

23. This description of the modernism/postmodernism debate follows the work of Timothy Reiss, *The Discourse of Modernism* (Ithaca: Cornell Univ., 1982), and Jean-Francois Lyotard, *The Postmodern Condition: A Report*

on Knowledge, trans. G. Bennington & B. Massumi (Minneapolis: Univ. of Minnesota, 1984). A broader consideration of recent philosophical turns is Philip Lewis, "The Post-Structuralist Condition," *Diacritics*, 12 (Spring 1982).

24. *The Content of the Form*, p. 65.

25. *Metahistory*, pp. 368–70.

26. *Metahistory*, p. 433.

27. *Tropics of Discourse*, p. 23.

28. *Metahistory*, pp. 433–4.

29. *Metahistory*, p. 56.

30. Paul Ricoeur's work is a prime example of this.

31. *The Content of the Form*, p. 87.

32. Cf. Paul Smith, "The Will to Allegory in Postmodernism," *Dalhousie Review*, 62 (1982), pp. 105–22.

33. *Tropics of Discourse*, p. 278.

34. *Metahistory*, p. 260

35. *Metahistory*, p. 372.

36. *Tropics of Discourse*, p. 117.

37. *Tropics of Discourse*, p. 216.

38. Frank Lentricchia, *After the New Criticism* (Chicago: Univ. of Chicago, 1980), pp. 39–44.

39. Lentricchia, p. 351.

40. See Lentricchia's highly determined vision of history in *Ariel and the Police* (Madison: Univ. of Wisconsin, 1988).

41. *Metahistory*, pp. 57–58.

42. *Tropics of Discourse*, p. 89.

43. *Tropics of Discourse*, p. 89.

44. *Tropics of Discourse*, p. 92.

45. *The Content of the Form*, p. 45.

46. *Tropics of Discourse*, p. 118.

47. *Tropics of Discourse*, ch. 11.

48. We should note that these distinctions, like all historical periods or stylistic terms, are drawn for a purpose, and may be justly questioned by someone with another purpose. As Paul de Man said: "The difficulty for me is that the 'postmodern approach' seems a somewhat naively historicist approach. The notion of modernity is already very dubious; the notion of postmodernity becomes a parody of the notion of modernity." Stephano Rosso, "An Interview with Paul de Man," *Critical Inquiry*, 12 (Summer 1986), p. 793.

49. *Tropics of Discourse*, p. 250.

50. *The Content of the Form*, p. x.

51. Lyotard, p. 77.

52. Lyotard, p. 79.

53. The Stendhal quotation, "All great writers were romantics in their own day," is from *Racine and Shakespeare* (1823); cited in *The Romantic Reader*, ed. H. Hugo. (New York: Viking, 1957), p. 60.

54. Lyotard, p. 81.

55. Lyotard, pp. 81–82.

56. *The Content of the Form*, p. 72.

57. "Historical Pluralism," p. 484.

58. *The Content of the Form*, p. 209.

59. "The Historian at the Bridge of Sighs," *Reviews in European History*, 1:4 (1975), p. 445.

60. Claudia J. Brodsky, *The Imposition of Form: Studies in Narrative Representation and Knowledge* (Princeton: Princeton Univ., 1987), p. 24. It should be added here that Kant makes heavy use of tropologically informed models in the *Critique of Pure Reason*. Cf. Kellner, *Language and Historical Representation: Getting the Story Crooked*, pp. 228–64.

61. Brodsky, p. 52.

62. Brodsky, p. 86.

63. See the discussion in Nancy F. Partner's "The New Cornificius: Medieval History and the Artifice of Words," in *Classical Rhetoric and Medieval Historiography*, ed. by E. Breisach, (Kalamazoo: Western Michigan Univ., 1985), pp. 5–60.

Contributors

Joseph J. Comprone, Professor and Head of the Department of Humanities, Michigan Technical Institute, has published four college composition textbooks and written numerous articles on composition theory, theories of literacy, literary theory, and film. He is currently working on a book on Kenneth Burke and a collection of essays on writers who combine literary and scientific genres in their work.

Mara Holt, Assistant Professor of English, Ohio University, has written articles on the role of pragmatism in histories of rhetoric and writing instruction.

David Ingram, Associate Professor of Philosophy, Loyola University of Chicago, has written *Habermas and the Dialectic of Reason* (Yale University Press, 1987) and *Critical Theory and Philosophy* (Paragon House, 1990) and edited *Critical Theory: The Essential Readings* (Paragon House, 1990). He has also published numerous articles on social and political philosophy and continental philosophy from Kant to the present.

Hans Kellner, Professor of History and Comparative Literature, Michigan State University, wrote *Language and Historical Representation: Getting the Story Crooked* (University of Wisconsin Press, 1989). He is also the author of numerous articles on historical discourse.

Michael Kleine, Associate Professor of English, University of Arkansas at Little Rock, has written on rhetorical theory, discourse analysis, and ethnographic approaches to the study of writing. His current work concerns the role of metaphor in virological discourse.

Charles I. Schuster, Associate Professor of English and Director of the Undergraduate and Graduate Writing Programs, University of Wisconsin at Milwaukee, is the general editor of *The Politics of Writing Instruction* (Boynton/Cook-Heinemann, 1991). He has also written numerous articles on composition and discourse theory.

Michael H. Shank, Associate Professor of the History of Science at the University of Wisconsin−Madison, is the author of *"Unless you Believe, You Shall Not Understand": Logic, University and Society in Late Medieval Vienna* (Princeton University Press, 1988). Although his research focuses on medieval natural philosophy, he retains an abiding interest in recent philosophy of science.

Peter Skagestad, Lecturer in Philosophy, University of Lowell, Massachusetts, wrote *Making Sense of History: the Philosophies of Popper and Collingwood* (Oslo, 1975) and *The Road of Inquiry: Charles Peirce's Pragmatic Realism*

(Columbia University Press, 1981). He is also the author of numerous articles on the philosophy of Charles Saunders Peirce.

John Trimbur, Associate Professor of English, Worcester Polytechnic Institute, has published a number of articles on collaborative learning, writing theory, and cultural studies. He has coedited *the Politics of Writing Instruction* (Boynton/ Cook-Heinemann, 1991) and is working on a composition textbook with Diana George.

David Vampola is completing a dissertation at the University of Pittsburgh on the changing and persisting characteristics of the German professoriate from 1860 to 1938. He is also working on the social and institutional foundations of German philosophy in the nineteenth and twentieth centuries.

Lambert Zuidervaart, Professor of Philosophy and Chair of the Philosophy Department, Calvin College, has written *Adorno's Aesthetic Theory: The Redemption of Illusion* (MIT Press, 1991) and coauthored *Dancing in the Dark: Youth, Popular Culture, and the Electronic Media* (Eerdmans, 1991). He is currently writing a book on postmodernism and the idea of artistic truth in German aesthetics.